ON

AW

By

Sheldon F. Kurtz
...an and Foundation Professor
Florida State University
College of Law
Percy Boardwell Professor
Univ. of Iowa
College of Law

Herbert Hovenkamp
Ben V. & Dorothy Willie Professor
Univ. of Iowa
College of Law

AMERICAN CASEBOOK SERIES

WEST PUBLISHING CO.
ST. PAUL, MINN. 1991

-2 DEC 1993

TABLE OF CONTENTS

AMERICAN PROPERTY LAW

CONTENTS

CONTENTS

CONTENTS

CONTENTS

Chapter 2

ACQUISITION OF PROPERTY RIGHTS:
A FIRST LOOK

§2.1 BY CAPTURE

Add as Problem 12 on Page 53:

12.   O attracted wild geese to a pond on her land.   The geese that were attracted to the pond would then eat the crops on land adjoining O's land that was owned by P.   If P sues O for the value of P's lost crops, can P prevail? See Andrews v. Andrews, 242 N.C. 382, 88 S.E.2d 88 (1955).

Suppose wild geese congregated on O's land.   O hired a pest control company to chase the birds away.   The company successfully drove the birds off O's land.   In doing so, however, the birds congregated on P's land causing him to contract histoplasmosis, a fungal infection.   P sues O for damages.   What result? See Glave v. Michigan Terminix Co., 159 Mich.App. 537, 407 N.W.2d 36 (1987).

§2.2 BY FIND

Add as New Principal Case Immediately Before Favorite v. Miller on Page 63:

GANTER v. KAPILOFF
Court of Special Appeals of Maryland (1986)
69 Md.App. 97, 516 A.2d 611

GILBERT, Chief Justice.

This appeal tests the truthfulness of the old saw "Finders keepers, losers weepers."   Our assay reveals the saw to be toothless, its mettle an alloy of "hot air," folklore, and wishful thinking.

The brothers Leonard and Bernard Kapiloff are philatelists. In approximately 1976 they purchased two sets of stamps from Robert A. Siegel, Inc., a New York corporation dealing in postage stamps.   That the stamps are of considerable value is reflected by their advertised price, $150,400.00.   As far as the brothers knew, those stamps remained in their possession until February 1, 1983.   On that date Bernard Kapiloff saw an advertisement, in a nationally circulated catalogue, offering the stamps for sale.

He contacted the alleged owner, Robert L. Ganter, and demanded return of the stamps. The demand was refused. The Kapiloffs notified the Federal Bureau of Investigation, and that agency took physical possession of the stamps from J. & H. Stolow, another New York stamp dealer. The stamps had been consigned to Stolow by Ganter, who asserted that they were his property.

Ganter related in a deposition that he acquired the stamps by finding them in a dresser he had purchased for thirty dollars in a used furniture store. The purchase was made, according to Ganter, in "the spring or summer of 1979 or 1980." When he "took the drawers out and started spraying [them] for roaches," Ganter "found a bunch of newspapers, magazines and the stamps." The stamps were in a glassine envelope and "looked very official" because they were accompanied by a certificate with "maybe a gold label on it." No appraisal of the stamps was sought by Ganter at that time because he had "no particular interest in the stamps." Subsequently, he visited someone in New York City who suggested the stamps be appraised. At Thanksgiving time 1982 Ganter took the stamps to the Stolow Auction House and was told that they were "a rather sensational find."

When Ganter refused the Kapiloffs' demand that he return the stamps to them, they sued him and J. & H. Stolow, Inc., in replevin in the District Court of Maryland for Baltimore City. The action was removed by Ganter to the Circuit Court for Baltimore City where it was amended to include a count seeking a declaratory judgment that the Kapiloffs were "the true owners of the ... stamps."

Following a hearing...summary judgment [was entered] in favor of the Kapiloffs on both counts.[1]

The Replevin Action

An action of replevin is designed to obtain possession of personal property that is wrongfully detained by the defendant.... Indubitably, the Kapiloffs had the right to assert an action in replevin since they averred that they

---

1. How one in a declaratory judgment action enters a summary judgment without declaring any rights or findings is not explained. In any event, that procedural aspect of this case is not an issue on appeal. We shall treat the matter as the parties seem to have done--a declaration by the trial court that the ownership of the stamps is in the Kapiloffs.

owned the stamps and that Ganter and Stolow had unauthorized possession of the stamps when the action was filed....

"Finders Keepers"

Having determined that the Kapiloffs could maintain an action of replevin and that the stamps were not in custodia legis, we turn now to Ganter's "Finders- Keepers Theory" of ownership.

The first reference that we have discovered to the adage about "finders keepers" appears in the writings of Plautus who penned in Trinummis 1. 63 (c. 194 B.C.), "Habeas ut nanctus: He keeps that finds." In Charles Reade's It is Never Too Late to Mend, Ch. 65 (1856), the saying was reported as "Losers seekers, finders keepers." That expression has evolved into the more familiar "Finders keepers, losers weepers." Whatever its origin, the maxim is legally unsound.

Historically, since at least March 25, 1634, the law of Maryland has been that he who finds lost personal property holds it against all the world except the rightful owner. Chief Justice Coke in Isaack v. Clark, 2 Bylstrode 306 (1615), wrote:

> "[W]hen a man doth finde goods, it hath been said, and so commonly held, that if he doth dis-possess himself of them, by this he shall be discharged, but this is not so, as appears by 12 E. 4 fol. 13. for he which findes goods, if bound to answer him for them who hath the property; and if he deliver them over to any one, unless it be unto the right owner, he shall be charged for them, for at the first it is in his election, whether he will take them or not into his custody, but when he hath them, one onely hath then right unto them, and therefore he ought to keep them safely; if a man therefore which findes goods, if he be wise, he will then search out the right owner of them, and so deliver them unto him...."

Isaack, however, is not generally recognized as the premier authority dealing with ownership of lost property. Usually that status is afforded to England's Chief Justice Pratt for his opinion in Armory v. Delamirie, 1 Strange 505 (1722). There a chimney sweep found a jewel and took it to a goldsmith. The jewel was delivered into the hands of an apprentice who took out the stones. The chimney sweep was offered a pittance for the socket minus the stones. The sweep sued the goldsmith. In allowing recovery from the goldsmith of the value of the gems, the court articulated the legal precept that the finder of lost property, while not acquiring an absolute ownership in it, does, nevertheless, hold the property "against all but the rightful owner...."

Even though Maryland was not settled at the time of the Isaack's decision, it was the law of the proprietory province from the time of its founding. Armory, likewise, was binding in the courts of Maryland. With the advent of the Revolutionary War and subsequent adoption of a State constitution, Maryland carried into its State law those laws of England which existed on July 4, 1776. There they remain except where they have been changed by the Legislature.... To date the General Assembly has not overruled, amended, altered, or changed, by one iota, the holdings of Isaack and Armory. Those decisions remain the law of this State.

Maryland is not alone in following Armory. Our sister states that have considered the issue also follow Armory...Generally, it may be said that the finder of lost property holds it as a bailee for the true owner. As to all others, the finder's rights "are tantamount to ownership, giving him the right to possess and hold the found goods." [citation omitted].

In the matter sub judice, Ganter, having found the stamps, had the right to exercise ownership over them against the whole world except the true owners, who were determined by Judge Hammerman to be the brothers Kapiloff. Once the true owners were determined, Ganter's possessory interest ceased....

Ganter asserts that the judge erred in granting summary judgment in favor of the Kapiloffs because there were genuine disputes of material fact.

Ganter is mistaken. The disputes he perceives as genuine and material are in actuality picayune and immaterial. We refer to but a few of them: To overcome the Kapiloffs' assertion of ownership, Ganter retorts that either of the brothers may have sold the stamps without the other's knowledge. That possibility, he avers, is sufficient to carry the question of ownership to a jury. We disagree. As we see it, Ganter's "dispute" is but sheer speculation entitled to no consideration.

Ganter alleges that because he says he possessed the stamps for a few years there is an inference that he owned them. We have already seen that the law is to the contrary, excepting, of course, where there is a possibility of adverse possession, which is not here applicable.[2]

Another "dispute" advanced by Ganter is that the stamps may not be the same ones that the Kapiloffs own. That theory, while interesting, lacks support in the record, particularly when the Kapiloffs maintain that the particular stamps in question are theirs and an expert, Robert A. Siegel, who sold the stamps to the Kapiloffs, supports their claim of ownership. Although an expert employed by Ganter opined that there were thousands of stamps circulated, his statement does not in any manner contest that of Siegel or the Kapiloffs that the stamps found by Ganter were the precise stamps owned by the Kapiloffs.

Ganter hypothesizes that because the Kapiloffs failed to insure their stamp collection they were not the true owners. The logic of that hypothesis totally and completely eludes us. It may have been an unwise business practice not to insure the stamps, but the lack of insurance is irrelevant to ownership. Ganter has advanced what appear to be ideas, notions, concepts, and fantasies of what might have been. However they are called, they are not genuine disputes of material facts.

Judgment Affirmed

NOTES AND QUESTIONS

1. The court found that the Kapiloffs were the true owners of the stamps. Could the Kapiloffs have prevailed in the absence of that finding? For example, suppose they had been mere finders or the stamps had been left with them by the true owner for safe keeping. Could they have prevailed?

Add as Problem 4(g) on Page 71:

Should artifacts buried with the dead in conformity with customary, religious or spiritual beliefs become the property

---

2. [Authors' Note: see, §4.4 for a discussion of adverse possession of chattels.

of a finder? See, e.g., Charrier v. Bell, 496 So.2d 601 (La. App. 1st Cir. 1986).

§2.5 BY GIFT

Add after Problem 2 on Page 124:

GRUEN v. GRUEN
Court of Appeals of New York (1986)
68 N.Y.2d 48, 505 N.Y.S.2d 849, 496 N.E.2d 869

SIMONS, JUDGE.

Plaintiff commenced this action seeking a declaration that he is the rightful owner of a painting which he alleges his father, now deceased, gave to him. He concedes that he has never had possession of the painting but asserts that his father made a valid gift of the title in 1963 reserving a life estate for himself. His father retained possession of the painting until he died in 1980. Defendant, plaintiff's stepmother, has the painting now and has refused plaintiff's requests that she turn it over to him. She contends that the purported gift was testamentary in nature and invalid insofar as the formalities of a will were not met or, alternatively, that a donor may not make a valid inter vivos gift of a chattel and retain a life estate with a complete right of possession. Following a seven-day nonjury trial, Special Term found that plaintiff had failed to establish any of the elements of an inter vivos gift and that in any event an attempt by a donor to retain a present possessory life estate in a chattel invalidated a purported gift of it. The Appellate Division held that a valid gift may be made reserving a life estate and, finding the elements of a gift established in this case, it reversed and remitted the matter for a determination of value. That determination has now been made and defendant appeals directly to this court...from the subsequent final judgment...awarding plaintiff $2,500,000 in damages representing the value of the painting, plus interest. We now affirm.

The subject of the dispute is a work entitled "Schloss Kammer am Attersee II" painted by a noted Austrian modernist, Gustav Klimt. It was purchased by plaintiff's father, Victor Gruen, in 1959 for $8,000. On April 1, 1963 the elder Gruen, a successful architect with offices and residences in both New York City and Los Angeles during most of the time involved in this action, wrote a letter to plaintiff, then an undergraduate student at Harvard, stating that he was giving him the Klimt painting for his birthday but that he wished to retain the possession of it for his lifetime. This letter is not in evidence, apparently because plaintiff destroyed it on instructions from his father. Two other letters were received, however, one dated May 22, 1963 and the other April 1, 1963. Both had been dictated by Victor Gruen and sent together to plaintiff on or about May 22, 1963. The letter dated May 22, 1963 reads as follows:

Dear Michael:

I wrote you at the time of your birthday about the gift of the painting by Klimt.

Now my lawyer tells me that because of the existing tax laws, it was wrong to mention in that letter that I want to use the painting as long as I live. Though I still want to use it, this should not appear in the letter. I am enclosing, therefore, a new letter and I ask you to send the old one back to me so that it can be destroyed.

I know this is all very silly, but the lawyer and our accountant insist that they must have in their possession copies of a letter which will serve the purpose of making it possible for you, once I die, to get this picture without having to pay inheritance taxes on it.

Love,
s/Victor.

Enclosed with this letter was a substitute gift letter, dated April 1, 1963, which stated:

Dear Michael:

The 21st birthday, being an important event in life, should be celebrated accordingly. I therefore wish to give you as a present the oil painting by Gustav Klimt of Schloss Kammer which now hangs in the New York living room. You know that Lazette and I bought it some 5 or 6 years ago, and you always told us how much you liked it.

Happy birthday again.
Love,

s/Victor.

Plaintiff never took possession of the painting nor did he seek to do so. Except for a brief period between 1964 and 1965 when it was on loan to art exhibits and when restoration work was performed on it, the painting remained in his father's possession, moving with him from New York City to Beverly Hills and finally to Vienna, Austria, where Victor Gruen died on February 14, 1980. Following Victor's death plaintiff requested possession of the Klimt painting and when defendant refused, he commenced this action.

The issues framed for appeal are whether a valid inter vivos gift of a chattel may be made where the donor has reserved a life estate in the chattel and the donee never has had physical possession of it before the donor's death and, if it may, which factual findings on the elements of a valid inter vivos gift more nearly comport with the weight of the evidence in this case, those of Special Term or those of the Appellate Division. The latter issue requires application of two general rules. First, to make a valid inter vivos gift there must exist the intent on the part of the donor to make a present transfer; delivery of the gift, either actual or constructive to the donee; and acceptance by the donee...Second, the proponent of a gift has the burden of proving each of these elements by clear and convincing evidence...

Donative Intent

There is an important distinction between the intent with which an inter vivos gift is made and the intent to make a gift by will. An inter vivos gift requires that the donor intend to make an irrevocable present transfer of ownership; if the intention is to make a testamentary disposition effective only after death, the gift is invalid unless made by will...

Defendant contends that the trial court was correct in finding that Victor did not intend to transfer any present interest in the painting to plaintiff in 1963 but only expressed an intention that plaintiff was to get the painting upon his death. The evidence is all but conclusive, however, that Victor intended to transfer ownership of the painting to plaintiff in 1963 but to retain a life estate in it and that he did, therefore, effectively transfer a remainder interest in the painting to plaintiff at that time. Although the original letter was not in evidence, testimony of its contents was received along with the substitute gift letter and its covering letter dated May 22, 1963. The three letters should be considered together as a single instrument...and when they are they unambiguously establish that Victor Gruen intended to make a present gift of title to the painting at that time. But there was other evidence for after 1963 Victor made several statements orally and in writing indicating that he had previously given plaintiff the painting and that plaintiff owned it. Victor Gruen retained possession of the property, insured it, allowed others to exhibit it and made necessary repairs to it but those acts are not inconsistent with his retention of a life estate....

Defendant contends that even if a present gift was intended, Victor's reservation of a lifetime interest in the painting defeated it. She relies on a statement from Young v. Young, 80 N.Y. 422 that " '[a]ny gift of chattels which expressly reserves the use of the property to the donor for a certain period, or * * * as long as the donor shall live, is ineffectual' " (id., at p. 436, quoting 2 Schouler, Personal Property, at 118). The statement was dictum, however, and the holding of the court was limited to a determination that an attempted gift of bonds in which the donor reserved the interest for life failed because there had been no delivery of the gift, either actual or constructive (see, id., at p. 434; see also, Speelman v. Pascal, 10 N.Y.2d 313, 319-320, 222 N.Y.S.2d 324, 178 N.E.2d 723). The court expressly left undecided the question "whether a remainder in a chattel may be created and given by a donor by carving out a life estate for himself and transferring the remainder" (Young v. Young, supra, at p. 440). We answered part of that question in Matter of Brandreth, 169 N.Y. 437, 441-442, 62 N.E. 563, supra) when we held that "[in] this state a life estate and remainder can be created in a chattel or a fund the same as in real property". The case did not require us to decide whether there could be a valid gift of the remainder.

Defendant recognizes that a valid inter vivos gift of a remainder interest can be made not only of real property but also of such intangibles as stocks and bonds. Indeed, several of the cases she cites so hold. That being so, it is difficult to perceive any legal basis for the distinction she urges which would permit gifts of remainder interests in those properties but not of remainder interests in chattels such as the Klimt painting here. The only reason suggested is that the gift of a chattel must include a present right to possession. The application of Brandreth to permit a gift of the remainder in this case, however, is consistent with the distinction, well recognized in the law of gifts as well as in real property law, between ownership and possession or enjoyment...Insofar as some of our cases purport to require that the donor intend to transfer both title and possession immediately to have a valid inter vivos gift...they state the rule too broadly and confuse the effectiveness of a gift with the transfer of the possession of the subject of that gift. The correct test is " 'whether the maker intended the [gift] to have no effect until after the maker's death, or whether he intended it to transfer some present interest...' " As long as the evidence establishes an intent to make a present and irrevocable transfer of title or the right of ownership, there is a present transfer of some interest and the gift is effective immediately... Thus, in Speelman v. Pascal..., we held valid a gift of a percentage of the future royalties to the play "My Fair Lady" before the play even existed. There, as in this case, the donee received title or the right of ownership to some property immediately upon the making of the gift but possession or enjoyment of the subject of the gift was postponed to some future time.

Defendant suggests that allowing a donor to make a present gift of a remainder with the reservation of a life estate will lead courts to effectuate otherwise invalid testamentary dispositions of property. The two have entirely different characteristics, however, which make them distinguishable. Once the gift is made it is irrevocable and the donor is limited to the rights of a life tenant not an owner. Moreover, with the gift of a remainder title vests immediately in the donee and any possession is postponed until the donor's death whereas under a will neither title nor possession vests immediately. Finally, the postponement of enjoyment of the gift is produced by the express terms of the gift not by the nature of the instrument as it is with a will...

Delivery

In order to have a valid inter vivos gift, there must be a delivery of the gift, either by a physical delivery of the subject of the gift or a constructive or symbolic delivery such as by an instrument of gift, sufficient to divest the donor of dominion and control over the property... As the statement of the rule suggests, the requirement of delivery is not rigid or inflexible, but is to be applied in light of its purpose to avoid mistakes by donors and fraudulent claims by donees... Accordingly, what is sufficient to constitute delivery "must be tailored to suit the circumstances of the case..." The rule requires that " '[t]he delivery necessary to consummate a gift must be as perfect as the nature of the property and the circumstances and surroundings of the parties will reasonably permit' " (citation omitted)

Defendant contends that when a tangible piece of personal property such as a painting is the subject of a gift, physical delivery of the painting itself is the best form of delivery and should be required. Here, of course, we have only delivery of Victor Gruen's letters which serve as instruments of gift. Defendant's statement of the rule as applied may be generally true, but it ignores the fact that what Victor Gruen gave plaintiff was not all rights to the Klimt painting, but only title to it with no right of possession until his death. Under these circumstances, it would be illogical for the law to require the donor to part with possession of the painting when that is exactly what he intends to retain.

Nor is there any reason to require a donor making a gift of a remainder interest in a chattel to physically deliver the chattel into the donee's hands only to have the donee redeliver it to the donor. As the facts of this case demonstrate, such a requirement could impose practical burdens on the parties to the gift while serving the delivery requirement poorly. Thus, in order to accomplish this type of delivery the parties would have been required to travel to New York for the symbolic transfer and redelivery of the Klimt painting which was hanging on the wall of Victor Gruen's Manhattan apartment. Defendant suggests that such a requirement would be stronger evidence of a completed gift, but in the absence of witnesses to the event or any written confirmation of the gift it would provide less protection against fraudulent claims than have the written instruments of gift delivered in this case.

Acceptance

Acceptance by the donee is essential to the validity of an inter vivos gift, but when a gift is of value to the donee, as it is here, the law will presume an acceptance on his part... Plaintiff did not rely on this presumption alone but also presented clear and convincing proof of his acceptance of a remainder interest in the Klimt painting by evidence that he had made several contemporaneous statements acknowledging the gift to his friends and associates, even showing some of them his father's gift letter, and that he had retained both letters for over 17 years to verify the gift after his father died. Defendant relied exclusively on affidavits filed by plaintiff in a matrimonial action with his former wife, in which plaintiff failed to list his interest in the painting as an asset. These affidavits were made over 10 years after acceptance was complete and they do not even approach the evidence in Matter of Kelly (285 N.Y. 139, 148-149, 33 N.E.2d 62 [dissenting in part], supra) where the donee, immediately upon delivery of a diamond ring, rejected it as "too flashy". We agree with the Appellate Division that interpretation of the affidavit was too speculative to support a finding of rejection and overcome the substantial showing of acceptance by plaintiff.

Accordingly, the judgment appealed from and the order of the Appellate Division brought up for review should be affirmed, with costs.

NOTES AND QUESTIONS

1. Property transferred during a donor life as a gift is subject to the federal estate tax (death tax) if the donor retained the right to the possession of the gifted property for her life. Int. Rev. Code § 2036(a). This provision causes such gifted property to be taxed in the same way as if the donor retained the property until death and bequeathed the property to the donee in the her will.

Although Victor clearly intended to retain possession of the painting for his life (and in fact did), his lawyer recommended that he "doctor up" the transaction in order to avoid a paper trail that would result in an adverse tax consequence. In your judgment, is this ethical? Is it legal?

If, as appears to be the case, the donor, acting under advice of counsel, executed instruments of gift which failed to reflect the actual fact that the donor retained possession of the painting for life, should that effect the validity of the gift for state law purposes.

2. Re-read Victor's letters to his son. Who do you think wrote them?

Add as Problems 7 and 8 on Page 125:

7. Andrew gave Bonnie an engagement ring as a symbol of their engagement. The ring was worth $1,400. Andrew later broke off the engagement and, in a fit of anger, Bonnie threw the ring into a field. Is Bonnie liable to Andrew for the value of the ring? See Harris v. Davis, 139

Ill.App.3d 1046, 487 N.E.2d 1204 (1986) (gift conditional on marriage).   Compare Wion v. Henderson, 24 Ohio App.3d 207, 494 N.E.2d 133 (1985) (no need to return ring if engagement broken by the donor) and Lyle v. Durham, 16 Ohio App.3d 1, 473 N.E.2d 1216 (1984) (must return ring regardless of who breaks the engagement).

8. Father gave Daughter a check in the amount of $20,000 intending to make an inter vivos gift.   Daughter forwarded the check to her bank with directions to purchase a certificate of deposit.   Before her bank was able to process the check for payment Father died.   When, after his death, the check was presented at the Father's bank for payment, that bank refused to honor the check on the grounds that the gift was revoked by the Father's death.   Is the bank correct? See In re Estate of Bolton, 444 N.W.2d 482 (Iowa 1989).

Chapter 3

SOME RIGHTS, POWERS AND OBLIGATIONS OF POSSESSORS

§3.2 POWERS

Add as Problem 6 Immediately Following Problem 5 on Page 155:

Owner left a bag of clothing with the local Goodwill store. Goodwill is a national organization which trains disabled persons in the sale and merchandizing of used goods, including clothing and silver. Mistakenly, silver flatware worth $3,500 was also included in the bag. Ms. Lucky purchased the silver from Goodwill. Thereafter, Owner sued to recover the silver from Ms. Lucky. What arguments might each of the parties raise in support of their claim to own the silver and if you were the judge in this case, how would you rule? See Kahr v. Markland, 187 Ill. App.3d 603, 543 N.E.2d 579 (1989).

§3.3 OBLIGATIONS

Add as New Case at the Beginning of § 3.3:

JONES v. YORK
U. S. Dist. Ct., Eastern Dist. Va. (1989)
717 F. Supp. 421

CLARKE, DISTRICT JUDGE.

... The plaintiffs' complaint in this case raises an issue of first impression in the rapidly developing field of human reproductive technology. The plaintiffs, Steven York, M.D. and Risa Adler-York (the Yorks), are the progenitors of the cryopreserved human pre-zygote (the pre-zygote) at issue in this case. The plaintiffs seek the release and transfer of the pre-zygote from the defendant The Howard and Georgeanna Jones Institute For Reproductive Medicine (Jones Institute) in Norfolk, Virginia to the Institute for Reproductive Research at the Hospital of the Good Samaritan located in Los Angeles, California. The defendants have refused to consent to an inter-institutional transfer of the pre-zygote.

... The plaintiffs' complaint in this matter is in four counts: breach of contract (Count I); quasi-contract (Count

II); detinue (Count III) and [fourth count based on Eleventh Amendment immunity omitted]. The plaintiffs seek declaratory, injunctive and compensatory relief....Because this matter is before the Court on defendants' Motion to Dismiss the Complaint for failure to state a claim upon which relief can be granted, the Court will construe the Complaint in a light most favorable to the plaintiffs....

The plaintiffs were married in 1983 and have been attempting to achieve a pregnancy since 1984. Because of damage to Mrs. York's remaining Fallopian tube, the Yorks are unable to achieve a pregnancy through normal coital reproduction. The plaintiffs were advised that through in vitro fertilization, plaintiffs would be able to become the parents of their own genetic child. The in vitro fertilization process involves removing one or more oocytes or eggs from the woman's body, fertilizing those eggs in vitro (outside the womb) with the husband's sperm, and then depositing the developing masses into the woman's uterus up to the eight-cell stage....

In the spring of 1986, plaintiffs consulted with Drs. Jones and Kreiner at the Jones Institute in Norfolk, Virginia in order to determine whether they were viable candidates for the in vitro fertilization (IVF) program, known as the Vital Initiation of Pregnancy (VIP) program. The Yorks were accepted into the IVF program and signed VIP Consent Form No. 6B....Consent Form 6B stated, and Dr. Kreiner assured the Yorks, that the expectation of pregnancy is about 20 percent after the transfer of one fertilized mature egg, about 28 percent after the transfer of two fertilized mature eggs and about 38 percent after the transfer of three fertilized mature eggs.... At the time the Yorks entered the IVF program in Norfolk, they were residents of New Jersey. During the course of treatment, the Yorks moved to California.

The Yorks returned to the Jones Institute on four separate occasions to undergo the in vitro fertilization process: August 22, 1986 to September 7, 1986; November 28, 1986 to December 7, 1986; February 12, 1987 to February 18, 1987; and May 17, 1987 to June 5, 1987. None of these in vitro fertilization attempts resulted in pregnancy. Prior to the attempt in May 1987, the plaintiffs signed a form entitled "Informed Consent: Human Pre- Zygotes Cryopreservation" (Cryopreservation Agreement)... The consent form outlined the procedure for cryopreservation or freezing of pre-zygotes and detailed the couple's rights in the frozen pre-zygote.

The Cryopreservation Agreement explained that the cryopreservation procedure is available in the event more than five pre-zygotes are retrieved during the IVF treatment. The Agreement further stated that the cryopreservation procedure is intended to reduce the risk of multiple births, while simultaneously "creating additional opportunities for the initiation of pregnancy with the transfer of concepti developed from frozen-thawed pre- zygotes." After signing the Agreement, the plaintiffs underwent the IVF process on May 17, 1987. On May 27, 1987, Dr. Kreiner removed six eggs from Mrs. York and fertilized those eggs with Dr. York's sperm, creating six embryos. On May 29, 1987, five embryos were transferred to Mrs. York's uterus. The remaining embryo, which is the subject of this litigation, was cryogenically preserved in accordance with the procedures outlined in the Cryopreservation Agreement.

In May of 1988, a year after the pre-zygote was frozen, the Yorks sought to have the pre-zygote transferred from the Jones Institute in Norfolk, Virginia to the Institute for Reproductive Research at the Hospital of the Good Samaritan in Los Angeles, California. At the Los Angeles clinic, Dr. Richard Marrs would thaw the embryo and insert it in Mrs. York through in vitro fertilization. The plaintiffs consulted two embryologists to arrange for proper cryogenic support in order to successfully transport the embryo. The plaintiffs planned to have Dr. York personally retrieve the embryo from Norfolk and transport it to California by commercial airliner. The pre-zygote would be housed in a biological dry shipper during the flight.

On May 28, 1988, the Yorks wrote Dr. Muasher and indicated their intent to retrieve and transfer the pre-zygote. By letter dated June 13, 1988, Dr. Muasher, writing on behalf of the Jones Institute, refused to allow such a transfer. On June 18, 1988, Dr. Richard Marrs, on behalf of the Yorks, sought consent to transfer the pre-zygote from physicians at the Jones Institute. By letter dated August 9, 1988, Dr. Jones refused to approve the transfer of the frozen pre-zygote....

Breach of Contract:

The plaintiffs allege that the defendants' continued dominion and control over the frozen pre-zygote is contrary to the language of the Cryopreservation Agreement. The pertinent provision of the Cryopreservation Agreement provides: We may withdraw our consent and discontinue participation at any time without prejudice and we understand our pre-zygotes will be stored only as long as we are active IVF patients at The Howard and Georgeanna Jones Institute For Reproductive Medicine or until the end of our normal reproductive years. We have the principle responsibility to decide the disposition of our pre- zygotes. Our frozen pre-zygotes will not be released from storage for the purpose of intrauterine transfer without the written consents of us both. In the event of divorce, we understand legal ownership of any stored pre-zygotes must be determined in a property settlement and will be released as directed by order of a court of competent jurisdiction. Should we for any reason no longer wish to attempt to initiate a pregnancy, we understand we may choose one of three fates for our pre-zygotes that remain in frozen storage. Our pre-zygotes may be: 1) donated to another infertile couple (who will remain unknown to us) 2) donated for approved research investigation 3) thawed but not allowed to undergo further development.

The defendants argue that plaintiffs' proprietary rights in the pre- zygote are limited to the "three fates" enumerated in this provision because there is no established protocol for the inter-institutional transfer of pre- zygotes.

The Court begins its analysis by noting that the Cryopreservation Agreement created a bailor-bailee relationship between the plaintiffs and defendants. While the parties in this case expressed no intent to create a bailment, under Virginia law, no formal contract or actual meeting of the minds is necessary. Morris v. Hamilton, 225 Va. 372, 302 S.E.2d 51, 52 (1983). Rather, all that is needed "is the element of lawful possession however created, and duty to account for the thing as the property of another that creates the bailment...." Crandall v. Woodard, 206 Va. 321, 143 S.E.2d 923, 927 (1965). The essential nature of a bailment relationship imposes on the bailee, when the purpose of the bailment has terminated, an absolute obligation to return the subject matter of the bailment to the bailor. 8 Am. Jur.2d Bailments § 178 (1980). The obligation to return the property is implied from the fact of lawful possession of the personal property of another. Id.

In the instant case, the requisite elements of a bailment relationship are present. It is undisputed that the Jones

Institutes' possession of the pre-zygote was lawful pursuant to the Cryopreservation Agreement. The defendants also recognized their duty to account for the pre-zygote by virtue of a paragraph in the Cryopreservation Agreement purporting to disclaim liability for any injury to the pre-zygote.[1] Finally, the defendants consistently refer to the pre-zygote as the "property" of the Yorks in the Cryopreservation Agreement. Although the Cryopreservation Agreement constitutes a bailment contract, the Agreement is nevertheless governed by the same principles as apply to other contracts.

The defendants assert that plaintiffs' property interest in the pre-zygote is limited by the Virginia Human Research statute. Va.Code § 37.1-234, et seq. Under Virginia law, relevant statutes and regulations existing at the time the contract was made become a part of the contract and must be read into it as if expressly referred to or incorporated. General Electric Co. v. Moretz, 270 F.2d 780, 787 (4th Cir.1959), cert. denied, 361 U.S. 964, 80 S.Ct. 593, 4 L.Ed.2d 545 (1960). The Human Research statute requires every institution which conducts human research to establish a human research review committee or institutional review board. The statute further provides: No human research shall be conducted or authorized by such institution or agency unless (a) such committee has reviewed and approved the proposed human research project giving consideration to ... whether the research conforms with such other requirements as the Board by regulation may establish.... The committee shall require periodic reports from each existing human research project to ensure that it is being carried out in conformity with the proposal as approved....

---

1. The disclaimer provision in the Cryopreservation Agreement provides: We understand that with any technique necessitating mechanical support systems, equipment failure can occur. Neither the Eastern Virginia Medical Authority (EVMA) nor The Howard and Georgeanna Jones Institute For Reproductive Medicine, its directors, employees or consultants are to be held liable for any destruction, damage, misuse or improper testing, freezing, maintenance storage, withdrawal, thawing and/or delivery caused by or resulting from any gross negligence, malfunction of the storage tank, any failure of utilities, any strike, cessation of services, or other labor disturbance, any war, acts of a public enemy, or other disturbance, any fire, wind, earthquake, water, or other acts of God, or the failure of any other laboratory. We are advised that EVMA provides no insurance coverage, compensation plan or free medical care plan to compensate us if we or our pre-zygotes are harmed in any way by this cryopreservation procedure.

Va.Code § 37.1-236(B). Defendants assert that the Cryopreservation Agreement contains all of the protocol currently approved by the human research review committee. Conspicuously absent from this protocol is any provision for the inter-institutional transfer of cryopreserved human pre-zygotes. Therefore, argue the defendants, because the review committee has not considered or issued guidelines concerning the ethical, medical and legal implications of inter-institutional transfer, the plaintiffs' proprietary interests in the pre-zygote are limited to the three choices for disposition currently recognized in the protocol.

The Court finds that the incorporation of the Virginia Human Research statute into the Cryopreservation Agreement has no affect on the dispute between the parties. The purpose of the Human Research statute is to ensure a complete disclosure of information between the researcher and the subject. The statute envisions that through the legal mechanism of informed consent a human research review committee will promulgate ethical guidelines which protect both scientist and subject from the legal claims of the other.[2] The Court finds that the terms of the statute, when made a part of the Agreement in dispute here, do not conflict with any other terms of the Agreement. The Court further finds that the failure of the human research review committee to consider the ramifications of the inter-institutional transfer of cryopreserved human pre-zygotes does not vitiate the contract between these parties nor does it usurp this Court's jurisdiction to settle a contractual dispute between these parties.

The Court notes the Cryopreservation Agreement should

---

2. The Ethics Committee of the American Fertility Society has found that an informed consent, [P]rotects the participants in the new reproductive technologies no matter what type of institution or clinic provides the service and no matter whether the procedure is experimental or standard practice.... Informed consent protects patients by giving them the opportunity to refuse treatments that they consider to be too risky.... The Committee also found that, The provision of information is also key with respect to risks in childbearing. Lawsuits have been brought against physicians by parents of children with genetic defects who claimed that their physicians did not advise them that genetic screening could have been done on them or the developing fetus, which would have given them the option of not giving birth to an affected child. The Ethics Committee of the American Fertility Society, Ethical Considerations of the New Reproductive Technologies, 46 Fertility and Sterility 105 (1986).

be more strictly construed against the defendants, the parties who drafted the Agreement. Winn v. Aleda Construction Co., 227 Va. 304, 315 S.E.2d 193, 195 (1984). The defendants have defined the extent of their possession interest as bailee of the pre-zygote by the following provision of the Agreement: "We may withdraw our consent and discontinue participation at any time without prejudice and we understand our pre-zygote will be stored only as long as we are active IVF patients at the [Jones Institute]...." The testimony at the hearing on plaintiffs' Motion for Temporary Injunction and the briefs submitted by the plaintiffs make it clear that plaintiffs wish to terminate their relationship with the Jones Institute and continue treatment at the fertility clinic in Los Angeles, California.

The defendants have further defined the limits of their possessory interest by recognizing the plaintiffs' proprietary rights in the pre-zygote. The Agreement repeatedly refers to "our pre-zygote," and explicitly provides that in the event of a divorce, the legal ownership of the pre-zygote "must be determined in a property settlement" by a court of competent jurisdiction. The Agreement further provides that the plaintiffs have "the principal responsibility to decide the disposition" of the pre-zygote and that the pre- zygote will not be released from storage without the written consent of both plaintiffs.[3] The Court finds that the inference to be drawn from these provisions of the Cryopreservation Agreement is that the defendants fully recognize plaintiffs' property rights in the pre-zygote and have limited their rights as bailee to exercise dominion and control over the pre-zygote.

The defendants take the position that the plain language of the Cryopreservation Agreement limits the plaintiffs' proprietary right to the pre- zygote to the "three fates" listed in the Agreement: (1) donation to another infertile couple; (2) donation for approved research; and (3) thawing. The Court finds, however, that the applicability

---

3. This provision of the Agreement is consistent with the position of the American Fertility Society in their Ethical Statement on in vitro fertilization. The American Fertility Society found: It is understood that the gametes and concepti are the property of the donors. The donors therefore have the right to decide at their sole discretion the disposition of these items, provided such disposition is within medical and ethical guidelines as outlined herein. The Ethics Committee of the American Fertility Society, Ethical Considerations of the New Reproductive Technologies, 46 Fertility and Sterility 895 (1986).

of the three fates is limited by the following language, "Should we [the Yorks] for any reason no longer wish to initiate a pregnancy, we understand we may chose one of three fates for our pre-zygotes that remain in frozen storage." The allegations of plaintiffs' Complaint, and the entire thrust of this litigation, suggest that plaintiffs continue to desire to achieve pregnancy. The Agreement does not state that the attempt to initiate a pregnancy is restricted to procedures employed at the Jones Institute. The "three fates" are therefore inapplicable to the case at bar.

For the reasons stated herein, the Court finds that Count I of plaintiffs' Complaint states a claim upon which relief can be granted. Count II is pled in the alternative alleging an action based on quasi-contract. Accordingly, defendants' Motion to Dismiss Counts I and II are denied.

Detinue:

In Count III of the Complaint, plaintiffs allege a cause of action in detinue. The requisite elements of a detinue action in Virginia are as follows: (1) plaintiff must have a property interest in the thing sought to be recovered; (2) the right to immediate possession; (3) the property is capable of identification; (4) the property must be of some value; and (5) defendant must have had possession at some time prior to the institution of the act. D.T. Vicars v. Atlantic Discount Co., 205 Va. 934, 140 S.E.2d 667, 670 (1965). Moreover, if the property is in the possession of a bailee, an action in detinue accrues upon demand and refusal to return the property or upon a violation of the bailment contract by an act of conversion. Gwin v. H.T.N. Graves, 230 Va. 34, 334 S.E.2d 294, 297 (1985).

After review of plaintiffs' Complaint, the Court finds that plaintiffs have properly alleged a cause of action in detinue. Accordingly, defendants' Motion to Dismiss Count III is Denied.

NOTES AND QUESTIONS

1. Suppose after the transfer of the embryo to the California clinic, the Yorks decided to divorce. Mr. York claims that as owner of a one half interest in the embryo he would like to have it thawed and not implanted. Mrs. York objects. If Mr. York's claim could be sustained as a matter of property law, could the court in a dispute between the

Yorks conclude the embryo was not property, or would collateral estoppel apply to bind the Yorks to the legal conclusion that it was?

Davis v. Davis, an unreported decision from the Circuit Court of Tennessee, Blount County, Equity Division, 1989 WL 140495 (Tenn. Cir. Ct. 1989), held that an embryo was human life from the moment of conception and therefore was not property subject to division between divorcing parties. The court held that custody of the embryos should be awarded to the wife but it reserved all matters concerning support, visitation, final custody and related issues.

Could the court have avoided the question of "when human life begins" but nonetheless conclude that the embryos were to be in the custody of Mrs. Davis? What are the implications of that determination? For example, suppose Mr. Davis dies shortly after the Davis' divorce becomes final and that under state law the property of a single person passes to that person's children. Does Mr. Davis' property pass to the embryos? Suppose following the decision Mrs. Davis directs that an embryo be "flushed." Has she committed murder? Would Mr. Davis be entitled to damages from her for the embryo's wrongful death?

Assume one of the embryos is successfully brought to live birth over Mr. Davis' objection. Would he be liable to provide that child with child support? Would he be entitled to visit that child from time to time? If you conclude he would not, then why did the court reserve these matters for later consideration?

2. The Davis court spent considerable time discussing evidence that the embryos represent "life." Assuming that they are life, does it necessarily follow they are "human life." In considering that question, is it sufficient merely to conclude the embryos are human because they come from the union of human sperm and ova or is there more that enters into the determination of when life is "human life." The noted bioethicist, Professor Fletcher observes that:

> Synthetic concepts such as human and man and person require operational terms spelling out the which and what and when. Only in that way can we get down to cases--to normative decisions. There are always some people who prefer to be visceral and affective in their moral choices, with no desire to have any rationale for what they do.

But <u>ethics</u> is precisely the business of rational, critical reflection (encephalic and not merely visceral) about the problems of moral agent--in biology and medicine as much as in law, government, education or anything else.

Fletcher, Indicators of Humanhood: A Tentative Profile of Man, 2 Hastings Cent. Rep. No. 5, 1 (1972). Professor Fletcher then catalogs characteristics of humanness. These are: (1) minimal intelligence (I.Q. 40 or over), (2) self-awareness, (3) self-control, (4) a sense of time, (5) a sense of futurity, (6) a sense of the past, (7) the capability to relate to others, (8) concern for others, (9) communication, (10) control of existence, (11) curiosity, (12) change and changeability, (13) balance of rationality and feeling, (14) idiosyncrasy, and (15) neo-corital function. How would Professor Fletcher likely have characterized the embryos in Davis?

3. O's blood and spleen were used by a group of scientists to develop a cell line to be used in extremely profitable research. O sued the scientists to recover a portion of the profits on the theory that they had converted his property. Does O have a property right in her spleen? See Moore v. Regents of the University of California, 51 Cal.3d 120, 271 Cal.Rptr. 146, 793 P.2d 479 (1990) (recover permitted for failure to obtain O's consent for use of the spleen but not on conversion theory). Suppose you conclude, as the California Supreme Court believed in *Moore*, that O has no property in her spleen, how would you decide the following case.

Child had her tooth removed by the dentist. That evening Child placed tooth under her pillow in hopes of an exchange for money with the tooth fairy. During the night, the tooth is stolen by a thief. Does Child (or her parent) have a cause of action for conversion?

Add to End of Note 2 on Page 170:

In Allen v. Hyatt Regency-Nashville Hotel, 668 S.W.2d
286 (1984), the court found a bailment under the following
facts:

Appellant is the owner and operator of a modern
high-rise hotel in Nashville fronting on the south side
of Union Street. Immediately to the rear, or south,
of the main hotel building there is a multi-story
parking garage with a single entrance and a single exit
to the west, on Seventh Avenue, North. As one
enters the parking garage at the street level, there is
a large sign reading "Welcome to Hyatt Regency-
Nashville." There is another Hyatt Regency sign inside
the garage at street level, together with a sign marked
"Parking." The garage is available for parking by
members of the general public as well as guests of the
hotel, and the public are invited to utilize it.

On the morning of February 12, 1981, appellee's
husband, Edwin Allen, accompanied by two passengers,
drove appellee's new 1981 automobile into the parking
garage. Neither Mr. Allen nor his passengers intended
to register at the hotel as a guest. Mr. Allen had
parked in this particular garage on several occasions,
however, testifying that he felt that the vehicle would
be safer in an attended garage than in an unattended
outside lot on the street. The single entrance was
controlled by a ticket machine. The single exit was
controlled by an attendant in a booth just opposite to
the entrance and in full view thereof. Appellee's
husband entered the garage at the street level and
took a ticket which was automatically dispensed by the
machine. The machine activated a barrier gate which
rose and permitted Mr. Allen to enter the garage. He
drove to the fourth floor level, parked the vehicle,
locked it, retained the ignition key, descended by
elevator to the street level and left the garage. When
he returned several hours later, the car was gone,
and it has never been recovered. Mr. Allen reported
the theft to the attendant at the exit booth, who
stated, "Well, it didn't come out here." The attendant
did not testify at the trial.

Mr. Allen then reported the theft to security
personnel employed by appellant, and subsequently
reported the loss to the police. Appellant regularly
employed a number of security guards, who were

dressed in a distinctive uniform, two of whom were on duty most of the time. These guards patrolled the hotel grounds and building as well as the garage and were instructed to make rounds through the garage, although not necessarily at specified intervals.

Do you agree that a bailment was created?

Chapter 4

ADVERSE POSSESSION

§4.2 THE ACTUAL, OPEN, CONTINUOUS, AND EXCLUSIVE REQUIREMENTS

Add at end of Carryover Paragraph on Page 188:

See also, In Re Estate of Wells, 576 A.2d 707 (1990)(tenant can adversely possess against landlord only after giving actual notice of intent to possess adversely).

Add on Page 188 Immediately Following the End of Note 4:

NOME 2000 v. FAGERSTROM
Supreme Court of Alaska (1990)
799 P.2d 304

MATTHEWS, JUDGE.

This appeal involves a dispute over a tract of land measuring approximately seven and one-half acres, overlooking the Nome River (hereinafter the disputed parcel).... Record title to a tract of land known as mineral survey 1161, which includes the disputed parcel, is held by Nome 2000. On July 24, 1987, Nome 2000 filed suit to eject Charles and Peggy Fagerstrom from the disputed parcel. The Fagerstroms counterclaimed that through their use of the parcel they had acquired title by adverse possession. A jury trial ensued and, at the close of the Fagerstroms' case, Nome 2000 moved for a directed verdict on two grounds. First, it maintained that the Fagerstroms' evidence of use of the disputed parcel did not meet the requirements of the doctrine of adverse possession. Alternatively, Nome 2000 maintained that the requirements for adverse possession were met only as to the northerly section of the parcel and, therefore, the Fagerstroms could not have acquired title to the remainder. The trial court denied the motion. After Nome 2000 presented its case, the jury found that the Fagerstroms had adversely possessed the entire parcel. The court then entered judgment in favor of the Fagerstroms.

On appeal, Nome 2000 contests the trial court's denial of its motion for a directed verdict and the sufficiency of the evidence in support of the jury verdict...

I. Factual Background

The disputed parcel is located in a rural area known as Osborn. During the warmer seasons, property in Osborn is suitable for homesites and subsistence and recreational activities. During the colder seasons, little or no use is made of Osborn property.

Charles Fagerstrom's earliest recollection of the disputed parcel is his family's use of it around 1944 or 1945. At that time, he and his family used an abandoned boy scout cabin present on the parcel as a subsistence base camp during summer months. Around 1947 or 1948, they moved their summer campsite to an area south of the disputed parcel. However, Charles and his family continued to make seasonal use of the disputed parcel for subsistence and recreation.

In 1963, Charles and Peggy Fagerstrom were married and, in 1966, they brought a small quantity of building materials to the north end of the disputed parcel. They intended to build a cabin.

In 1970 or 1971, the Fagerstroms used four cornerposts to stake off a twelve acre, rectangular parcel for purposes of a Native Allotment application....The northeast and southeast stakes were located on or very near mineral survey 1161. The northwest and southwest stakes were located well to the west of mineral survey 1161. The overlap constitutes the disputed parcel. The southeast stake disappeared at an unknown time.

Also around 1970, the Fagerstroms built a picnic area on the north end of the disputed parcel. The area included a gravel pit, beachwood blocks as chairs, firewood and a 50-gallon barrel for use as a stove.

About mid-July 1974, the Fagerstroms placed a camper trailer on the north end of the disputed parcel. The trailer was leveled on blocks and remained in place through late September. Thereafter, until 1978, the Fagerstroms parked their camper trailer on the north end of the disputed parcel from early June through September. The camper was equipped with food, bedding, a stove and other household items.

About the same time that the Fagerstroms began parking the trailer on the disputed parcel, they built an outhouse and a fish rack on the north end of the parcel. Both fixtures remained through the time of trial in their original locations.[1] The Fagerstroms also planted some spruce trees, not indigenous to the Osborn area, in 1975-76.

During the summer of 1977, the Fagerstroms built a reindeer shelter on the north end of the disputed parcel. The shelter was about 8x8 feet wide, and tall enough for Charles Fagerstrom to stand in. Around the shelter, the Fagerstroms constructed a pen which was 75 feet in diameter and 5 feet high. The shelter and pen housed a reindeer for about six weeks and the pen remained in place until the summer of 1978.

During their testimony, the Fagerstroms estimated that they were personally present on the disputed parcel from 1974 through 1978, "every other weekend or so" and "[a] couple times during the week ... if the weather was good." When present they used the north end of the parcel as a base camp while using the entire parcel for subsistence and recreational purposes. Their activities included gathering berries, catching and drying fish and picnicking. Their children played on the parcel. The Fagerstroms also kept the property clean, picking up litter left by others.

While so using the disputed parcel, the Fagerstroms walked along various paths which traverse the entire parcel. The paths were present prior to the Fagerstroms' use of the parcel and, according to Peggy Fagerstrom, were free for use by others in connection with picking berries and fishing. On one occasion, however, Charles Fagerstrom excluded campers from the land. They were burning the Fagerstroms' firewood.

Nome 2000 placed into evidence the deposition testimony of Dr. Steven McNabb, an expert in anthropology, who stated that the Fagerstroms' use of the disputed parcel was consistent with the traditional Native Alaskan system of land use. According to McNabb, unlike the non-Native system, the traditional Native system does not recognize exclusive ownership of land. Instead, customary use of land, such as the Fagerstroms' use of the disputed parcel, establishes only a first priority claim to the land's resources. The claim is not exclusive and is not a matter of ownership, but is more in the nature of a stewardship. That is, other members of

---

1. The outhouse was blown over one winter by strong winds, but was re-erected the following summer with additional supports.

the claimant's social group may share in the resources of the land without obtaining permission, so long as the resources are not abused or destroyed. McNabb explained that Charles' exclusion of the campers from the land was a response to the campers' use of the Fagerstroms' personal property (their firewood), not a response to an invasion of a perceived real property interest.[2]

Nevertheless, several persons from the community testified that the Fagerstroms' use of the property from 1974 through 1977 was consistent with that of an owner of the property. For example, one Nome resident testified that since 1974 "[the Fagerstroms] cared for [the disputed parcel] as if they owned it. They made improvements on it as if they owned it. It was my belief that they did own it."

During the summer of 1978, the Fagerstroms put a cabin on the north end of the disputed parcel. Nome 2000 admits that from the time that the cabin was so placed until the time that Nome 2000 filed this suit, the Fagerstroms adversely possessed the north end of the disputed parcel. Nome 2000 filed its complaint on July 24, 1987.

II. Discussion

A.

The Fagerstroms' claim of title by adverse possession is governed by AS 09.10.030, which provides for a ten-year limitations period for actions to recover real property.[3] Thus, if the Fagerstroms adversely possessed the disputed parcel, or any portion thereof, for ten consecutive years, then they have acquired title to that property.... Because the Fagerstroms' use of the parcel increased over the years, and because Nome 2000 filed its complaint on July 24, 1987, the relevant period is July 24, 1977 through July 24, 1987. We recently described the elements of adverse possession as follows: "In order to acquire title by adverse possession, the

---

2. However, Charles Fagerstrom testified that when he excluded the campers he felt that they were "on our property." He also testified that during the mid to late 70's he would have "frown[ed]" upon people camping on "my property."

3. A seven-year period is provided for by AS 09.25.050 when possession is under "color and claim of title." The Fagerstroms do not maintain that their possession was under color of title.

claimant must prove, by clear and convincing evidence, ...
that for the statutory period 'his use of the land was
continuous, open and notorious, exclusive and hostile to the
true owner.' " Smith v. Krebs, 768 P.2d 124, 125 (Alaska
1989) (citations omitted).   The first three conditions--
continuity, notoriety and exclusivity-- describe the physical
requirements of the doctrine. See R. Cunningham, W.
Stoebuck and D. Whitman, The Law of Property § 11.7 at
758-60, 762-63 (1984). The fourth condition, hostility, is
often imprecisely described as the "intent" requirement. Id.
at 761.

On appeal, Nome 2000 argues that as a matter of law the
physical requirements are not met absent "significant physical
improvements" or "substantial activity" on the land. Thus,
according to Nome 2000, only when the Fagerstroms placed
a cabin on the disputed parcel in the summer of 1978 did
their possession become adverse. For the prior year, so the
argument goes, the Fagerstroms' physical use of the property
was insufficient because they did not construct "significant
structure[s]" and their use was only seasonal. Nome 2000
also argues that the Fagerstroms' use of the disputed parcel
was not exclusive because "[o]thers were free to pick the
berries, use the paths and fish in the area." We reject these
arguments.

Whether a claimant's physical acts upon the land are
sufficiently continuous, notorious and exclusive does not
necessarily depend on the existence of significant
improvements, substantial activity or absolute exclusivity.
Indeed, this area of law is not susceptible to fixed standards
because the quality and quantity of acts required for
adverse possession depend on the character of the land in
question. Thus, the conditions of continuity and exclusivity
require only that the land be used for the statutory period
as an average owner of similar property would use it.
Alaska National Bank v. Linck, 559 P.2d 1049, 1052 (Alaska
1977) (One test for determining continuity of possession is
to ask whether the land was used as an average owner would
use it.); Peters v. Juneau-Douglas Girl Scout Council, 519
P.2d 826, 831 (Alaska 1974) ("[P]ossession need not be
absolutely exclusive; it need only be a type of possession
which would characterize an owner's use."). Where, as in
the present case, the land is rural, a lesser exercise of
dominion and control may be reasonable. See Linck, 559
P.2d at 1052 (citing Cooper v. Carter Oil Co., 316 P.2d 320
(Utah 1957) for the proposition that "pasturing of sheep for
three weeks a year is sufficient where land is suitable only

for grazing"), 1053 (citing Monroe v. Rawlings, 49 N.W.2d 55, 56 (Mich.1951) for the proposition that "6 visits per year to hunting cabin plus some timber cutting found sufficient where land was wild and undeveloped"); Peters, 519 P.2d at 831 (citing Pulcifer v. Bishop, 225 N.W. 3 (Mich.1929) for the proposition that exclusivity is not destroyed as to beach property commonly used by others). The character of the land in question is also relevant to the notoriety requirement. Use consistent with ownership which gives visible evidence of the claimant's possession, such that the reasonably diligent owner "could see that a hostile flag was being flown over his property," is sufficient. Shilts v. Young, 567 P.2d 769, 776 (Alaska 1977). Where physical visibility is established, community repute is also relevant evidence that the true owner was put on notice.[4]

Applying the foregoing principles to this case, we hold that the jury could reasonably conclude that the Fagerstroms established, by clear and convincing evidence, continuous, notorious and exclusive possession for ten years prior to the date Nome 2000 filed suit... We point out that we are concerned only with the first year, the summer of 1977 through the summer of 1978, as Nome 2000 admits that the requirements of adverse possession were met from the summer of 1978 through the summer of 1987.

The disputed parcel is located in a rural area suitable as a seasonal homesite for subsistence and recreational activities. This is exactly how the Fagerstroms used it during the year in question. On the premises throughout the entire year were an outhouse, a fish rack, a large reindeer pen (which, for six weeks, housed a reindeer), a picnic area, a small quantity of building materials and some trees not indigenous to the area. During the warmer season, for about 13 weeks, the Fagerstroms also placed a camper trailer on blocks on the disputed parcel. The Fagerstroms and their children visited the property several times during the warmer season to fish, gather berries, clean the premises, and play. In total, their conduct and improvements went well beyond "mere casual and occasional trespasses" and instead "evince[d] a purpose to exercise exclusive dominion over the property." See Peters, 519 P.2d

---

4. The function of the notoriety requirement is to afford the true owner an opportunity for notice. However, actual notice is not required; the true owner is charged with knowing what a reasonably diligent owner would have known...

at 830.   That others were free to pick berries and fish is
consistent with the conduct of a hospitable landowner, and
undermines neither the continuity nor exclusivity of their
possession.   See id. at 831 (claimant "merely acting as any
other hospitable landowner might" in allowing strangers to
come on land to dig clams).

With respect to the notoriety requirement, a quick
investigation of the premises, especially during the season
which it was best suited for use, would have been sufficient
to place a reasonably diligent landowner on notice that
someone may have been exercising dominion and control over
at least the northern portion of the property.   Upon such
notice, further inquiry would indicate that members of the
community regarded the Fagerstroms as the owners.
Continuous, exclusive, and notorious possession were thus
established.

[The court's discussion of the hostility requirement is
omitted.   It is entirely consistent with the court's prior
holding in Peters v. Juneau-Douglas Girl Scout Council, on
page 188 of this book].

Having concluded that the Fagerstroms established the
elements of adverse possession, we turn to the question
whether they were entitled to the entire disputed parcel.
Specifically, the question presented is whether the jury could
reasonably conclude that the Fagerstroms adversely possessed
the southerly portion of the disputed parcel...

Absent color of title,[5] only property actually possessed
may be acquired by adverse possession....Here, from the
summer of 1977 through the summer of 1978, the
Fagerstroms' only activity on the southerly portion of the
land included use of the pre-existing trails in connection
with subsistence and recreational activities, and picking up
litter.   They claim that these activities, together with their
placement of the cornerposts, constituted actual possession
of the southerly portion of the parcel.   Nome 2000 argues
that this activity did not constitute actual possession and, at

---

5.   "Color of title exists only by virtue of a written instrument which
purports to pass title to the claimant, but which is ineffective because of a
defect in the means of conveyance or because the grantor did not actually
own the land he sought to convey." Hubbard, 684 P.2d at 847. As noted
above...the Fagerstroms do not claim the disputed parcel by virtue of a
written instrument. [Authors' Note: See also pgs. 207-209 of casebook].

most, entitled the Fagerstroms to an easement by prescription across the southerly portion of the disputed parcel.

Nome 2000 is correct. The Fagerstroms' use of the trails and picking up of litter, although perhaps indicative of adverse use, would not provide the reasonably diligent owner with visible evidence of another's exercise of dominion and control. To this, the cornerposts add virtually nothing. Two of the four posts are located well to the west of the disputed parcel. Of the two that were allegedly placed on the parcel in 1970, the one located on the southerly portion of the parcel disappeared at an unknown time. The Fagerstroms maintain that because the disappearing stake was securely in place in 1970, we should infer that it remained for a "significant period." Even if we draw this inference, we fail to see how two posts on a rectangular parcel of property can, as the Fagerstroms put it, constitute "[t]he objective act of taking physical possession" of the parcel. The two posts simply do not serve to mark off the boundaries of the disputed parcel and, therefore, do not evince an exercise of dominion and control over the entire parcel. Thus, we conclude that the superior court erred in its denial of Nome 2000's motion for a directed verdict as to the southerly portion. This case is remanded to the trial court, with instructions to determine the extent of the Fagerstroms' acquisition in a manner consistent with this opinion....

§4.3 HOSTILITY AND OTHER CONFUSIONS

Add on Page 212 Immediately Following First Paragraph:

CARPENTER v. RUPERTO
Supreme Court of Iowa (1982)
315 N.W.2d 782

McCORMICK, JUSTICE.

Plaintiff Virginia Carpenter appeals from an adverse decree in her action to quiet title to land adjacent to her residential premises based on a theory of adverse possession... We affirm on the merits of the appeal and dismiss the cross-appeal for want of jurisdiction...

Plaintiff and her husband moved in 1951 to a home which they purchased in southeast Des Moines. Plaintiff's husband subsequently died, but plaintiff has lived on the premises continuously. Her lot has a frontage of 40 feet and is 125 feet long.   It is legally described as:

> Lot One Hundred Forty-Four (144) in Gray's
> Subdivision of Lots Fifty (50) and Sixty-Two (62)
> in BROOKS AND COMPANY, an Addition, now
> included in and forming a part of the City of Des
> Moines, Iowa.

A larger undeveloped lot bounded plaintiff's property to the
north.   It is described as:

> The East 125 Feet of the North 474 Feet of Lot
> Sixty-Two (62) in BROOKS AND COMPANY'S
> ADDITION TO THE CITY OF DES MOINES, now
> included in and forming a part of the City of Des
> Moines, Iowa.

Defendants and their predecessors have held record title
to this lot at all material times.

The property which plaintiff claims to have acquired by
adverse possession is the south 60 feet of defendants' lot.
Thus, the property in dispute is a 60 by 125 foot parcel
adjacent to the north boundary of plaintiff's lot.

When plaintiff and her husband moved into their home in
July 1951, the lot north of their property was a cornfield.
Although plaintiff was not certain of the location of the
northern boundary of her lot, she knew her lot's dimensions,
and she knew it did not include the cornfield.   In 1952 the
corn was not planted as far south on the adjacent lot.
Concerned about rats and the threat of fire, and desiring
additional yard for their children, plaintiff and her husband
cleared several feet of the property to the north, graded it,
and planted grass seed on it.   Since that time plaintiff has
used the land as an extension of her yard.   She planted
peony bushes on it during the 1950's, installed a propane
tank on it approximately 30 feet north of her lot in 1964,
constructed a dirt bank on the city right of way to divert
water from that parcel in 1965, and put in a driveway
infringing five feet onto the land in 1975.

The remainder of defendants' lot was planted in corn until
approximately 1957.   The lot was owned by Abraham and
Beverly Rosenfeld from July 1960 until February 1978.
During that period the only use Rosenfelds made of the
property was to store junk and debris on it.   Except for the
strip used by plaintiff, the lot was overgrown with brush

and weeds. The Rosenfelds paid all taxes and special assessments on the property. Plaintiff and her husband at one time obtained the Rosenfelds' permission to keep a horse on the lot. On one occasion in the 1960's plaintiff examined the plat of defendants' lot in the courthouse to see if it ran all the way to a street to the north. When defendant McCormick purchased his interest in the lot in 1978, he was aware of the possibility of a boundary dispute because of the location of plaintiff's propane tank and driveway. He and the other defendants were unsuccessful in their efforts to settle the dispute with plaintiff, who subsequently brought this action.

In seeking to establish her ownership of the disputed parcel, plaintiff alleged she had "for more than thirty (30) years last past been in open, exclusive, hostile, adverse and actual possession under claim of right." The trial court held in part that she did not establish her possession was under a claim of right. The court reasoned that a claim of right must be made in good faith and that plaintiff was not in good faith because she knew someone else had title to the land. Although the court found plaintiff had not proved her claim of adverse possession, it ordered defendants to "do equity" by deeding to her the strip of land her driveway was on and to pay the costs of moving the propane tank to her lot. The appeal and cross-appeal followed...

The doctrine of adverse possession is based on the ten-year statute of limitations for recovery of real property in section 614.1(5), The Code. One claiming title by adverse possession must establish hostile, actual, open, exclusive and continuous possession, under a claim of right or color of title, for at least ten years, by clear and positive proof. Because the law presumes possession under regular title, the doctrine is strictly construed. These and other governing principles are explained in I-80 Associates, Inc. v. Chicago, Rock Island and Pacific Railroad, 224 N.W.2d 8, 10-11 (Iowa 1974).

As permitted, plaintiff relied on claim of right rather than color of title. In contending the trial court erred in finding she failed in her proof of this element, she attacks the viability of the principal case relied on by the trial court, Goulding v. Shonquist, 159 Iowa 647, 141 N.W. 24 (1913). Its facts are analogous to those here.

In *Goulding* the individual also cleared land adjacent to his house. The land was overrun with brush and willows

and was frequented by hunters.   After clearing it, the
individual used the land as a pasture and garden.   In
finding he did not establish good faith claim of right, the
court said:

> When he moved into his present property, the
> lands in question were objectionable because they
> were frequented by hunters, and for that reason
> he and his wife thought they ought to clear them
> up.   He says he supposed they were part of the
> old river bed or waste land upon which anyone
> could enter.   No other facts are offered by
> defendant as a reason for entering into the
> possession of the land at that time.   Whether the
> title to the land was in the state or some other
> person, the defendant knew that he had no title
> and that he had no claim of title, and no right
> whatever to enter into the possession, and his
> possession was not in good faith for that reason.

Id. at 651, 141 N.W. at 25.   The court quoted a statement
from Litchfield v.   Sewell, 97 Iowa 247, 251, 66 N.W. 104,
106 (1896), that "that there can be no such thing as adverse
possession where the party knows he has no title, and that,
under the law, he can acquire none by his occupation."

Plaintiff argues that it is inconsistent to say ownership
can be acquired by claim of right as an alternative to color
of title and at the same time say ownership cannot be
acquired by a person who knows he does not have title.
She also argues that the good faith requirement was
eliminated by the court's decision in I-80 Associates, Inc.
Although we agree it is an overstatement to say ownership
cannot be acquired by a person who knows he does not have
title, plaintiff is incorrect in her argument that good faith
is not an essential component of claim of right.   Moreover,
we agree with the trial court that plaintiff did not prove this
element of her adverse possession claim.

The overbreadth of the statement that title cannot be
obtained through adverse possession by one who knows he
has no title is demonstrated in Litchfield, Goulding and
subsequent decisions.   In Litchfield the court rejected the
adverse possession claim of a person in possession of land
under a quitclaim deed from a squatter.   In finding an
absence of good faith, the court noted the adverse
possession doctrine "has no application to one who actually
knows that he has no claim, or title, or right to a title." 97

Iowa at 250, 66 N.W. at 106. Under this holding a mere squatter or one who claims under a squatter cannot have a good faith claim of right to the property, but mere knowledge by the person that he has no title is not preclusive. A claim of right by a squatter is a false claim. To permit a squatter to assert a claim of right would put a premium on dishonesty. *See* 4 H. Tiffany, *Real Property* § 1147 at 792 (3d ed. 1975). One of the main purposes of the claim of right requirement is "to bar mere squatters from the benefits of adverse possession." 7 R. Powell, *Real Property* ¶ 1015 (Rohan ed. 1981). As in *Litchfield*, the possessor in Goulding not only knew that he had no title but that he had no claim of title or any right to enter into possession of the property. He was a mere squatter.

Knowledge of a defect in title is not alone sufficient to preclude proof of good faith:

> One is not deprived of the benefit of the statute of limitations merely because his claim of right is unenforceable or his title is known to be defective. The doctrine of adverse possession presupposes a defective title. It is not based on, but is hostile to, the true title. If the statute were to run only in favor of a valid title, it would serve no purpose. The holder of such a title has no need to invoke the statute. Where bad faith is held to negative an alleged claim of right, it is only another way of saying that such claim has been disproved.

Creel v. Hammans, 234 Iowa 532, 535, 13 N.W.2d 305, 307 (1944).

Nevertheless, when knowledge of lack of title is accompanied by knowledge of no basis for claiming an interest in the property, a good faith claim of right cannot be established. For example, a mere exchange of quitclaim deeds by persons who know legal title is in another will not support a claim of right:

> It is evident the claim and possession of George C. Abel could not have been in good faith. There was no reason why he and his brother should believe they had any right to divide and apportion between themselves the real estate of their father while he was an insane patient in the state hospital. They must be held to have known

the quitclaim deeds they exchanged gave them no
title. At best, they proceeded upon what proved
to be an unfounded assumption that their father
would never be discharged from the adjudication
of insanity. No claim of ownership by adverse
possession will be sustained upon such a
foundation. Plaintiff's position at this point does
not appeal to a court of equity.

Abel v. Abel, 245 Iowa 907, 920, 65 N.W.2d 68, 75 (1954).

The good faith requirement was not an issue in *I-80
Associates, Inc.* The discussion of claim of right in that
case concerned mode of proof and did not include a
comprehensive definition of the element. The requirement of
good faith was implicitly reaffirmed in a subsequent case,
Pearson v. City of Guttenberg, 245 N.W.2d 519, 532 (Iowa
1976). We now confirm that good faith, as explained in this
case, is essential to adverse possession under a claim of
right.

We believe plaintiff failed to prove a good faith claim of
right in the present case. She knew her lot did not include
the cornfield north of it. She knew someone else had title
to it and she had no interest in it or claim to it. This is
not a case of confusion or mistake. At the time she entered
possession of the disputed land, plaintiff knew she had no
legal right to do so. To say that one can acquire a claim
of right by merely entering possession would recognize
squatter's rights. Possession for the statutory period cannot
be bootstrapped into a basis for claiming a right to
possession.

We hold that the trial court was right in rejecting
plaintiff's claim...

Affirmed on the appeal; dismissed on the cross-appeal.

NOTES AND QUESTIONS

1. Under what circumstances could a possessor in a
mistaken boundary line case establish a "good faith" claim?

2. Does the holding in *Carpenter* place Iowa in the Maine
or the Connecticut camp?

3. Does the holding of *Carpenter* apply as well to non-
mistaken boundary line cases? If so, how could the possessor

in such case establish "good faith"?

§4.4 ADVERSE POSSESSION OF CHATTELS

Add as New Case following Problem 4 on Page 226:

SOLOMON R. GUGGENHEIM FOUNDATION v. LUBELL
Court of Appeals of New York (1991)
1991 WL 17119

WACHTLER, JUDGE.

The backdrop for this replevin action (see, CPLR art. 71) is the New York City art market, where masterpieces command extraordinary prices at auction and illicit dealing in stolen merchandise is an industry all its own. The Solomon R. Guggenheim Foundation, which operates the Guggenheim Museum in New York City, is seeking to recover a Chagall gouache worth an estimated $200,000. The Guggenheim believes that the gouache was stolen from its premises by a mailroom employee sometime in the late 1960s. The appellant Rachel Lubell and her husband, now deceased, bought the painting from a well-known Madison Avenue gallery in 1967 and have displayed it in their home for more than 20 years. Mrs. Lubell claims that before the Guggenheim's demand for its return in 1986, she had no reason to believe that the painting had been stolen.

On this appeal, we must decide if the museum's failure to take certain steps to locate the gouache is relevant to the appellant's statute of limitations defense. In effect, the appellant argues that the museum had a duty to use reasonable diligence to recover the gouache, that it did not do so, and that its cause of action in replevin is consequently barred by the statute of limitations. The Appellate Division rejected the appellant's argument. We agree with the Appellate Division that the timing of the museum's demand for the gouache and the appellant's refusal to return it are the only relevant factors in assessing the merits of the statute of limitations defense. We see no justification for undermining the clarity and predictability of this rule by carving out an exception where the chattel to be returned is a valuable piece of art. Appellant's affirmative defense of laches remains viable, however, and her claims that the museum did not undertake a reasonably diligent search for the missing painting will enter into the trial court's evaluation of the merits of that defense. Accordingly, the order of the Appellate Division should be

affirmed.   The gouache, known alternately as "Menageries"
or "Le Marchand de Bestiaux" ("The Cattle Dealer"), was
painted by Marc Chagall in 1912, in preparation for an oil
painting also entitled "Le Marchand de Bestiaux." It was
donated to the museum in 1937 by Solomon R. Guggenheim.

The museum keeps track of its collection through the use
of "accession cards," which indicate when individual pieces
leave the museum on loan, when they are returned and when
they are transferred between the museum and storage.   The
museum lent the painting to a number of other art museums
over the years.   The last such loan occurred in 1961-62.
The accession card for the painting indicates that it was
seen in the museum on April 2, 1965.   The next notation on
the accession card is undated and indicates that the painting
could not be located.

Precisely when the museum first learned that the gouache
had been stolen is a matter of some dispute.   The museum
acknowledges that it discovered that the painting was not
where it should be sometime in the late 1960s, but claims
that it did not know that the painting had in fact been
stolen until it undertook a complete inventory of the museum
collection beginning in 1969 and ending in 1970.   According
to the museum, such an inventory was typically taken about
once every ten years.   The appellant, on the other hand,
argues that the museum knew as early as 1965 that the
painting had been stolen.   It is undisputed, however, that
the Guggenheim did not inform other museums, galleries or
artistic organizations of the theft, and additionally, did not
notify the New York City Police, the FBI, Interpol or any
other law enforcement authorities. The museum asserts that
this was a tactical decision based upon its belief that to
publicize the theft would succeed only in driving the gouache
further underground and greatly diminishing the possibility
that it would ever be recovered.   In 1974, having concluded
that all efforts to recover the gouache had been exhausted,
the museum's Board of Trustees voted to "deaccession" the
gouache, thereby removing it from the museum's records.

Mr. and Mrs. Lubell had purchased the painting from the
Robert Elkon Gallery for $17,000 in May of 1967.   The
invoice and receipt indicated that the gouache had been in
the collection of a named individual, who later turned out
to be the museum mailroom employee suspected of the theft.
They exhibited the painting twice, in 1967 and in 1981, both
times at the Elkon Gallery.   In 1985, a private art dealer
brought a transparency of the painting to Sotheby's for an

auction estimate. The person to whom the dealer showed the transparency had previously worked at the Guggenheim and recognized the gouache as a piece that was missing from the museum. She notified the museum, which traced the painting back to the defendant. On January 9, 1986, Thomas Messer, the museum's director, wrote a letter to the defendant demanding the return of the gouache. Mrs. Lubell refused to return the painting and the instant action for recovery of the painting, or, in the alternative, $200,000, was commenced on September 28, 1987. In her answer, the appellant raised as affirmative defenses the statute of limitations, her status as a good faith purchaser for value, adverse possession, laches, and the museum's culpable conduct. The museum moved to compel discovery and inspection of the gouache and the defendant cross-moved for summary judgment. In her summary judgment papers, the appellant argued that the replevin action to compel the return of the painting was barred by the three year statute of limitations because the museum had done nothing to locate its property in the twenty year interval between the theft and the museum's fortuitous discovery that the painting was in Mrs. Lubell's possession. The trial court granted the appellant's cross motion for summary judgment, relying on DeWeerth v. Baldinger (836 F.2d 103), an opinion from the United States Court of Appeals for the Second Circuit. The trial court cited New York cases holding that a cause of action in replevin accrues when demand is made upon the possessor and the possessor refuses to return the chattel. The court reasoned, however, that in order to avoid prejudice to a good faith purchaser, demand cannot be unreasonably delayed and that a property owner has an obligation to use reasonable efforts to locate its missing property to ensure that demand is not so delayed. Because the museum in this case had done nothing for twenty years but search its own premises, the court found that its conduct was unreasonable as a matter of law. Consequently, the court granted Mrs. Lubell's cross motion for summary judgment on the grounds that the museum's cause of action was time-barred.

The Appellate Division modified, dismissing the statute of limitations defense and denying the appellant's cross motion for summary judgment. The Appellate Division held that the trial court had erred in concluding that "delay alone can make a replevin action untimely" (153 A.D.2d 143, 149). The court stated that the appellant's lack of diligence argument was more in the nature of laches than the statute of limitations and that as a result, the appellant needed to show that she had been prejudiced by the museum's delay in demanding return of the gouache (Id.) The court also held that summary judgment was inappropriate because several issues of fact existed, including whether the museum's response to the theft was unreasonable, when the museum first realized that the gouache was missing, when the museum should have realized that the gouache had been stolen, whether it was unreasonable for the museum not to have taken certain steps after it realized that the gouache was missing but before it realized that it had been stolen, and when the museum learned of the defendant's possession of the gouache (id., at 151-52).   The Appellate Division granted leave to this court, certifying the following question: "Was the Order of this Court, which modified the Order of the Supreme Court, properly made?" We answer this certified question in the affirmative.   New York case law has long protected the right of the owner whose property has been stolen to recover that property, even if it is in the possession of a good faith purchaser for value (see, Saltus v. Everett, 20 Wend. [NY] 267, 282).   There is a three year statute of limitations for recovery of a chattel (CPLR § 214[3]).   The rule in this state is that a cause of action for replevin against the good faith purchaser of a stolen chattel accrues when the true owner makes demand for return of the chattel and the person in possession of the chattel refuses to return it... Until demand is made and refused, possession of the stolen property by the good faith purchaser for value is not considered wrongful... Although seemingly anomalous, a different rule applies when the stolen object is in the possession of the thief.   In that situation, the statute of limitations runs from the time of the theft... even if the property owner was unaware of the theft at the time that it occurred...

In DeWeerth v. Baldinger [(836 F.2d 103 (198_)] which the trial court in this case relied upon in granting Mrs. Lubell's summary judgment motion, the Second Circuit took note of the fact that New York case law treats thieves and good faith purchasers differently and looked to that difference as a basis for imposing a reasonable diligence requirement on the owners of stolen art.   Although the court acknowledged that the question posed by the case was an open one, it declined to certify it to this Court (see, 22 NYCRR § 500.17), stating that it did not think that it "[would] recur with sufficient frequency to warrant use of the certification procedure" (836 F.2d at 108).   Actually, the issue has recurred several times in the three years since DeWeerth was decided (see, e.g., The Republic of Turkey v The Metropolitan Museum of Art, No. 87 Civ. 3750 [VLB], slip op. [SDNY July 16, 1990]), including the case now before us. We have reexamined the relevant New York case law and we conclude that the Second Circuit should not have imposed a duty of reasonable diligence on the owners of stolen art work for purposes of the statute of limitations.

While the demand and refusal rule is not the only possible method of measuring the accrual of replevin claims, it does appear to be the rule that affords the most protection to the true owners of stolen property. Less protective measures would include running the three year statutory period from the time of the theft even where a good faith purchaser is in possession of the stolen chattel, or, alternatively, calculating the statutory period from the time that the good faith purchaser obtains possession of the chattel (see generally, Weil, Repose, 8 IFAR reports, at 6-7 [August-September 1987]). Other states that have considered this issue have applied a discovery rule to these cases, with the statute of limitations running from the time that the owner discovered or reasonably should have discovered the whereabouts of the work of art that had been stolen (see, e.g., O'Keefe v. Snyder, 83 NJ 478, 416 A.2d 862; Cal.Civ.Proc.Code § 338[c]).

New York has already considered--and rejected--adoption of a discovery rule. In 1986, both houses of the New York State Legislature passed Assembly Bill 11462-A (Senate Bill 3274-B), which would have modified the demand and refusal rule and instituted a discovery rule in actions for recovery of art objects brought against certain not-for-profit institutions. This bill provided that the three year statute of limitations would run from the time these institutions gave notice, in a manner specified by the statute, that they were in possession of a particular object. Governor Cuomo vetoed the measure, however, on advice of the United States Department of State, the United States Department of Justice and the United States Information Agency (see, 3 U.S. Agencies Urge Veto of Art-Claim Bill, N.Y. Times, July 23, 1986, C15, col. 1). In his veto message, the Governor expressed his concern that the statute "[did] not provide a reasonable opportunity for individuals or foreign governments to receive notice of a museum's acquisition and take action to recover it before their rights are extinguished." The Governor also stated that he had been advised by the State Department that the bill, if it went into effect, would have caused New York to become "a haven for cultural property stolen abroad since such objects [would] be immune from recovery under the limited time periods established by the bill."

The history of this bill and the concerns expressed by the Governor in vetoing it, when considered together with the abundant case law spelling out the demand and refusal rule, convince us that that rule remains the law in New York and that there is no reason to obscure its straightforward protection of true owners by creating a duty of reasonable diligence. Our case law already recognizes that the true owner, having discovered the location of its lost property, cannot unreasonably delay making demand upon the person in possession of that property... Here, however, where the demand and refusal is a substantive and not a procedural element of the cause of action (see, Solomon R. Guggenheim Foundation v Lubell, 153 A.D.2d, at 147; Menzel v. List, 22 A.D.2d 647; compare, CPLR § 206 [where a demand is necessary to entitle a person to commence an action, the time to commence that action is measured from when the right to make demand is complete]), it would not be prudent to extend that case law and impose the additional duty of diligence before the true owner has reason to know where its missing chattel is to be found.

Further, the facts of this case reveal how difficult it would be to specify the type of conduct that would be required for a showing of reasonable diligence. Here, the parties hotly contest whether publicizing the theft would have turned up the gouache. According to the museum, some members of the art community believe that publicizing a theft exposes gaps in security and can lead to more thefts; the museum also argues that publicity often pushes a missing painting further underground. In light of the fact that members of the art community have apparently not reached a consensus on the best way to retrieve stolen art (see, B. Burnham, Art Theft: Its Scope, Its Impact and Its Control), it would be particularly inappropriate for this Court to spell out arbitrary rules of conduct that all true owners of stolen art work would have to follow to the letter if they wanted to preserve their right to pursue a cause of action in replevin. All owners of stolen property should not be expected to behave in the same way and should not be held to a common standard. The value of the property stolen, the manner in which it was stolen, and the type of institution from which it was stolen will all necessarily affect the manner in which a true owner will search for missing property. We conclude that it would be difficult, if not impossible, to craft a reasonable diligence requirement that could take into account all of these variables and that would not unduly burden the true owner.

Further, our decision today is in part influenced by our recognition that New York enjoys a worldwide reputation as a preeminent cultural center. To place the burden of locating stolen artwork on the true owner and to foreclose the rights of that owner to recover its property if the burden is not met would, we believe, encourage illicit trafficking in stolen art. Three years after the theft, any purchaser, good faith or not, would be able to hold onto stolen art work unless the true owner was able to establish that it had undertaken a reasonable search for the missing art. This shifting of the burden onto the wronged owner is inappropriate. In our opinion, the better rule gives the owner relatively greater protection and places the burden of investigating the provenance of a work of art on the potential purchaser.

Despite our conclusion that the imposition of a reasonable diligence requirement on the museum would be inappropriate for purposes of the statute of limitations, our holding today should not be seen as either sanctioning the museum's conduct or suggesting that the museum's conduct is no longer an issue in this case. We agree with the Appellate Division that the arguments raised in the appellant's summary judgment papers are directed at the conscience of the court and its ability to bring equitable considerations to bear in the ultimate disposition of the painting. As noted above, although appellant's statute of limitations argument fails, her contention that the museum did not exercise reasonable diligence in locating the painting will be considered by the trial judge in the context of her laches defense. The conduct of both the appellant and the museum will be relevant to any consideration of this defense at the trial level, and as the Appellate Division noted, prejudice will also need to be shown (153 A.D.2d at 149). On the limited record before us there is no indication that the equities favor either party. Mr. & Mrs. Lubell investigated the provenance of the gouache before the purchase by contacting the artist and his son-in-law directly. The Lubells displayed the painting in their home for more than 20 years with no reason to suspect that it was not legally theirs. These facts will doubtless have some impact on the final decision regarding appellant's laches defense. Because it is impossible to conclude from the facts of this case that the museum's conduct was unreasonable as a matter of law, however, Mrs. Lubell's cross motion for summary judgment was properly denied.

We agree with the Appellate Division, for the reasons stated by that court, that the burden of proving that the painting was not stolen properly rests with the appellant Mrs. Lubell. We have considered her remaining arguments, and we find them to be without merit. Accordingly, the order of the Appellate Division should be affirmed, with costs, and the certified question answered in the affirmative.

JUDGES SIMONS, KAYE, ALEXANDER, TITONE, HANCOCK AND BELLACOSA, concur.

NOTES AND QUESTIONS

1. Analyzed from the perspective of the requirements of adverse possession, would the display of the painting on the walls in the home of the Lubells be sufficiently open? See DeWeerth v. Baldinger, 658 F.Supp. 1987 (1987), rev'd, 836 F.2d 103 (2d Cir. 1987)

Add as Problem 1 in §4.5 on Page 226:

Although a person cannot acquire title by adverse possession against the government, is the government required to compensate a landowner for improvements made on the property if the improvements were made under the good faith belief that the party owned the real property? United States v. Hato Rey Building Co., Inc., 660 F.Supp. 1340 (D.Puerto Rico 1987).

Chapter 5

ESTATES IN LAND AND FUTURE INTERESTS

§5.2 THE FEE SIMPLE ABSOLUTE

Add As Note 1a Immediately Following Note 1 on Page 250:

In *White*, the statute provided that a devise passes the devisor's entire interest in the property "unless the intent to pass a less estate or interest shall appear by express terms, or be necessarily implied in the terms of the instrument." Furthermore, the court noted that in construing wills doubts about the meaning of language that might create a limitation should be resolved in favor of finding an absolute estate. How is the statutory language and the principal of will construction implicated in White v. Brown.

Add Following Note 7 on Page 254:

Courts have generally assumed there is no constitutional right to inherit property. For example, consider the following statement by the Iowa Supreme Court:

The right to take property by devise or descent is a statutory privilege, and not a natural right. Such matters are strictly within legislative control...Neither our state nor our Federal Constitution secures the right to anyone to control or dispose of his property after his death, nor the right to anyone, whether of kin or not, to take it by inheritance...The legislature may restrict the succession of estates or decedents in any manner, and, if it pleased, could absolutely repeal the statute of wills and of descent and distribution. It could, in the exercise of its sovereignty, take any or all property, upon the death of the owner, for the payment of decedent's debts, and apply the residue to public uses." In re Estate of Emerson, 191 Iowa 900, 905, 183 N.W. 327, 329 (1921).

Compare the preceding view with that of the United States Supreme Court in Hodel v. Irving, 481 U.S. 704, 705 (1987), holding that a federal statute preventing an American Indian from disposing of property by will was unconstitutional:

...Appellees here do not assert that their own property rights have been taken unconstitutionally, but rather that their decedents' right to pass the property at death has been taken. Nevertheless, we have no difficulty in finding the concerns of the prudential standing doctrine met here.

For obvious reasons, it has long been recognized that the surviving claims of a decedent must be pursued by a third party. At common law, a decedent's surviving claims were prosecuted by the executor or administrator of the estate. For Indians with trust property, statutes require the Secretary of the Interior to assume that general role. 25 U.S.C. §§ 371-380. The Secretary's responsibilities in that capacity, however, include the administration of the statute that the appellees claim is unconstitutional, see 25 U.S.C. §§ 2202, 2209, so that he can hardly be expected to assert appellees' decedents' rights to the extent that they turn on that point. Under these circumstances, appellees can appropriately serve as their decedents' representatives for purposes of asserting the latters' Fifth Amendment rights. They are situated to pursue the claims vigorously, since their interest in receiving the property is indissolubly linked to the decedents' right to dispose of it by will or intestacy. A vindication of decedents' rights would ensure that the fractional interests pass to appellees; pressing these rights unsuccessfully would equally guarantee that appellees take nothing. In short, permitting appellees to raise their decedents' claims is merely an extension of the common law's provision for appointment of a decedent's representative. It is therefore a 'settled practice of the courts' not open to objection on the ground that it permits a litigant to raise third parties' rights...

§5.6 THE CLASSIFICATION OF FUTURE INTERESTS IN TRANSFEREES

Add as New Principal Case on Page 303 Immediately Before § 5.7:

ROWETT v. McFARLAND
Supreme Court of South Dakota (1986)
394 N.W.2d 298

HERTZ, ACTING JUSTICE

Rowetts appeal from the trial court's entry of summary judgment in favor of appellees McFarland, et al. We reverse and remand.

Facts

This appeal concerns the determination of the consistently troubling question of whether a remainder is vested or contingent. In assessing case authority from foreign jurisdictions, the only conclusion which may be safely entertained is that the opinions are in conflict.

The focal point of this action is approximately 3,000 acres of real property located in Meade County, South Dakota. The conflict arises from its disputed ownership. Ewell Hanks (Hanks), owned this land and referred to it as the "home place." Hanks died on April 25, 1936. By paragraph six of his Last Will and Testament dated December 17, 1935, Hanks gave his wife, Lena Hanks, a life estate in the "home place" for her lifetime, or until she should remarry, and without power of sale. Hanks disposed of the remainder of this property by paragraph seven of the will, which sets forth the following:

> SEVENTH: That upon the death of my said wife, without issue, or if she should re-marry, at the time of her re-marriage, all of the said land herein referred to as "approximately 3000 acres belonging to my home place" shall revert to my estate and shall be divided equally between my son, Harvey Hanks, and my daughter, Frances Rowett, or their heirs. (emphasis added)

A Decree of Distribution for the Ewell Hanks estate was entered by the Meade County Court on November 27, 1937. This decree restates the will in its entirety, and thus reaffirms the life estate in Lena Hanks. It also adopts paragraph seven stated above, however, the last phrase reads, "or to their heirs", rather than "or their heirs", as was written in the will.[1] (emphasis added).

Lena Hanks had no children by Ewell Hanks and she never remarried. She died on November 3, 1983.

At the time of his death, Hanks left two surviving

---

1. We consider this inconsistency immaterial to the disposition of this case. We note, however, that a final decree of distribution controls the will even if it is erroneous, so long as the decree was rendered with due process. Miller v. Thode, 372 N.W.2d 459, 462 (S.D.1985).

children: Harvey Hanks (Harvey) and Frances Rowett (Frances). Harvey died on April 13, 1942. The Decree of Distribution entered in connection with his estate distributed Harvey's one-half remainder interest in the "home place" to Solomon Wartti and to attorney H.F. Fellows (Fellows), an assignee of Wartti.

Frances and her husband Raymond (Ray) Rowett conveyed her remainder interest in the "home place" to George McFarland by warranty deed dated December 28, 1953, for the sum of $8,000. Frances died intestate on October 27, 1975, and left the following heirs: her husband Ray, and her children, appellants Sidney W. Rowett, Elsie E. Rowett Kosnoski and Ethel L. Posch (Rowetts). Frances' estate was not probated.

Ray died intestate February 10, 1980, and left as his heirs the three appellants, and four other children from a previous marriage. These four children were brought into the action as third party defendants after their existence was discovered during the taking of the Rowetts depositions. Ray's estate was not probated.

Through a series of conveyances, Fellows and another attorney, Percy H. Helm (Helm), owned as assignees Harvey's undivided one-half remainder interest in the "home place" which they sold to George McFarland by contract dated December 23, 1953. After abstracts of title showed the title to be free, clear, and merchantable, Fellows, Helm, and their respective spouses conveyed their interest in the "home place" by warranty deed to George McFarland on January 3, 1955.

George McFarland conveyed his interest in the "home place" to appellee David A. McFarland on October 4, 1976. Lena Hanks and her son, Lloyd Marcotte, a lessee of the "home place", quit claimed their interest in the "home place" to appellees Gregor B. McFarland... and David A. McFarland on October 29, 1976. David A. McFarland and his wife, Delores,2 sold and conveyed their interest in the subject property to the appellees Snyder 2 on July 9, 1982.

On September 25, 1983, Snyder received a letter from one of the Rowetts which indicated a possible claim of ownership in the "home place", which Snyder had purchased some fourteen months earlier. This litigation followed.

Initially, Rowetts prayed for a judgment quieting title to

their undivided one-half interest in the "home place." McFarlands denied the validity of Rowetts claim and requested the quieting of title to the one-half interest in themselves. Certain additional parties were joined who are not material to this discussion. Both sides moved for summary judgment.

In granting McFarlands motion for summary judgment, the trial court determined that paragraph seven of Hanks' will was ambiguous. As such, it recognized the presumption of vesting unless clearly designated otherwise, and held that paragraph seven vested the remainder interest in the "home place" to Harvey Hanks and Frances Rowett as of the death of Ewell Hanks. Rowetts appeal to this court.

Claims of the Parties

Rowetts claim ownership of an undivided one-half interest in the "home place" by virtue of paragraph seven in Hanks' will. They contend that this provision unambiguously created a life estate in Lena Hanks, upon whose death, a contingent remainder passed to their mother, Frances Rowett, or if she failed to survive the life tenant, then to her heirs who take the share their mother would have taken if living. (emphasis added). Rowetts contend that Frances' interest, at most, was vested subject to divestment, in the event she predeceased Lena Hanks. Therefore, Rowetts claim that their mother, as well as Harvey Hanks, conveyed nothing to the McFarlands because the remaindermen had no vested interest in the "home place."

McFarlands argue that paragraph seven's use of the phrase "or their heirs" was ambiguous because Hanks failed to use any specific words of survivorship or a time reference, to provide for the event of the remaindermen predeceasing the life tenant. They claim that the ambiguity, coupled with the presumption of vesting, created an indefeasibly vested remainder in Harvey Hanks and Frances Rowett upon the death of Ewell Hanks. As such, McFarlands contend that the respective deeds from Lena Hanks, Frances (and Ray) Rowett, and the assignees of Harvey Hanks, resulted in a complete fee title to the McFarlands, and ultimately, the Snyders, despite the fact that Harvey and Frances predeceased Lena Hanks....

Were Frances and Harvey's[2] interests vested remainders as claimed by the McFarlands, or were they contingent remainders, or at most, vested subject to divestment as claimed by the Rowetts? The resolution of this question turns on the application of the following guiding principles.

The process of will construction has as its sole purpose the discovery of the testator's intent.... For it is the testator's intention which is used as a polestar to guide in the interpretation of all wills, and, when ascertained, effect will be given to it unless it violates some rule of law, or is contrary to public policy. Tiffany v. Thomas, 190 S.E. 101, 103 (Va. 1937). "In ascertaining this intention the language used, and the sense in which it is used by the testator, is the primary source of information, as it is the expressed intention of the testator which is sought." Id. If that intention is clearly manifested by the language of the will, it is the duty of this court to declare and enforce it...

In construing a will, it is an elementary rule that effect must be given to every word of the will, rather than an interpretation which will render any of its expressions inoperative.... Generally, ordinary words are given their usual and ordinary meaning, and technical words are presumed to be used in a technical sense, unless the context clearly indicates otherwise... "Words are not to be changed or rejected unless they manifestly conflict with the plain intention of the testator, or unless they are absurd, unintelligible or unmeaning for want of any subject to which they can be applied." Tiffany, 190 S.E. at 103.

In Taylor v. Taylor, 118 Iowa 407, 92 N.W. 71 (1902), the Supreme Court of Iowa was faced with a similar factual situation, (discussed more fully, infra), and wrote:

> Courts of justice will transpose the clauses of a will and construe 'or' to be 'and' and 'and' to be 'or' only in such cases when it is absolutely necessary so to do to support the evident meaning of the testator. But they cannot arbitrarily expunge or alter words without such apparent necessity.

Id. at 72. Henkel v. Auchstetter, 240 Iowa 1367, 39 N.W.2d

---

2. No party to this proceeding is making claim to the one-half interest of Harvey Hanks.

650, 654 (1949).

The law favors the early vesting of devised estates and it presumes that words of survivorship relate to the death of the testator, if fairly capable of such construction; and that no estate will be held contingent unless positive terms are employed in the will indicating the testator's intent to annex futurity to the substance of the devise... But this rule, like other rules of construction applicable to wills, is intended for use in doubtful cases when the language used is unclear and must give way to any lawful intention of the testator which may be gathered from the four corners of the will... Thus, the rule favoring early vesting must yield to the principle that the testator's intention as expressed in the will must prevail, if it can be ascertained with reasonable certainty....

In order for this court to hold that Frances Rowett took an absolute vested remainder, it necessarily follows that we interpret "or," appearing in paragraph seven of Hanks' will, to mean "and." McFarlands claim that the phrase "or their heirs" is ambiguous because Hanks failed to use any specific words of survivorship or a time reference. Rowetts claim that the word "or" should be read in its usual disjunctive sense as indicating substitution.

In Ebey v. Adams, 135 Ill. 80, 25 N.E. 1013 (1890), the testator, by clause two of his will, gave his entire estate which consisted of both real and personal property, to his widow for life or until her remarriage. Clause three stated that upon the widow's death or remarriage, the property should be sold by the testator's executors, from which proceeds they should pay $1,000 each to two of his grandchildren, and then distribute the residue among the testator's six children "or their heirs." Id. at 1014. One of testator's children, a daughter, conveyed her interest in the land, and then died before the termination of the life estate. The court held that the daughter's heirs, and not her grantees, took her share of the estate because the devise over did not vest until the death of testator's widow. Id. at 1016. The court stated:

> The words "heir," or "their heirs," are technically words of limitation; but in this and other cases they are used as words of purchase, and always have that operation when it sufficiently appears that the term is used to designate a particular person, or particular

persons, who may stand in that relation at the
happening of a certain event, or at a certain
period, and not to the whole line of heirs in
succession. No one can have heirs while living.
The word "or," therefore, as here used, indicates
substitution; and the payment or distribution is
to be made at a fixed period, i.e., upon the sale
by the executors, after the termination of the
intermediate estate. It would seem clear,
therefore, that the persons who are to take are
such of the children as might be living at the
time of the distribution, and the heirs of such as
might have predeceased. It follows, when this
language is considered in connection with the
context, that there was here created an
alternative devise.

Id.

In Taylor, supra, the testator's will devised all of his
real and personal property to his wife for life, and at her
death or remarriage, the property was to be equally divided
"between [testator's] children or their heirs as the law
directs." 92 N.W. at 71. Inasmuch as the Iowa Code made
technical words unnecessary in creating a fee... the court
stated that to construe "or" as "and" would render the
clause meaningless, as without it, the fee would have passed
to the children anyway. Id. at 72. The court further
stated that there appeared no reason to believe "or" was
intended for "and," nor that it was not designedly employed
to express the testator's real intention. Id. Therefore,
regarding the words "or their heirs" as words of purchase,
the court held that the heirs of a child dying before the life
tenant took under the will, and not by descent, and thus,
the remainder was contingent. Id. at 73.

McFarlands insist that without specific words of
survivorship, Frances' interest must have vested at the time
of Ewell Hanks' death.... However, in Schaeffer's Adm'r v.
Schaeffer's Adm'r, 54 W.Va. 681, 46 S.E. 150 (1903), the
court stated:

... [T]he rule that reads a gift to survivors
simply as applying to objects living at the death
of the testator is confined to those cases in which
there is no other period to which survivorship
can be referred, and that, where such gift is
preceded by a life or other prior interest, it
takes effect in favor of those who survive the

period of distribution, and of those only.
(citation omitted)

Id. at 151.   In this case, a will gave testator's widow a life
estate, with power to sell some realty as well as consume its
proceeds, and then it directed: "At the death of my wife
what real estate and personal property may be left shall be
sold, and divided equally among my children, or their
children, or their representatives." Id. at 150.   The testator
died leaving his widow.   Two of his sons gave deeds of
trust to secure debts on their interest in their father's
estate.   Each son predeceased the widow, and both of them
were survived by children.   Id.   In a contest between the
(deceased) sons' creditors and the sons' children,
respectively, the court stated:

> ... [T]he force of 'or their children' is
> equivalent to 'in case of their death'; that they
> provide those who take in place of the first
> legatee; that they make a condition on which the
> vesting of any estate depends; that they have the
> effect to give only a contingent remainder to
> [testator's] children, preventing any estate in
> them at the testator's death.

Id. at 152.   The court thus held that the deeds of trust
given for the debts of the testator's two sons, both of whom
died before the life tenant, had no effect upon the testator's
property as against the children of such sons.   Id.   at 153.

In Mercer v. Downs, 191 N.C. 203, 131 S.E. 575 (1926),
the testator's will gave a life estate in a 500 acre tract of
land to his wife for her lifetime, "and at her death to go to
our surviving children or their heirs." Id. 131 S.E. at 576.
The court characterized the remainder interests as
contingent, and held that the language of the will created
substitute or alternate remainders which were contingent on
the death of any of testator's children during his wife's
lifetime.   Id. 131 S.E. at 577.   "[T]he remaindermen could
not be ascertained with certainty until the termination of the
life estate." Id. ...

However, in some cases involving a testamentary gift of
an estate to A for life, remainder to B "or his heirs," the
quoted or similar words were treated, under the
circumstances, as merely descriptive of the interest of B, as
words of limitation, as equivalent to "and his heirs," or as
surplusage, so that B had an indefeasibly vested remainder

at the testator's death. See cases cited at 128 A.L.R. at 325-331. There is additional support for the supposition that when a testator manifests no expressed intent to use the word "heirs" as a word of purchase, then it is construed as a word of limitation, and thus, remainder to B "or his heirs" vests in B at the testator's death....[Tunnell v. Berry, 73 N.C.App. 222, 326 S.E.2d 288, 310- 311.]

As was said in Wyman...[Wyman v. Kinney, 111 Vt. 94, 10 A.2d 191 (1940):

> There is also a class of cases, somewhat numerous, where the word "or" is interposed between the name of the first legatee or devisee and the heirs of such person,--as, to A. or his heirs, forever, or in tail,--in regard to which there has been considerable discussion, and where there does not seem to be perfect coincidence. Some of the earlier cases where this occurs incline to treat the variation from the usual form of creating such limitations as merely accidental, and as not being intended to create any different estates. The cases where the word "or" being interposed between the name of the first devisee or legatee and his heirs [has] been held to indicate the intention of substituting the latter in place of the ancestor are numerous, and, being more recent, as a general thing, and more in consonance with the words used, must be regarded as defining the most reliable rule. (citation omitted).

10 A.2d at 194.

Here, nothing in Hanks' will indicates that it was unskillfully drafted which may have otherwise prompted us to construe "or" as "and," with the result that "or their heirs" become words of limitation. On the contrary, paragraph three of the will devised some 320 acres of land to Frances Rowett and provided: "to her and her heirs forever, ..." Similarly, paragraph four gave Hanks' wife certain described personal property by providing: "I give, devise and bequeath unto my wife, Lena Hanks, to her and her heirs, ..." By using the words "and her heirs " in paragraphs three and four, Hanks demonstrated his ability to create an absolute fee limited to the named devisee or legatee.

In paragraph six, Hanks gave his wife a life estate in the "home place" for her lifetime, or until remarriage, and without power of sale. No words of gift were used to indicate the final vesting of the residuary estate until the seventh paragraph of the will. There we find the time fixed when the division was to be made, not upon Hanks death, but after the death of the life tenant....By restricting the life tenant's use of the property to "without power of sale," we find that Hanks intended to retain the "home place" in his own bloodline, by disposing of it to those who would be the natural objects of his bounty.... Paragraph seven is the only one in which Hanks used substitutional language to dispose of the residue by providing that it should be divided equally between his two children, "or their heirs." Inasmuch as no one can have heirs while living, Ebey, supra, we find the word "or," as used here, indicative of substitution. We further find that Hanks intended to use the word "heirs" as a word of purchase in view of his intent to finally vest the "home place" in the objects of his bounty: his children, or their heirs...[Tillotson v. Carpenter, 61 S.D. 570, 570, 250 N.W. 339 (1933); George v. Widemire, 242 Ala. 579, 7 So.2d 269, 273 (1942)]

McFarlands contend that paragraph nine conclusively shows that Hanks knew how to devise a contingent remainder by using appropriate language to designate a time reference. As such, they claim his failure to use similar language in paragraph seven militates against interpreting the phrase "or their heirs" as words of purchase. Paragraph nine states the following:

> NINTH: That upon the death of my said wife, Lena Hanks, without issue, or upon her re-marriage, that the home in Sturgis, South Dakota, shall be sold and the money received from the sale of said home shall be divided equally between Frances Rowett and any children that she may have at that time; Harvey Hanks and any children that he may have at that time; Alden Marcotte, Laura Marcotte and Lloyd Marcotte, in equal proportions to each of said persons, it being the intention that the children if any of Harvey Hanks and Frances Rowett shall share equally with the persons named in this devise.

We are not persuaded by this argument. Thus, we do not find paragraph nine determinative of Hanks' ability to

create contingent remainders especially in light of paragraphs
three and four, and his use of the word "or" in the
disputed paragraph. Hanks intention, as ascertained by the
language employed in the four corners of the will, does not
justify attributing the meaning of "and" to "or" in paragraph
seven.

> In the absence of any showing to the contrary,
> we are to assume that the testator selected
> language adapted to express his meaning, and
> that he knew and appreciated the effect of the
> language used in the will." (citations omitted).
> Henkel, 39 N.W.2d at 653. Therefore, having
> determined that Hanks intended to use "or" in its
> usual disjunctive sense of substitution, and
> "heirs" as a word of purchase, we next turn to
> the nature of the remainder interests he intended
> to create in his children and heirs by the use of
> said word.

In Wyman, supra, the devise was strikingly similar to the
case before us. The testatrix died in July, 1901. By the
terms of her will she disposed of her property as follows:

> I give, devise and bequeath to my husband ...
> all my real estate and personal estate ... during
> his natural life for his use and benefit, and after
> his decease I give and devise the same to my
> three daughters, Hattie, Libbie and Nellie to be
> equally divided among them, or their heirs.

10 A.2d at 193.

> After the testatrix's death, her husband occupied the
> land until his death in 1938. During the life tenancy,
> the husband and three daughters gave mortgages on
> the real estate. Libbie and Hattie predeceased their
> father, and each of them left children who survived
> him. In reversing a decree of foreclosure, the court
> said:

> From our examination of the matter it seems clear
> that the testatrix intended to impose the condition
> that the named children be living at the death of
> the life tenant in order that their estates vest in
> them in interest as well as possession and that
> otherwise the heirs of such as may have deceased
> prior to that time would take in possession what

their ancestors would have taken if they had survived the life tenant. In other words it must be considered that the testatrix intended to create as to the named children contingent and not vested remainders for when a condition of survivorship of the life tenant is imposed, the remainder thus created is one of contingency. * * *

This is so because in such a case time is of the substance of the devise and the event upon which it is limited to take effect, the survivorship of one over another, is always an uncertain and dubious event. (emphasis added).

Id. at 195.

The opinion quotes extensively from the Ebey and Taylor cases, discussed supra, and concluded the following:

It follows from what we have said that the named daughters had, during the life of the life tenant, only contingent remainders. The vesting of the estates in interest, as well as in possession depended upon their surviving the life tenant. As both Libbie and Hattie died before the termination of the life estate leaving heirs, it also follows that said daughters took no interest under the will which they could convey or encumber as against their heirs. The persons standing in relation of heirs to them took under the will as purchasers and not by descent the shares that the deceased daughters would have taken had they survived, unencumbered by the mortgages in question.

Id. 10 A.2d at 196....

The foregoing authorities convince us that Hanks intended to impose a condition precedent... upon Frances and Harvey, to-wit: that they be living at the death of the life tenant. As such, the vesting of their remainder interests in the "home place," as well as their possession, depended upon them surviving Lena Hanks. Where a testamentary disposition is made upon a condition precedent, nothing vests until the condition is fulfilled....When survivorship is a condition precedent to the taking of a remainder, the remainder is contingent....A future interest entitles the owner to possession of the property only at a future period...A future interest is contingent while the person in whom it is limited to take effect remains uncertain....At the time of Hanks' death, whether Frances would take her interest in the "home place" was an uncertain and dubious event because her ability to do so was contingent upon her surviving the life tenant.

Although paragraph seven does not contain words like "surviving" or "then living," the factor of survivorship is nevertheless implicit in the language used and the thought expressed. The day of distribution was marked by the death of Lena Hanks. By using the word "or" in its usual sense of substitution, paragraph seven unambiguously provided for the reversion of the "home place," (following termination of the preceding life interest), back to Hanks' estate where it should be equally divided between his children who might be living at the time of distribution, or the children of such who might be predeceased....

It being shown that Hanks' daughter, Frances Rowett, failed to meet the contingency set forth in paragraph seven by dying before the termination of the precedent life estate, it follows that she took no interest in the "home place" under her father's will. But Frances' heirs, the Rowetts, were entitled upon the death of Lena Hanks to take under the will, and as purchasers, the one-half remainder share Frances would have taken had she survived the day of distribution.... Thus, Frances' contingent remainder vested in the Rowetts when the contingency was removed by the death of Lena Hanks....

Having held that Frances had no interest in the "home place," we further hold that her conveyance by warranty deed to George McFarland was void ab initio.[3] Accordingly, we reverse the trial court's entry of summary judgment in favor of the McFarlands, and hold that Frances Rowett's remainder interest was contingent.

All the Justices concur.

---

3. As noted supra, Hanks explicitly stated that Lena Hanks' life use of the "home place" was "without power of sale." He similarly designated her life use of the Sturgis home in paragraph eight. Therefore, we would also hold Lena Hanks' quit claim deed for the "home place" to McFarlands as void ab initio.

§5.8 THE RULE IN SHELLEY'S CASE

Add as Problem 6 Immediately After Problem 5 on Page 312:

6. In 1940 O, a resident of State X, conveys Blackacre to A for life, then to A's heirs. In 1947, State X enacts the following statute: "The Rule in Shelley's Case is hereby abolished." A dies in 1950 leaving a last will bequeathing all of her property to X. A's sole heir is H. As between X and H, who owns Blackacre? See Society National Bank v. Jacobson, 54 Ohio St.3d 15, 560 N.E.2d 217 (1990).

§5.9 THE DOCTRINE OF WORTHIER TITLE

Add as New Case Immediately before Notes and Questions on Page 316:

HARRIS TRUST AND SAVINGS BANK v. BEACH
Supreme Court of Illinois (1987)
118 Ill.2d 1, 513 N.E.2d 833

JUSTICE SIMON delivered the opinion of the court:

In construing either a trust or a will the challenge is to find the settlor's or testator's intent and, provided that the intention is not against public policy, to give it effect. (See Hull v. Adams (1948), 399 Ill. 347, 352, 77 N.E.2d 706.) Courts search for intent by analyzing both the words used in the instrument and the circumstances under which they were drafted, including: "the state of the testator's property, his family, and the like." (Armstrong v. Barber (1909), 239 Ill. 389, 404, 88 N.E.2d 246.) When, however, the instrument fails to make the settlor's or testator's intention clear, courts often resort to rules of construction to determine the meaning of the terms used in the document. (Hull v. Adams (1948), 399 Ill. 347, 352, 77 N.E.2d 706.) Rules of construction, which are applied in the same manner to both wills and trusts, are court created presumptions of what the ordinary settlor or testator would have intended the ambiguous terms to mean; they are merely the court's own assessments of what the person probably meant when the provision was drafted. (Harris Trust & Savings Bank v. Jackson (1952), 412 Ill. 261, 266-67, 106 N.E.2d 188.) Such rules should not be allowed to defeat what the ordinary settlor would have intended. When a rule of construction tends to subvert intentions, the rule is no longer legitimate and must be discarded. H. Carey and D. Schuyler, Illinois Law of Future Interests 190-93 (Cum. Pocket Part 1954).

In this case Harris Trust and Savings Bank, Robert Hixon Glore and William Gray III, trustees of two trusts, sought instructions from the circuit court of Cook County regarding to whom and in what manner the trusts should be distributed. The central controversy is over the proper construction of the remainder over to the heirs following the death of a life tenant: specifically, the question is whether the settlor intended that his heirs be ascertained at his death, or whether he desired that they be determined after the death of his wife, who was the life tenant.

The pertinent facts in this case are as follows: Frank P. Hixon and Alice Green entered into an antenuptial agreement dated March 30, 1921, and following that, they were married. The agreement created a trust consisting of 200 shares of preferred stock of Pioneer Investment Company, a Hixon family holding company. The trust provided that Alice was to receive the net income of the trust for life and that she could "dispose of Fifty Thousand ($50,000) Dollars of said fund in such a manner as she" deemed fit and proper. In exchange for the provisions made for her in the trust, Alice surrendered any interest, including dower, which she might have had in Hixon's estate. If Hixon survived Alice, the trust property was to be reconveyed to him. If Alice survived Hixon, the trust provided that on her death "the balance of said trust fund shall be divided among the heirs of the party of the first part [Hixon], share and share alike."

On May 31, 1926, Hixon created a second trust to provide for Alice. The principal of this trust consisted of 300 shares of stock of Pioneer Investment Company. This trust provided that Alice was to receive the income from the principal for life and upon her death "this trust shall terminate, and the trust fund shall be distributed equally among my [Hixon's] heirs."

In 1930, Hixon executed his will, which was interpreted by our appellate court and is not at issue in this case (Harris Trust & Savings Bank v. Beach (1985), 145 Ill.App.3d 682, 99 Ill.Dec. 438, 495 N.E.2d 1173), leaving gifts to specific individuals and charities. He divided the residue of his estate equally among his daughters, Ellen Glore and Dorothy Clark and in trust for Alice. Hixon died in 1931, when he was 69 years old. He was survived by Alice, who was then 49, by Dorothy and Ellen, who were then 38 and 36, respectively, and by his grandchildren,

Frances Glore Beach, Charles F. Glore, Jr., and Robert Hixon Glore, who were then minors.

Alice lived for 51 more years. Both the 1921 and the 1926 trusts continued for her benefit until she died in February 1982. At that time, Hixon's then living descendants were his grandchildren, Frances Glore Beach and Robert Hixon Glore (the grandchildren), and the children of his deceased grandchild, Charles F. Glore, Jr.--Charles F. Glore III, Sallie Glore Farlow, and Edward R. Glore (the great-grandchildren). The parties agree that both the 1921 and the 1926 trust should be distributed in the same manner.

If Hixon's heirs are those surviving at his death, the trust estates will pass under the wills of his two daughters, Ellen H. Glore and Dorothy H. Clark, who both died in 1973. Ellen had three children. One child, as noted above-- Charles F. Glore, Jr.--is deceased and survived by three children, Hixon's great-grandchildren. Ellen's other two children--the grandchildren Robert and Frances--are living and are parties to this suit. Dorothy had no children. The devisees under her will are defendants California Institute of Technology, Santa Barbara Foundation, Santa Barbara Cottage Hospital and the Kansas Endowment Association (collectively the charities), and her husband Alfred. Alfred is deceased and his portion of the assets would be distributed to his devisees, Frederick Acker, as special trustee under the will of Charles F. Glore, Jr., and Robert Hixon Glore. On the other hand, if the heirs are determined at the time of Alice's death, the trust estates will be divided among Hixon's now-living descendants--the two grandchildren and three great- grandchildren.

The four charities assert that the heirs should be those heirs alive at Hixon's death; this determination would include them since they were devisees under Dorothy's will. The grandchildren and the great-grandchildren argue that the heirs should be those who were surviving at Alice's death, but they disagree over whether the trust should be divided per stirpes (by each share) or per capita (by each head).

All parties seeking distribution in their favor filed motions for summary judgment, and the circuit court granted the motion in favor of the charities. That court held that the class of heirs should be ascertained at Hixon's death. The court concluded that the heirs would be only Hixon's two daughters, since Alice was excluded under the terms of the

antenuptial agreement. The circuit court also decided that
the Doctrine of Worthier Title (the doctrine), which is
discussed more fully below, was an anachronism, and should
not be applied to this case. The court observed that
although the doctrine was abolished prospectively by statute
in 1955 (see Ill.Rev.Stat.1985, ch. 30, par. 188), it would
still be applicable here since both trusts were executed prior
to that date. However, because the doctrine consistently
thwarted settlors' and testators' intentions, the circuit judge
determined that if the doctrine applied at all, it would be
applied only as a rule of construction and not as a rule of
law; hence, he was not constrained to follow it....

The grandchildren and great-grandchildren appealed, and
the appellate court held that the doctrine applied as a matter
of law. (145 Ill.App.3d 673, 99 Ill.Dec. 435, 495 N.E.2d
1170.) The appellate court consequently voided the remainder
in Hixon's heirs, ruling that the trust reverted to Hixon's
estate and passed under the residuary clause of his will.
Because the appellate court did not give any effect to the
remainder in Hixon's heirs, it was unnecessary for that court
to decide whether the class of heirs should be considered at
Hixon's or at Alice's death....

Three issues are presented on review: (1) whether the
heirs are those surviving Hixon's death or Alice's death; (2)
whether the doctrine [of worthier title] is applicable, and if
so, whether it applies as a rule of construction or a rule of
law; and (3) whether, if the heirs are determined at Alice's
death, the shares should be distributed per stirpes or per
capita. Since the meaning of the word "heirs" as used in
the trust is a necessary predicate to the applicability of the
doctrine to this case, we begin by deciding at what point
the heirs are to be determined.

The word "heirs" refers to "those persons appointed by
the law to inherit an estate in case of intestacy." (Le Sourd
v. Leinweber (1952), 412 Ill. 100, 105, 105 N.E.2d 722.)
When used in its technical sense, the testator's or settlor's
heirs are, of course, determined at the time of his or her
death. (Hull v. Adams (1948), 399 Ill. 347, 352, 77 N.E.2d
706.) This court, however, has never adopted the technical
meaning of the word "heirs" as a rule of law. We have
observed that " 'heirs' when used in a will does not
necessarily have a fixed meaning. It may mean children or,
where there are no children, it may mean some other class
of heirs * * * if the context of the entire will plainly shows
such to have been the intention of the testator." (Emphasis

added.) (Stites v. Gray (1955), 4 Ill.2d 510, 513, 123 N.E.2d 483.) A determination of the class of heirs, therefore, is governed by the settlor's or testator's intention rather than by a fixed rule of law. The rule in Illinois, however, has been that, unless the settlor's intention to the contrary is "plainly shown" in the trust document, courts will rely upon the technical meaning of the term "heirs" by applying it as a rule of construction. (Harris Trust & Savings Bank v. Jackson (1952), 412 Ill. 261, 266, 106 N.E.2d 188.) The charities are, therefore, correct in their observation that presently our rule of construction requires us to determine heirs at the settlor's death unless the trust or will provides clear evidence to the contrary. (See, e.g., Stites v. Gray (1955), 4 Ill.2d 510, 513, 123 N.E.2d 483; Le Sourd v. Leinweber (1952), 412 Ill. 100, 105, 105 N.E.2d 722; Hull v. Adams (1948), 399 Ill. 347, 352, 77 N.E.2d 706.) The initial question we must address is whether we should continue to adhere to this standard of proof.

The charities contend that this high degree of proof is necessary to rebut the rule of construction because of the policy favoring early vesting of remainders. They refer to one leading commentator's views on implied survivorship and its detrimental effects on early vesting (see Halbach, Future Interests: Express and Implied Conditions of Survival, 49 Cal.L.Rev. 297, 304- 07 (1961)), as well as to Evans v. Giles (1980), 83 Ill.2d 448, 47 Ill.Dec. 349, 415 N.E.2d 354, and to Dyslin v. Wolf (1950), 407 Ill. 532, 96 N.E.2d 485, which are factually distinguishable from this case, to bolster their position. However, they overlook that two eminent scholars in the field of Illinois future interest law revised their views regarding the policy in favor of early vesting. In the supplement to their treatise entitled the Illinois Law of Future Interests, Carey and Schuyler observe that "it was the rule regarding the destructibility of contingent remainders that caused courts to favor the early vesting of estates. * * * But now, in this state and in many others, there is no rule of destructibility. If the original reason for favoring early vesting is gone, why continue to favor it?" H. Carey and D. Schuyler, Illinois Law of Future Interests 190 (Cum. Pocket Part 1954); Ill.Rev.Stat.1985, ch. 30, par. 40.

Briefly stated, the destruction of contingent remainders was an archaic device which frequently frustrated grantors' intentions by prematurely defeating an interest subject to a condition. By vesting remainders as quickly as possible the drastic effects of destructibility "could be contained by a rule of construction which resulted in declaring that future interests were vested and hence indestructible." (H. Carey and D. Schuyler, Illinois Law of Future Interests 190 (Cum. Pocket Part 1954)). Our legislature abolished destructibility when it passed "An Act concerning future interests" in 1921 (Ill. Rev. Stat. 1985, ch. 30, par. 40). However, despite the passage of this statute, vesting remainders as quickly as possible was such an imbedded rule of construction that in many cases courts continued to adhere to it without question and regardless of the consequences.

Early vesting frequently frustrates intentions by casting property to strangers. (H. Carey and D. Schuyler, Illinois Law of Future Interests 193 (Cum. Pocket Part 1954); see also DeKowin v. First National Bank of Chicago (N.D. Ill. 1949), 84 F. Supp. 918, rev'd on other grounds (C.A. Ill. 1949), 179 F.2d 347 (property goes to second wife of son-in-law); Peadro v. Peadro (1948), 81 N.E.2d 192, 400 Ill. 482 (property falls into the hands of the second wife of the testator's niece's widower).) Carey and Schuyler observe that if interests following life estates "are said to be contingent on survivorship, * * * children of the life tenant will take all the property, which seems to accord more with what the testator wanted." H. Carey and D. Schuyler, Illinois Law of Future Interests 192 (Cum. Pocket Part 1954).

In their 1954 supplement to their treatise on future interests, Professors Carey and Schuyler re-examined their earlier view that early vesting is axiomatic. (See H. Carey and D. Schuyler, Illinois Law of Future Interests 399 (1941); H. Carey and D. Schuyler, Illinois Law of Future Interests 190-93 (Cum. Pocket Part 1954). They state:

> One does not readily differ from men so learned as Professor Gray and Professor Kales, both of whom seemed satisfied with the axiom that 'the law favors the early vesting of estates.' Accordingly, at the time the principal text was written, and even in 1947, when the first supplement to this was published, the authors were much inclined unquestioningly to accent this ancient dogma. But subsequent further reflection causes one to wonder if the maxim has lost much, if not most of its utility." (H. Carey and D. Schuyler, Illinois Law of Future Interests 190 (Cum. Pocket Part 1954).)

They conclude that "the desirability of retaining the rule of early vesting as a rule of construction * * * warrant[s] a microscopic scrutiny of it by those charged with the administration of justice." (H. Carey and D. Schuyler, Illinois Law of Future Interest 193 (Cum. Pocket Part (1954).) In the instant case, we have an interest following a life estate. If we follow both the circuit and appellate court's decision and vest the heirs' interest as quickly as possible, a large portion of the estate will fall into the hands of strangers. If we reduce the burden of proving that a grantor intended to use "heirs" in a nontechnical sense and if that vests the gift at the termination of the life estate, obviously only those heirs surviving the life tenant will share in the remainder.

Whether survivorship ought to be implied is not a case of first impression before this court. A rule of construction regarding implied survivorship was set forth in Drury v. Drury (1915), 271 Ill. 336, 111 N.E. 140, where this court held that when a gift to a class was "postponed pending the termination of the life estate * * * only those took who were in existence at the termination of the life estate." (Emphasis added.) (271 Ill. 336, 341, 111 N.E. 140.) The effect of Drury was to delay the vesting of the gift by adding or implying survivorship for the class of remaindermen to share in the estate.

Hofing v. Willis (1964), 31 Ill.2d 365, 373, 201 N.E.2d 852, clarified Drury by stating that implied survivorship was not a mandatory rule of construction. Rather, according to the court in Hofing, the grantor's intent regarding this issue should remain paramount. While a later case, Evans v. Giles (1980), 83 Ill.2d 448, 456, 47 Ill.Dec. 349, 415 N.E.2d 354, also criticized the Drury rule, the rationale in that case was that implied survivorship defeated the policy against early vesting. In neither Hofing nor Evans did this court hold that it was inappropriate to imply survivorship when there was evidence that the grantor intended to do so. Further, Hofing, Evans and Dyslin are distinguishable in an important respect: the gift was not to a class of heirs--a term which is vague and imports futurity--but rather in Hofing to a group of sisters, in Giles to a specific individual, and in Dyslin to the grandchildren.

We agree with Professors Carey and Schuyler that early vesting of remainders should no longer be followed in this State without question. Early vesting is an axiom which must not get in the way when a contrary intent is demonstrated by a preponderance of the evidence.

Requiring clear and convincing evidence or a plain showing
to rebut the presumption in favor of the technical meaning
of the term "heirs" (see Stites v. Gray (1955), 4 Ill.2d 510,
513, 123 N.E.2d 483; Le Sourd v. Leinweber (1952), 412 Ill.
100, 105, 105 N.E.2d 722; Hull v. Adams (1948), 399 Ill.
347, 352, 77 N.E.2d 706), has its roots in the maxim
favoring early vesting of remainders. Frequently this
policy, as is the case here, frustrates what the ordinary
settlor would have intended. We hold that because the
primary reason for early vesting is no longer as important
as it formerly was, proof by the preponderance of the
evidence that the settlor, testator, or donor intended to use
the term "heirs" in its nontechnical sense is sufficient to
delay the vesting of a gift to a time other than at the
grantor's death.

The result of delaying a gift to the heirs is not dramatic.
The fear that a contingent remainder could be prematurely
destroyed no longer exists. Further, should a predeceased
member of the class be excluded from the gift, the result is
not drastic. If the predeceased "heir" leaves issue, as is
the case here, the settlor's own blood still enjoys the gift.
If, on the other hand, a predeceased member fails to leave
issue, as also occurred here, the gift is prevented from
falling into the hands of strangers. In sum, by altering the
degree of proof necessary to delay the vesting of a gift to
the heirs, we do no harm. Instead, we further the ordinary
grantor's intent, which is exactly what a proper rule of
construction ought to do. Consequently, in this case we
must determine which parties have offered the preponderant
proof as to Hixon's intent--the charities or the grandchildren
and great-grandchildren.

Hixon's trusts, as the charities stress, do not explicitly
state the point at which his heirs should be determined.
The 1921 trust provides that the "balance of said trust fund
shall be divided among the heirs," and the 1926 trust states
that "the trust shall be distributed equally among my
[Hixon's] heirs." When the trusts are considered as a whole,
however, it becomes apparent that the documents revolve
totally around Alice's life and death; Hixon's life and death
play only secondary roles. As the grandchildren and great-
grandchildren note, the trusts were created for Alice's
benefit in exchange for her rights to dower or any other
portion of Hixon's estate. The trusts were intended to last
throughout her life, and depending upon when she died, the
trust principal would either revert to Hixon or be distributed
to his heirs. Alice's central role in the trust is indicative

of Hixon's intent to make her and not himself the point of reference for determining the heirs. Under similar circumstances, our appellate court found the testator's frequent reference to the life tenant's death to be evidence of his intent to look towards the future and to ascertain the heirs at the life tenant's death rather than at his own. (See Handy v. Shearer (1967), 81 Ill.App.2d 461, 464, 225 N.E.2d 414.) In that case the court stated that the frequent references to the life tenant's death suggested "that it was an event and a point of time that weighed heavily in the testator's plan and in his thinking. * * * By using the date of the widow's remarriage or death as a date for the determination of 'my legal heirs,' testator's plan is complete." 81 Ill.App.2d 461, 464, 225 N.E.2d 414.

The circumstances under which Hixon created the trust provide additional evidence of his intent to vest the gift at Alice's death. Hixon was 20 years older than Alice and he would consequently have expected her trusts to last for a considerable time after his own death. During this time, changes in the family through births and deaths would certainly occur. Rather than leave the remainder of the principal to his daughters, as he left the residue of his estate in his will, his use of an indefinite term such as "heirs" covered the inevitable changes in family circumstances that might occur.

Alice's power of appointment over $50,000 of the trust principal is also evidence of Hixon's intent to ascertain the heirs at her death. The grandchildren and great-grandchildren observe that this power might prevent the heirs from ever enjoying the trust principal; the trust could be worth $50,000 or less when Alice exercised her power of appointment and thus there would be no trust principal left to distribute. The grandchildren's and great-grandchildren's claim that it would be senseless to vest the gift upon Hixon's death when one could not be certain until Alice exercised her power of appointment whether or not there were any assets left for the heirs to possess and enjoy, certainly has merit.

The charities assert that under the common law gifts subject to powers of appointment are always considered to vest at the testator's or settlor's death even though they may be subject to complete or partial divestment. In other words, the charities argue that the remaindermen, in this case Hixon's heirs, would still have a vested right in the trust principal whether or not at the time of distribution it contained any assets. The charities are correct in their interpretation of the common law. (See Moynihan, Introduction to Real Property 120 (1962).) However, they refer to no decision in our State that adopts this position.

Our court has consistently held that the time at which a gift vests ultimately turns upon a "consideration of the whole instrument[, its] creation and by the intent apparently in the mind of their creator as gathered from such instrument." (Jones v. Miller (1918), 283 Ill. 348, 356, 119 N.E. 324; see also Fuller v. Black (1921), 298 Ill. 351, 353, 131 N.E. 641.) As we have already noted, Hixon must have anticipated that the trusts for Alice's benefit would last for some time. The value of the trust principal--stock--was likely to fluctuate during this period. The logical conclusion is that Hixon desired to wait before "dividing and distributing" his assets to see if they had any value; it is unlikely that Hixon would have intended to vest a gift which might be worth nothing. While the possibility that there might be nothing left for the remaindermen to take, standing by itself, would not be determinative; it is a factor to be considered along with the other circumstances presented in searching for Hixon's intent...

Because we have concluded that it was Hixon's intention that the heirs were to be ascertained at Alice's death, the doctrine of worthier title is not applicable. The doctrine, which was developed in medieval England but abolished there in 1833, voids a gift to the grantor's heirs. It was premised on the notion that it was worthier to take by descent than by devise. (Moynihan, Introduction to the Law of Real Property 152 (1962).)...

In Illinois, the doctrine applies only where the devisees would take exactly the same estate by devise as they would by descent. (McNeilly v. Wylie (1945), 389 Ill. 391, 393, 59 N.E.2d 811.) It "is not applicable where there is a difference in kind or quality of the estate or property to be passed under the devise from that which would descend under the statute [the laws of descent and distribution]." (389 Ill. 391, 393, 59 N.E.2d 811, accord Darst v. Swearingen (1906), 224 Ill. 229, 79 N.E. 635; Boldenweck v. City National Bank & Trust Co. (1951), 343 Ill.App. 569, 99 N.E.2d 692.) Therefore, under Illinois law the doctrine is not likely to operate when the heirs are determined after the termination of a life estate; when vesting is postponed the devisees rarely receive either the same amount or the same estate as they would had their gift taken effect at the testator's death.

Having already concluded that Hixon's heirs are to be determined at Alice's and not at Hixon's death, those who would take Hixon's estate under the laws of descent and distribution had Hixon died intestate--Alice and the two daughters--are not the same as those who will take after Alice's death--the grandchildren and great-grandchildren. As a result, the doctrine is not relevant and therefore we need not reach the other issues briefed before this court: whether the doctrine is a rule of construction or rule of law and whether the doctrine is an anachronism which should be abandoned in the case of trusts established in Illinois prior to our 1955 statutory abolition of the doctrine....

Judgments reversed; cause remanded.

Add as Note 7 on Page 317:

William conveyed Blackacre to himself for life, then to his daughter Emma for life, and then to her children, the children of any deceased child to take his or her parent's share. The deed further provided that if Emma died without any children or more remote issue, then Blackacre "shall descend to the heirs of said William, the children of any deceased child taking only the share which their parent would inherit if living".

William had four children, Able, Baker, Carrie and Emma and they died in that order. Emma devised her interest, if any, in Blackacre to Tom. Only Baker had issue who survived Emma. Baker's issue claim to own all of Blackacre; Tom claims to own one-fourth.

What result? See Warren Boynton State Bank v. Wallbaum, 143 Ill.App.3d 628, 493 N.E.2d 21 (1986).

Chapter 6

CONCURRENT ESTATES

§6.4 BANK ACCOUNTS

Add as new paragraph at end of Note 1 on Pg. 360:

In Estate of Propst v. Stillman, 50 Cal.3d 448, 788 P.2d 628, 268 Cal. Rptr. 114 (1990) the California Supreme Court held that a joint bank account co-tenant could unilaterally sever the joint tenancy by withdrawing the funds and depositing them in a new account in his name alone. The court indicated that some duty to account would arise if the joint tenants had an agreement against a unilateral severance but did not apply that duty as one that arises by law. While the court appeared to liken its rule to that involving real property, it also observed that a unilateral severance of a joint tenancy in real property leaves the co-tenants as tenants in common and does not result in the non-severing co-tenant being deprived of all interest in the property.

Chapter 7

PROPERTY AND COHABITANTS

§7.3 THE PROPERTY RIGHTS OF A SURVIVING SPOUSE: MODERN APPROACHES

Add at end of First Full Paragraph in § 7.3 on Page 364:

Under a typical forced share statute, the surviving spouse is entitled to a fixed share of the deceased spouse's estate. Therefore, a surviving spouse who had been married to the decedent for 20 years would be treated identically with a surviving spouse who had been married to the decedent for 2 years. It has been suggested that the size of the forced share should vary depending upon the length of the marriage. See, Langbein & Waggoner, Redesigning the Spouse's Forced Share, 22 Real Prop. Prob. & Tr. J. 303 (1987).

§7.6 IS EDUCATION A MARITAL ASSET?

Add as New Case on Page 404:

NELSON v. NELSON
Supreme Court of Alaska 1987
736 P.2d 1145

MATTHEWS, JUSTICE.

In this divorce case the trial court valued the marital property subject to division at $196,343 and divided it equally. On appeal, ...[the following question is raised:] (1) whether the court erred in failing to recognize the "human capital asset of the marriage," a bachelor's degree, and divide it by property division or alimony...

Clairborne had attended two years of college before the parties were married in 1967. At the time of their marriage June was working as a quality control inspector in electronics and Clairborne was working as an assistant manager of a pizza parlor. In 1968 Clairborne returned to college and completed his education in business accounting, obtaining a bachelor's degree in 1970. During most of this time June worked full-time and Clairborne worked part-time and received tuition aid because of his prior military service. Since graduation Clairborne has worked for ARCO. June has cared for the parties' three children and worked from time to time outside the home as well. She obtained a commercial pilot's license in 1981 and has been intermittently employed as an airline pilot with a local airline. However, at the time of trial she was unemployed. The parties separated in November of 1983 and were divorced in August of 1985. The alleged human capital asset is Clairborne's bachelor's degree in business accounting.

There are cases where courts have recognized that one spouse has a compensable property interest in the enhanced earning potential arising out of the other spouse's degree. E.g. In re Marriage of Horstmann, 263 N.W.2d 885, 891 (Iowa 1978); Woodworth v. Woodworth, 126 Mich.App. 258, 337 N.W.2d 332, 334 (1983). Those cases arise out of circumstances which are not present in the case at hand.

> Typically, one spouse attains a degree while the other provides support; then a divorce occurs soon after graduation. Usually there are few assets immediately available, but one spouse leaves the marriage with an education and increased earning potential, while the other spouse is given nothing for her efforts.

C. Bruch, The Definition of Marital Property in California: Toward Parity and Simplicity, 62-63 (1981). See also Lesman v. Lesman, 88 A.D.2d 153, 452 N.Y.S.2d 935, 939 (1982) ("It is the hard case, typified by the sacrificing wife who is deserted by her ungrateful husband shortly after he achieves his educational goal."). Such a case usually involves a graduate degree or a professional license. Further, the passage of time reduces and eventually eliminates the need to award the supporting spouse a share of the degree or the enhanced earning potential, because in such cases

> the wife's expectation is realized, in part at least, and by participating in her husband's income, she receives a return which may exceed the amount of her contributions to his education. It is also probable that at the time of the divorce, as the result of the husband's enhanced earnings, the parties will have accumulated marital property in which the divorced wife will share and thereby receive a return of her investment.

Lesman, 452 N.Y.S.2d at 939.

Most courts hold that a professional degree is not property subject to division. E.g., In re Marriage of Graham, 194 Colo. 429, 574 P.2d 75 (1978); Lesman v.

Lesman, 452 A.D.2d 153, 452 N.Y.S.2d 935 (1982); Washburn v. Washburn, 677 P.2d 152 (Wash.1984). We agree with these authorities. As the Colorado court explained in In re Marriage of Graham, 574 P.2d at 77:

[a]n educational degree, such as an M.B.A., is simply not encompassed even by the broad views of the concept of "property." It does not have an exchange value or any objective transferable value on an open market. It is personal to the holder. It terminates on death of the holder and is not inheritable. It cannot be assigned, sold, transferred, conveyed, or pledged. An advanced degree is a cumulative product of many years of previous education, combined with diligence and hard work. It may not be acquired by the mere expenditure of money. It is simply an intellectual achievement that may potentially assist in the future acquisition of property. In our view, it has none of the attributes of property in the usual sense of that term.

This does not mean that the spouse who has worked and made other sacrifices while the other spouse has obtained a potentially lucrative professional degree is without a remedy. The earning ability of the parties and their conduct during the marriage are relevant to a property division. Merrill v. Merrill, 368 P.2d 546, 548 (Alaska 1962). The fact that the work of one spouse has contributed to the earning potential of the other may justify a favorable award of property to the supporting spouse:

When a person supports a spouse through professional school in the mutual expectation of future financial benefit to the community, but the marriage ends before that benefit can be realized, that circumstance is a "relevant factor" which must be considered in making a fair and equitable division of property....

Washburn, 677 P.2d at 158.

Although we have previously adopted the view that divorcing spouses' financial needs should generally be secured by an appropriate property division rather than by alimony, when there is no substantial property to divide the supporting spouse may be entitled to alimony if it is both "just and necessary." AS 25.24.160(3); Bussell v. Bussell, 623 P.2d 1221, 1224 (Alaska 1981) (rehabilitative alimony allowed for the education of the supporting spouse); Messina

v. Messina, 583 P.2d 804 (Alaska 1978). Where there is no
substantial property and alimony is not reasonably necessary
to maintain the supporting spouse, a harder question is
presented. This is not the occasion to attempt to determine
whether the supporting spouse in such circumstances has
another available remedy, for those circumstances are not
present here.

We hold that the trial court did not abuse its discretion
in dividing the marital assets of the parties equally. The
two years at the outset of this seventeen year marriage
during which June worked and Clairborne went to school do
not compel an unequal property division. Both June and
Clairborne have benefitted from the increased earning
capacity gained by Clairborne during those two years.
Further, Clairborne's degree was not a specialized post-
graduate degree. Moreover, Clairborne also supported his
educational efforts by working part-time and through the
receipt of benefits because of his past military service....

Judgment affirmed.

NOTES AND QUESTIONS

There is a growing awareness that judicial awards of
either alimony or an equitable distribution of property likely
are biased in favor of the husband. These findings from
the Executive Summary of the Report of the Florida Supreme
Court Gender Bias Study Commission 4-7 (1990) illustrate the
point:

Men customarily retain more than half of the assets of
the marriage and leave with an enhanced earning
capacity. The remaining family members are left with
less than half of the marital assets and a severely
diminished earning capacity.

A homemaker's contributions of time and energy, as
well as the opportunities she has foregone, often are
minimized by Florida courts. Many judges are
especially reluctant to acknowledge that these
contributions are a genuine resource of the marriage.

Post-divorce families headed by women are the
fastest growing segment of those living in poverty.

Older women whose marriages end in divorce are
most likely either to have abandoned their own

aspirations or to have devoted their lives to furthering their husbands' careers. They are not adequately compensated by application of the present system of alimony and equitable division of marital assets.

In many areas of the state, the courts have virtually abandoned permanent alimony or substituted in its place unrealistic rehabilitative alimony awards.

Many judges fail to award permanent alimony, preferring instead to use the vehicle of equitable distribution. Yet, because men usually have a greater earning potential, women are disadvantaged by "equitable" distribution when marital assets are too slight to provide sufficient income.

In equitable distribution, men generally receive sixty-five to seventy-five percent of the marital assets compared to twenty-five to thirty-five percent for women.

The major asset of most marriages is the earning capacities of the partners.

The Commission recommended that Florida adopt a community property system as a way of rectifying this discriminatory treatment. It further recommends that presumptively property should be divided evenly upon divorce; that spousal awards for marriages of long duration should be designed to equalize the standards of living of post-divorce households at the time of dissolution rather than merely maintaining the standard of living established during the marriage. The Commission also recommends that periodic alimony for equitable distribution purposes should not end upon remarriage or death.

§7.7 PROPERTY RIGHTS OF UNMARRIED COHABITANTS

Add as New Case on Page 412:

BRASCHI v. STAHL ASSOCIATES COMPANY
Court of Appeals of New York (1989)
544 N.Y.S.2d 784, 74 N.Y.2d 201, 543 N.E.2d 49

TITONE, JUDGE.

In this dispute over occupancy rights to a rent-controlled apartment, the central question to be resolved on this request for preliminary injunctive relief ... is whether appellant has demonstrated a likelihood of success on the merits ... by showing that, as a matter of law, he is entitled to seek protection from eviction under New York City Rent and Eviction Regulations 9 NYCRR 2204.6(d)...That regulation provides that upon the death of a rent-control tenant, the landlord may not dispossess "either the surviving spouse of the deceased tenant or some other member of the deceased tenant's family who has been living with the tenant..." Resolution of this question requires this court to determine the meaning of the term "family" as it is used in this context.

I.

Appellant, Miguel Braschi, was living with Leslie Blanchard in a rent-controlled apartment located at 405 East 54th Street from the summer of 1975 until Blanchard's death in September of 1986. In November of 1986, respondent, Stahl Associates Company, the owner of the apartment building, served a notice to cure on appellant contending that he was a mere licensee with no right to occupy the apartment since only Blanchard was the tenant of record. In December of 1986 respondent served appellant with a notice to terminate informing appellant that he had one month to vacate the apartment and that, if the apartment was not vacated, respondent would commence summary proceedings to evict him.

Appellant then initiated an action seeking a permanent injunction and a declaration of entitlement to occupy the apartment. By order to show cause appellant then moved for a preliminary injunction...enjoining respondent from evicting him until a court could determine whether he was a member of Blanchard's family within the meaning of 9 NYCRR 2204.6(d). After examining the nature of the relationship between the two men, Supreme Court concluded that appellant was a "family member" within the meaning of the regulation and, accordingly, that a preliminary injunction should be issued. The court based this decision on its finding that the long-term interdependent nature of the 10-year relationship between appellant and Blanchard "fulfills any definitional criteria of the term 'family.' "

The Appellate Division reversed, concluding that section 2204.6(d) provides noneviction protection only to "family members within traditional, legally recognized familial relationships" (143 A.D.2d 44, 45, 531 N.Y.S.2d 562). Since appellant's and Blanchard's relationship was not one given formal recognition by the law, the court held that appellant could not seek the protection of the noneviction ordinance. After denying the motion for preliminary injunctive relief, the Appellate Division granted leave to appeal to this court, certifying the following question of law: "Was the order of this Court, which reversed the order of the Supreme Court, properly made?" We now reverse. * * *

It is fundamental that in construing the words of a statute "[t]he legislative intent is the great and controlling principle" ... [citations omitted] Indeed, "the general purpose is a more important aid to the meaning than any rule which grammar or formal logic may lay down" (United States v. Whitridge, 197 U.S. 135, 143, 25 S.Ct. 406, 408, 49 L.Ed. 696). Statutes are ordinarily interpreted so as to avoid objectionable consequences and to prevent hardship or injustice ... Hence, where doubt exists as to the meaning of a term, and a choice between two constructions is afforded, the consequences that may result from the different interpretations should be considered... In addition, since rent-control laws are remedial in nature and designed to promote the public good, their provisions should be interpreted broadly to effectuate their purposes... Finally, where a problem as to the meaning of a given term arises, a court's role is not to delve into the minds of legislators, but rather to effectuate the statute by carrying out the purpose of the statute as it is embodied in the words chosen by the Legislature...

The present dispute arises because the term "family" is not defined in the rent-control code and the legislative history is devoid of any specific reference to the noneviction provision. All that is known is the legislative purpose underlying the enactment of the rent-control laws as a whole. Rent control was enacted to address a "serious public emergency" created by "an acute shortage in dwellings," which resulted in "speculative, unwarranted and abnormal increases in rents" (L.1946 ch. 274, codified, as amended, at McKinney's Uncons.Laws of N.Y. § 8581 et seq). These measures were designed to regulate and control the housing market so as to "prevent exactions of unjust, unreasonable and oppressive rents and rental agreements and to forestall profiteering, speculation and other disruptive practices tending to produce threats to the public health * * * [and] to prevent uncertainty, hardship and dislocation" (id.). Although initially designed as an emergency measure to alleviate the housing shortage attributable to the end of

World War II, "a serious public emergency continues to exist
in the housing of a considerable number of persons" (id.).
Consequently, the Legislature has found it necessary to
continually reenact the rent-control laws, thereby providing
continued protection to tenants.

To accomplish its goals, the Legislature recognized that
not only would rents have to be controlled, but that
evictions would have to be regulated and controlled as well
(id.). Hence, section 2204.6 of the New York City Rent and
Eviction Regulations (9 NYCRR 2204.6), which authorizes the
issuance of a certificate for the eviction of persons
occupying a rent-controlled apartment after the death of the
named tenant, provides, in subdivision (d), noneviction
protection to those occupants who are either the "surviving
spouse of the deceased tenant or some other member of the
deceased tenant's family who has been living with the tenant
[of record]..." The manifest intent of this section is to
restrict the landowners' ability to evict a narrow class of
occupants other than the tenant of record. The question
presented here concerns the scope of the protections
provided. Juxtaposed against this intent favoring the
protection of tenants, is the over-all objective of a gradual
"transition from regulation to a normal market of free
bargaining between landlord and tenant" (see, e.g.,
Administrative Code of City of New York § 26-401). One way
in which this goal is to be achieved is "vacancy decontrol,"
which automatically makes rent-control units subject to the
less rigorous provisions of rent stabilization upon the
termination of the rent-control tenancy...

Emphasizing the latter objective, respondent argues that
the term "family member" as used in 9 NYCRR 2204.6(d)
should be construed, consistent with this State's intestacy
laws, to mean relationships of blood, consanguinity and
adoption in order to effectuate the over-all goal of orderly
succession to real property. Under this interpretation, only
those entitled to inherit under the laws of intestacy would be
afforded noneviction protection... Further, as did the
Appellate Division, respondent relies on our decision in
Matter of Robert Paul P., 63 N.Y.2d 233, 481 N.Y.S.2d 652,
471 N.E.2d 424, arguing that since the relationship between
appellant and Blanchard has not been accorded legal status
by the Legislature, it is not entitled to the protections of
section 2204.6(d), which, according to the Appellate
Division, applies only to "family members within traditional,
legally recognized familial relationships" (143 A.D.2d 44, 45,
531 N.Y.S.2d 562)....

Respondent's reliance on Matter of Robert Paul P. (supra) is also misplaced, since that case, which held that one adult cannot adopt another where none of the incidents of a filial relationship is evidenced or even remotely intended, was based solely on the purposes of the adoption laws...and has no bearing on the proper interpretation of a provision in the rent control laws.

We also reject respondent's argument that the purpose of the noneviction provision of the rent-control laws is to control the orderly succession to real property in a manner similar to that which occurs under our State's intestacy laws... The noneviction provision does not concern succession to real property but rather is a means of protecting a certain class of occupants from the sudden loss of their homes. The regulation does not create an alienable property right that could be sold, assigned or otherwise disposed of and, hence, need not be construed as coextensive with the intestacy laws. Moreover, such a construction would be inconsistent with the purposes of the rent-control system as a whole, since it would afford protection to distant blood relatives who actually had but a superficial relationship with the deceased tenant while denying that protection to unmarried lifetime partners. Finally, the dissent's reliance on Hudson View Props. v. Weiss, 59 N.Y.2d 733, 463 N.Y.S.2d 428, 450 N.E.2d 234 is misplaced. In that case we permitted the eviction of an unrelated occupant from a rent-controlled apartment under a lease explicitly restricting occupancy to "immediate family." However, the tenant in Hudson View conceded "that an individual not part of her immediate family" occupied the apartment (Id., at 735, 463 N.Y.S.2d 428, 450 N.E.2d 234), and, thus, the sole question before us was whether enforcement of the lease provision was violative of the State or City Human Rights Law. Whether respondent tenant was, in fact, an "immediate family" member was neither specifically addressed nor implicitly answered....

Contrary to all of these arguments, we conclude that the term family, as used in 9 NYCRR 2204.6(d), should not be rigidly restricted to those people who have formalized their relationship by obtaining, for instance, a marriage certificate or an adoption order. The intended protection against sudden eviction should not rest on fictitious legal distinctions or genetic history, but instead should find its foundation in the reality of family life. In the context of eviction, a more realistic, and certainly equally valid, view of a family includes two adult lifetime partners whose relationship is long term and characterized by an emotional and financial commitment and interdependence. This view comports both with our society's traditional concept of "family" and with the expectations of individuals who live in such nuclear units...[1] In fact, Webster's Dictionary defines "family" first as "a group of people united by certain convictions or common affiliation" (Webster's Ninth New Collegiate Dictionary 448 [1984]; see, Ballantine's Law Dictionary 456 [3d ed. 1969] ["family" defined as "(p)rimarily, the collective body of persons who live in one house and under one head or management"]; Black's Law Dictionary 543 [Special Deluxe 5th ed. 1979]). Hence, it is reasonable to conclude that, in using the term "family," the Legislature intended to extend protection to those who reside in households having all of the normal familial characteristics.[2] Appellant Braschi should therefore be afforded the opportunity to prove that he and Blanchard had such a household.

This definition of "family" is consistent with both of the competing purposes of the rent-control laws: the protection of individuals from sudden dislocation and the gradual transition to a free market system. Family members, whether or not related by blood, or law who have always treated the apartment as their family home will be protected against the hardship of eviction following the death of the named tenant, thereby furthering the Legislature's goals of preventing dislocation and preserving family units which might otherwise be broken apart upon eviction.[3] This approach will foster the

---

1. Although the dissent suggests that our interpretation of "family" indefinitely expands the protections provided by section 2204.6(d)...its own proposed standard--legally recognized relationships based on blood, marriage or adoption--may cast an even wider net, since the number of blood relations an individual has will usually exceed the number of people who would qualify by our standard.

2. We note that the concurrer apparently agrees with our view of the purposes of the noneviction ordinance (concurring op., at p. 215, at p. 791 of 544 N.Y.S.2d, at p. 56 of 543 N.E.2d), and the impact this purpose should have on the way in which this and future cases should be decided.

3. We note, however, that the definition of family that we adopt here for purposes of the noneviction protection of the laws is completely unrelated to the concept of "functional family," as that term has developed under this court's decisions in the context of zoning ordinances...[citations omitted] Those decisions focus on a locality's power to use its zoning powers in such a way

transition from rent control to rent stabilization by drawing a distinction between those individuals who are, in fact, genuine family members, and those who are mere roommates...or newly discovered relatives hoping to inherit the rent-controlled apartment after the existing tenant's death.[4]

The determination as to whether an individual is entitled to noneviction protection should be based upon an objective examination of the relationship of the parties. In making this assessment, the lower courts of this State have looked to a number of factors, including the exclusivity and longevity of the relationship, the level of emotional and financial commitment, the manner in which the parties have conducted their everyday lives and held themselves out to society, and the reliance placed upon one another for daily family services...These factors are most helpful, although it should be emphasized that the presence or absence of one or more of them is not dispositive since it is the totality of the relationship as evidenced by the dedication, caring and self-sacrifice of the parties which should, in the final analysis, control. Appellant's situation provides an example of how the rule should be applied.

Appellant and Blanchard lived together as permanent life partners for more than 10 years. They regarded one another, and were regarded by friends and family, as spouses. The two men's families were aware of the nature of the relationship, and they regularly visited each other's families and attended family functions together, as a couple.

---

as to impinge upon an individual's ability to live under the same roof with another individual. They have absolutely no bearing on the scope of noneviction protection provided by section 2204.6(d).

4. Also unpersuasive is the dissent's interpretation of the "roommate" law which was passed in response to our decision in Hudson View Props. v. Weiss, 59 N.Y.2d 733, 463 N.Y.S.2d 428, 450 N.E.2d 234. That statute allows roommates to live with the named tenant by making lease provisions to the contrary void as against public policy ... The law also provides that "occupant's" (roommates) do not automatically acquire "any right to continued occupancy in the event that the tenant vacates the premises"... Occupant is defined as "a person, other than a tenant or a member of a tenant's immediate family"... However, contrary to the dissent's assumption that this law contemplates a distinction between related and unrelated individuals, no such distinction is apparent from the Legislature's unexplained use of the term "immediate family."

Even today, appellant continues to maintain a relationship with Blanchard's niece, who considers him an uncle. In addition to their interwoven social lives, appellant clearly considered the apartment his home. He lists the apartment as his address on his driver's license and passport, and receives all his mail at the apartment address. Moreover, appellant's tenancy was known to the building's superintendent and doormen, who viewed the two men as a couple. Financially, the two men shared all obligations including a household budget. The two were authorized signatories of three safe-deposit boxes, they maintained joint checking and savings accounts, and joint credit cards. In fact, rent was often paid with a check from their joint checking account. Additionally, Blanchard executed a power of attorney in appellant's favor so that appellant could make necessary decisions--financial, medical and personal--for him during his illness. Finally, appellant was the named beneficiary of Blanchard's life insurance policy, as well as the primary legatee and coexecutor of Blanchard's estate. Hence, a court examining these facts could reasonably conclude that these men were much more than mere roommates.

Inasmuch as this case is before us on a certified question, we conclude only that appellant has demonstrated a likelihood of success on the merits, in that he is not excluded, as a matter of law, from seeking noneviction protection. Since all remaining issues are beyond this court's scope of review, we remit this case to the Appellate Division so that it may exercise its discretionary powers in accordance with this decision. Accordingly, the order of the Appellate Division should be reversed and the case remitted to that court for a consideration of undetermined questions. The certified question should be answered in the negative.

BELLACOSA, JUDGE (concurring).

My vote to reverse and remit rests on a narrower view of what must be decided in this case than the plurality and dissenting opinions deem necessary. The issue is solely whether petitioner qualifies as a member of a "family", as that generic and broadly embracive word is used in the anti-eviction regulation of the rent-control apparatus. The particular anti- eviction public policy enactment is fulfilled by affording the remedial protection to this petitioner on the facts advanced on this record at this preliminary injunction stage. The competing public policy of eventually restoring rent-controlled apartments to decontrol, to stabilization and even to arm's length market relationships is eclipsed in this instance, in my view, by the more pertinently expressed and clearly applicable anti-eviction policy. Courts, in circumstances as are presented here where legislative intent is completely indecipherable (Division of Housing and Community Renewal, the agency charged with administering the policy, is equally silent in this case and on this issue), are not empowered or expected to expand or to constrict the meaning of the legislatively chosen word "family," which could have been and still can be qualified or defined by the duly constituted enacting body in satisfying its separate branch responsibility and prerogative. Construing a regulation does not allow substitution of judicial views or preferences for those of the enacting body when the latter either fails or is unable or deliberately refuses to specify criteria or definitional limits for its selected umbrella word, "family", especially where the societal, governmental, policy and fiscal implications are so sweeping... For then, "the judicial function expands beyond the molecular movements, in Holmes' figure, into the molar"...[citation omitted]...

The application of the governing word and statute to reach a decision in this case can be accomplished on a narrow and legitimate jurisprudential track. The enacting body has selected an unqualified word for a socially remedial statute, intended as a protection against one of the harshest decrees known to the law-- eviction from one's home. Traditionally, in such circumstances, generous construction is favored. Petitioner has made his shared home in the affected apartment for 10 years. The only other occupant of that rent-controlled apartment over that same extended period of time was the tenant-in-law who has now died, precipitating this battle for the apartment. The best guidance available to the regulatory agency for correctly applying the rule in such circumstances is that it would be irrational not to include this petitioner and it is a more reasonable reflection of the intention behind the regulation to protect a person such as petitioner as within the regulation's class of "family". In that respect, he qualifies as a tenant in fact for purposes of the interlocking provisions and policies of the law. Therefore, under CPLR 6301, there would unquestionably be irreparable harm by not upholding the preliminary relief Supreme Court has decreed; the likelihood of success seems quite good since four Judges of this court, albeit by different rationales, agree at least that petitioner fits under the beneficial umbrella of the regulation; and the balance of equities would appear to favor petitioner.

SIMONS, JUDGE (dissenting).

I would affirm. The plurality has adopted a definition of family which extends the language of the regulation well beyond the implication of the words used in it. In doing so, it has expanded the class indefinitely to include anyone who can satisfy an administrator that he or she had an emotional and financial "commitment" to the statutory tenant. Its interpretation is inconsistent with the legislative scheme underlying rent regulation, goes well beyond the intended purposes of 9 NYCRR 2204.6(d), and produces an unworkable test that is subject to abuse. The concurring opinion fails to address the problem. It merely decides, ipse dixit, that plaintiff should win. Preliminarily, it will be helpful to briefly look at the legislative scheme underlying rent regulation....

Rent regulation in New York is implemented by rent control and rent stabilization. rent control is the stricter of the two programs. In 1946 the first of many "temporary" measures was enacted to address a public emergency created by the shortage of residential accommodations after World War II. That statute, and the statutes and regulations which followed it, were designed to monitor the housing market to prevent unreasonable and oppressive rents. These laws regulate the terms and conditions of rent-controlled tenancies exclusively; owners can evict tenants or occupants only on limited specified grounds... and only with the permission of the administrative agency....

Central to any interpretation of the regulatory language is a determination of its purpose. There can be little doubt that the purpose of section 2204.6(d) was to create succession rights to a possessory interest in real property where the tenant of record has died or vacated the apartment... It creates a new tenancy for every surviving family member living with decedent at the time of death who then becomes a new statutory tenant until death or until he or she vacates the apartment. The State concerns underlying this provision include the orderly and just succession of property interests (which includes protecting a deceased's spouse and family from loss of their longtime home) and the professed State objective that there be a gradual transition from government regulation to a normal market of free bargaining between landlord and tenant. Those objectives require a weighing of the interests of certain individuals living with the tenant of record at his or her death and the interests of the landlord in regaining possession of its property and rerenting it under the less onerous rent-stabilization laws. The interests are properly balanced if the regulation's exception is applied by using objectively verifiable relationships based on blood, marriage and adoption, as the State has historically done in the estate succession laws, family court acts and similar legislation... The distinction is warranted because members of families, so defined, assume certain legal obligations to each other and to third persons, such as creditors, which are not imposed on unrelated individuals and this legal interdependency is worthy of consideration in determining which individuals are entitled to succeed to the interest of the statutory tenant in rent-controlled premises. Moreover, such an interpretation promotes certainty and consistency in the law and obviates the need for drawn out hearings and litigation focusing on such intangibles as the strength and duration of the relationship and the extent of the emotional and financial interdependency...So limited, the regulation may be viewed as a tempered response, balancing the rights of landlords with those of the tenant. To come within that protected class, individuals must comply with State laws relating to marriage or adoption. Plaintiff cannot avail himself of these institutions, of course, but that only points up the need for a legislative solution, not a judicial one ...

Aside from these general considerations, the language itself suggests the regulation should be construed along traditional lines. Significantly, although the problem of unrelated persons living with tenants in rent- controlled apartments has existed for as long as rent control, there has been no effort by the State Legislature, the New York City Council or the agency charged with enforcing the statutes to define the word "family" contained in 9 NYCRR 2204.6(d) and its predecessors and we have no direct evidence of the term's intended scope. The plurality's response to this problem is to turn to the dictionary and select one definition, from the several found there, which gives the regulation the desired expansive construction.[5] I would

---

5. For example, the definitions found in Black's Law Dictionary 543 (Special Deluxe 5th ed.) are: "family. The meaning of word 'family' necessarily depends on field of law in which word is used, purpose intended to be accomplished by its use, and facts and circumstances of each case * * * Most commonly refers to group of persons consisting of parents and children; father, mother and their children; immediate kindred, constituting fundamental social unit in civilized society * * * A collective body of persons who live in one house and under one head or

search for the intended meaning by looking at what the
Legislature and the Division of Housing and Community
Renewal (DHCR), the agency charged with implementing rent
control, have done in related areas. These sources produce
persuasive evidence that both bodies intend the word family
to be interpreted in the traditional sense.

The legislative view may be found in the "roommate" law
enacted in 1983 (Real Property Law § 235-f, L.1983, ch.
403). That statute granted rights to persons living with, but
unrelated to, the tenant of record. The statute was a
response to our unanimous decision in Hudson View Props.
v. Weiss, 59 N.Y.2d 733, 463 N.Y.S.2d 428, 450 N.E.2d 234;
see, legislative findings to ch. 403, set out as note after
Real Property Law § 226-b, McKinney's Cons. Laws of N.Y.,
Book 49, at 130. In Hudson View the landlord, by a
provision in the lease, limited occupancy to the tenant of
record and the tenant's "immediate family". When the landlord
tried to evict the unmarried heterosexual partner of the
named tenant of record, she defended the proceeding by
claiming that the restrictive covenant in the lease violated
provisions of the State and City Human Rights Laws
prohibiting discrimination on the basis of marital status. We
held that the exclusion had nothing to do with the tenants'
unmarried status but depended on the lease's restriction of
occupancy to the tenant and the tenant's "immediate family".
Implicitly, we decided that the term "immediate family" did
not include individuals who were unrelated by blood,
marriage or adoption, notwithstanding "the close and loving
relationship" of the parties.   The Legislature's response to
Weiss was measured. It enacted Real Property Law § 235-
f(3), (4) which provides that occupants of rent-controlled
accommodations, whether related to the tenant of record or
not, can continue living in rent-controlled and rent-stabilized
apartments as long as the tenant of record continues to
reside there. Lease provisions to the contrary are rendered
void as against public policy (subd. [2]). Significantly, the
statute provides that no unrelated occupant "shall * * *
acquire any right to continued occupancy in the event the
tenant vacates the premises or acquire any other rights of

---

management. A group of blood-relatives; all the relations who descend from
a common ancestor, or who spring from a common root. A group of
kindred persons * * * Husband and wife and their children, wherever they
may reside and whether they dwell together or not" (citations omitted). The
term is similarly defined in the other dictionaries cited in the plurality
opinion.

tenancy" (subd. [6]). Read against this background, the statute is evidence the Legislature does not contemplate that individuals unrelated to the tenant of record by blood, marriage or adoption should enjoy a right to remain in rent-controlled apartments after the death of the tenant (see, Rice, The New Morality and Landlord-Tenant Law, 55 N.Y.S. Bar J. [No. 6] 33, 41 [postscript]).

There is similar evidence of how DHCR intends the section to operate. Manifestly, rent stabilization and rent control are closely related in purpose. Both recognize that, because of the serious ongoing public emergency with respect to housing in the City of New York, restrictions must be placed on residential housing. The DHCR promulgates the regulations for both rent-regulation systems, and the eviction regulations in rent control and the exceptions to them share a common purpose with the renewal requirements contained in the Rent Stabilization Code (compare, 9 NYCRR 2204.6[d], with 9 NYCRR 2523.5[b]). In the Rent Stabilization Code, the Division of Housing and Community Renewal has made it unmistakably clear that the definition of family includes only persons related by blood, marriage or adoption. Since the two statutes and the two regulations share a common purpose, it is appropriate to conclude that the definition of family in the regulations should be of similar scope.

Specifically, the rent-stabilization regulations provide under similar circumstances that the landlord must offer a renewal lease to "any member of such tenant's family * * * who has resided in the housing accommodation as a primary resident from the inception of the tenancy or commencement of the relationship" (9 NYCRR 2523.5[b][1]; see also, 2523.5[b][2]). family for purposes of these two provisions is defined in section 2520.6(o) as: "A husband, wife, son, daughter, stepson, stepdaughter, father, mother, stepfather, stepmother, brother, sister, nephew, niece, uncle, aunt, grandfather, grandmother, grandson, granddaughter, father-in-law, mother-in- law, son-in-law, or daughter-in-law of the tenant or permanent tenant". All the enumerated relationships are traditional, legally recognized relationships based on blood, marriage or adoption. That being so, it would be anomalous, to say the least, were we to hold that the agency, having intentionally limited succession rights in rent-stabilized accommodations to those related by blood, marriage or adoption, intended a different result for rent-controlled accommodations; especially so when it is recognized that rent control was intended to give way to rent stabilization and that the broader the definition of family adopted, the longer rent-controlled tenancies will be perpetuated by sequentially created family members entitled to new tenancies. These expressions by the Legislature and the DHCR are far more probative of the regulation's intended meaning than the majority's selective use of a favored dictionary definition.

Finally, there are serious practical problems in adopting the plurality's interpretation of the statute. Any determination of rights under it would require first a determination of whether protection should be accorded the relationship (i.e., unmarrieds, nonadopted occupants, etc.) and then a subjective determination in each case of whether the relationship was genuine, and entitled to the protection of the law, or expedient, and an attempt to take advantage of the law. Plaintiff maintains that the machinery for such decisions is in place and that appropriate guidelines can be constructed. He refers particularly to a formulation outlined by the court in 2-4 Realty Assocs. v. Pittman, 137 Misc.2d 898, 902, 523 N.Y.S.2d 7, which sets forth six different factors to be weighed. The plurality has essentially adopted his formulation. The enumeration of such factors, and the determination that they are controlling, is a matter best left to Legislatures because it involves the type of policy making the courts should avoid (see, People v. Allen, 27 N.Y.2d 108, 112-113, 313 N.Y.S.2d 719, 261 N.E.2d 637, supra), but even if these considerations are appropriate and exclusive, the application of them cannot be made objectively and creates serious difficulties in determining who is entitled to the statutory benefit. Anyone is potentially eligible to succeed to the tenant's premises and thus, in each case, the agency will be required to make a determination of eligibility based solely on subjective factors such as the "level of emotional and financial commitment" and "the manner in which the parties have conducted their everyday lives and held themselves out to society" (plurality opin.).

By way of contrast, a construction of the regulation limited to those related to the tenant by blood, marriage or adoption provides an objective basis for determining who is entitled to succeed to the premises. That definition is not, contrary to the claim of the plurality, "inconsistent with the purposes of the system" and it would not confer the benefit of the exception on "distant blood relatives" with only superficial relationships to the deceased (plurality opin.). Certainly it does not "cast an even wider net" than does the plurality's definition (plurality opin.). To qualify, occupants must not only be related to the tenant but must also "[have] been living with the tenant" (see, 22 NYCRR 2204.6[d]). We applied the "living with" requirement in 829 Seventh Ave. Co. v. Reider, 67 N.Y.2d 930, 502 N.Y.S.2d 715, 493 N.E.2d 939, when construing the predecessor to section 2204.6(d), and refused to extend the exception to a woman who occupied an apartment for the five months before the death of her grandmother, the statutory tenant, because she was not "living with" her grandmother. We held that the granddaughter, to be entitled to the premises under the exception, was required to prove more than blood relationship and cooccupancy; she also had to prove an intention to make the premises her permanent home. Since she had failed to establish that intention, she was not entitled to succeed to her grandmother's tenancy. That ruling precludes the danger the plurality foresees that distant relatives will be enabled to take advantage of the exception contained in section 2204.6(d) (cf., 9 NYCRR 2523.5[b][1], [2]).

Rent control generally and section 2204.6, in particular, are in substantial derogation of property owners' rights. The court should not reach out and devise an expansive definition in this policy-laden area based upon limited experience and knowledge of the problems. The evidence available suggests that such a definition was not intended and that the ordinary and popular meaning of family in the traditional sense should be applied. If that construction is not favored, the Legislature or the agency can alter it...

Accordingly, I would affirm the order of the Appellate Division.

Chapter 8

LEASEHOLD ESTATES

§8.2 CLASSIFICATION OF TENANCIES

Add as Note 6 on Page 418:

6. Robert signed a printed form lease providing that Lou was granted a term to commence on May 1 and to end when Lou terminates the lease. Three years later Robert notifies Lou to vacate the premises within thirty days. Lou claims he has a determinable life estate. Robert claims the lease created a tenancy at will. Who is correct? See Garner v. Gerrish, 63 N.Y.2d 575, 483 N.Y.S.2d 973, 473 N.E.2d 223 (1984).

§8.4 FORMAL REQUIREMENTS OF A LEASE

Add as Note 5 on Page 430:

5. A lease must include a reasonably definite description of the leased premises. "A description of land is sufficient if it 'provides, when applied to the physical features of the surrounding terrain, a reasonably certain guide or means for identifying such land.'" Crown Coco, Inc. v. Red Fox Restaurant of Royalton, Inc., 409 N.W.2d 919, 921 (Minn. Ct. App. 1987). Would a defense based upon the failure to set forth a reasonably definite description in the lease be waived if the lessee took actual possession of the premises? Id. at 922.

§8.5 THE NECESSITY OF DELIVERING POSSESSION

Add as New Case Immediately Following Note 10 on Page 438:

COLLEGE BLOCK v. ATLANTIC RICHFIELD COMPANY
Court of Appeals, Second District (1988)
206 Cal.App.3d 1376, 254 Cal. Rptr. 179

ASHBY, Acting Presiding Justice.

In this matter the trial court held as a matter of law that in the parties' lease there was an implied covenant of continued operation. We find that although the parties intended the lessee to continually operate a gasoline service station for the entire leasehold period, the trial court acted prematurely and a further factual determination must be made before the covenant is implied.

Statement of Case and Facts

In 1965, respondent, The College Block (College Block) owned a parcel of undeveloped real property. College Block signed a 20-year lease with appellant Atlantic Richfield Company (ARCO) in which ARCO agreed to build and operate a gasoline service station on the property.... Other provisions of the lease allowed ARCO to build, maintain and replace any buildings ARCO desired in operating a station, obligated ARCO to pay all applicable taxes, prohibited College Block from operating a gasoline station on other properties it owned or controlled, limited ARCO's use of the property to that of a service station, and allowed ARCO the right to cancel the lease if it could not obtain permits required in running a station. Pursuant to the lease, ARCO constructed and then operated for approximately 17 years a gasoline service station on the property.

The rent, pursuant to the lease, was determined by a percentage of the gasoline delivered, and irrespective of the gallons delivered, College Block was to receive a minimum of $1,000 per month.[1]

On January 1, 1983, 39 months prior to the expiration of

---

1. Article 3 of the lease states, in pertinent part, as follows:

"Lessee shall pay as full rental for the premises during the effective term of this lease the following amounts at the following times:

"A sum equal to ONE AND ONE-QUARTER CENTS (1 1/4 cents) per gallon for each gallon of gasoline, irrespective of grade, delivered to the herein described premises; or

"A sum equal to SIX AND FIVE-TENTHS PER CENT (6.5%) of the gross price ... of all gasoline delivered to the demised premises; WHICHEVER IS GREATER provided, however, that in no event, and irrespective of the number of gallons of gasoline so delivered, shall Lessor receive less than ONE THOUSAND DOLLARS ($1,000.00) per month for each month during which this lease remains in effect. For fractional monthly periods the minimum guaranteed rental herein specified shall be duly prorated. All rent shall be paid on or about the 20th day of each calendar month following the calendar month in which deliveries are made."

the lease, ARCO closed the station. When ARCO ceased operations, it paid College Block $1,000 per month for the months remaining on the lease. ARCO contended that it was responsible only for the minimum monthly rental because the lease did not contain an express covenant requiring it to operate the station. College Block brought suit alleging that ARCO was also responsible for additional sums College Block would have received had the station remained in business. College Block contended that it was entitled to damages because as a matter of law a covenant of continued operation was implied into the lease.[2]

College Block presented its case. There was no evidence presented as to whether, at the time the lease was entered into, the parties considered the $1,000 minimum rent to be a "substantial" minimum. Before ARCO proceeded, the court ruled as a matter of law that there was an implied covenant in the lease which required ARCO to operate a gasoline station for the entire twenty (20) year lease period. Based upon this ruling, the parties subsequently stipulated that had the station been in operation, College Block would have received approximately $3,250 per month.[3] A judgment based on this amount was subsequently entered.

On appeal, ARCO contends that the court erred in concluding that the lease contained an implied covenant of continued operation. After independently evaluating and interpreting the lease...we disagree with ARCO's contention that the language of the lease is ambiguous, but agree that further evidence must be considered before implying the covenant of continued operation into the lease.

---

2. College Block also sued for specific performance and damages for alleged breach of an implied covenant of good faith and fair dealing. These claims were dismissed upon ARCO's motion for nonsuit.

3. This sum is determined by adding the principal amount of the judgment ($87,696.14) to the $39,000 paid during the thirty-nine (39) month period of time remaining on the lease and dividing the total by thirty-nine (39).

Discussion

The issue of whether there is an implied covenant of continued operation arises because the lease did not fix the rent, but guaranteed a minimum payment plus a percentage based upon the gasoline delivered. In having a percentage lease, the parties contemplated a lengthy association (20 years) during which rents would periodically be established by the market place.

A percentage lease provides a lessor with a hedge against inflation and automatically adjusts the rents if the location becomes more valuable...It is advantageous to the lessee if the "location proves undesirable or his enterprise proves unsuccessful." (...citation omitted) Thus, both parties share in the inherent business risk...Inherent within all percentage leases is the fundamental idea that the business must continually operate if it is to be successful. To make a commercial lease mutually profitable when the rent is a minimum plus a percentage, or is based totally on a percentage, a covenant to operate in good faith will be implied into the contract if the minimum rent is not substantial....

In interpreting contracts, "[t]he whole of a contract is to be taken together, so as to give effect to every part ... each clause helping to interpret the other." (Civ.Code, § 1641.) Further, contracts are to be interpreted so as to make them reasonable without violating the intention of the parties. (Civ.Code, § 1643.) To effectuate the intent of the parties, implied covenants will be found if after examining the contract as a whole it is so obvious that the parties had no reason to state the covenant, the implication arises from the language of the agreement, and there is a legal necessity....A covenant of continued operation can be implied into commercial leases containing percentage rental provisions in order for the lessor to receive that for which the lessor bargained....

We first examine the lease to determine that to which the parties bargained. The lease between ARCO and College Block required ARCO to build and operate a gasoline service station on the undeveloped property owned by College Block. Other provisions in the lease allowed ARCO to build and maintain any edifices ARCO desired in operating a service station, obligated ARCO to pay all applicable property and taxes and insurance, prohibited College Block from

conducting a gasoline station on other properties College
Block owned or controlled, gave ARCO the right of first
refusal if College Block received an offer to sell the
property, and limited ARCO's use of the property to that of
the gasoline service station.[4]

In addition, the rent was tied to the operation of the
station. The rent provision, an essential part of the lease,
did not set a minimum payment irrespective of whether the
property was utilized as a service station, but rather
"irrespective of the number of gallons ... delivered."
"Without an on-going service station operation, no basis
would exist to calculate the rent." (Continental Oil Co. v.
Bradley (1979) 198 Colo. 331, 602 P.2d 1, 2.)[5] The wording
of this provision suggests that continued operation of the
business was contemplated.

Further, it is incongruent to limit College Block's abilities
to lease properties it owned or controlled for use as another
gasoline station under the noncompetition clause, thus
foreclosing College Block from securing another station if

---

4.   Article 6 of the lease grants ARCO the right and privilege of erecting
and maintaining structures for the purpose of operating a gasoline service
station. The original draft of the lease contained a provision which would
have allowed ARCO to utilize the property for a gasoline station as well as
for any lawful purpose. This provision was deleted by the parties. We need
not consider the deleted provision to conclude that ARCO was prohibited
from utilizing the property for any purpose other than a gasoline station.
Even though "a statement as to the purpose for which premises are leased
does not imply a covenant by the lessee that he will engage in that use...."
(Lippman v. Sears, Roebuck & Co., supra, 44 Cal.2d at p. 142, 280 P.2d
775), here the parties' intent to limit Arco's use of the property is implicit
within the totality of the contract. In examining the contract as a whole, all
important provisions refer to a gasoline station. For example, the contract
provisions required ARCO to build a station, allowed ARCO the option of
canceling the lease if ARCO could not obtain permits necessary to run the
station and determined the amount of rent based upon the number of gallons
delivered. To suggest that ARCO   could utilize the property for any other
purpose would be contrary to the spirit of the entire contract.

5.   ARCO was to construct the station within 120 days. Article 30 provided
that in the event construction was not completed within the 120 days, the
rent would be $1,000 per month or any fraction of a month to be prorated.
This provision was intended to encompass situations in which construction was
not timely. It cannot, as ARCO suggests, be utilized to suggest that there
was no obligation to continuously operate the station.

ARCO abandoned the premises, and to limit ARCO's ability to operate any other type of business on the property, yet to conclude that ARCO could cease operations when it desired. Contrary to ARCO's suggestion, the fact that ARCO and not College Block was obligated to build the gasoline service station is not controlling. Both parties were entitled to the expectations as bargained for in the lease.

ARCO's contention that there is no implied covenant of continued operation is based on Article 7 of the lease. ARCO's two arguments based upon this provision have no merit. Article 7 allows ARCO "[a]t any time during the term of this lease ... [to] remove from said premises any and all buildings, structures, improvements, ..." ARCO argues that "[s]ince it is impossible for ARCO to operate a service station while simultaneously exercising its right to remove all buildings and equipment from the leased property" it therefore could cease operating the station at any time as long as College Block was paid the specified minimum rent. ARCO's interpretation of this provision is inconsistent with the spirit of the entire contract. Article 7 is the only contract clause which raises a hint of ambiguity. As shown above, when this provision is viewed in conjunction with all other provisions of the contract, the party's intent becomes evident--ARCO was expected to continually operate a station for the entire length of the lease.... Article 7 was an obvious recognition that ARCO would need the right to refurbish, replace, and upgrade its station over the 20-year lease period. However, leaving this property idle was not in the contemplation of the parties. ARCO could tear down the gasoline station, replace it, and refurbish it. However, ARCO was still obligated to operate a station for the entire leasehold period.[6]

Article 6 gave ARCO the "right and privilege of erecting

---

6. ARCO cites three cases from other jurisdictions to support its argument that a removal provision indicates that a lessee may cease operations. Williams v. Safeway Stores, Incorporated (1967) 198 Kan. 331, 424 P.2d 541 is inapplicable because the case deals with a lessee's right to sublet property. Stevens v. Mobil Oil Corp. (Mich.1976) 412 F.Supp. 809 is inapplicable because a removal clause included in the pertinent lease only mentions the business purpose (gasoline station) in two other places and provides a maximum rental in addition to the guaranteed minimum rental payment. Stemmler v. Moon Jewelry Company (Fla.1962) 139 So.2d 150 is inapplicable because it deals with a short lease (five years) and the removal provision relates to fixtures.

... structures ... that it may require or desire to use in operating ... and conducting ... business of ... a gasoline and oil filling and service station...." Relying on Hicks v. Whelan Drug Co. (1955) 131 Cal.App.2d 110, 280 P.2d 104, ARCO contends that this language did not obligate ARCO to maintain a station, but merely gave it the "privilege" of doing so. In Hicks the court held that a tenant who leased property to operate a drug store and in addition had the "privilege" of operating a restaurant or soda fountain within the drug store could not be forced to operate the soda fountain. The court based its ruling on the fact that the soda fountain was an incidental function of the primary purpose of the lease, i.e., the drug store. Unlike Hicks and another case relied upon by appellant, Masciotra v. Harlow (1951) 105 Cal.App.2d 376, 233 Cal.Rptr. 586, when ARCO closed the gasoline service station it completely frustrated the purpose of the contract. The entire purpose of the lease between College Block and ARCO was to enable ARCO to operate a gasoline station on property owned by College Block. Thus, neither Hicks nor Masciotra is controlling....

We now turn to whether the $1,000 rent minimum was "substantial." Contracts which determine rents by a percentage of sales inherently contain uncertainties. As discussed above, this type of contract is designed to adjust to the commercial realities of the day by reconciling the rent to the amount of sales. If a business is not profitable, courts are reluctant to force the lessee to continue to operate the business. However, as in all contracts, both parties are entitled to their reasonable expectations at the time the contract was entered into.... If both parties contemplated continued operations of the business, a covenant of continued operation will be implied into commercial lease containing a specified minimum plus a percentage when the guaranteed minimum is not substantial or adequate.... In this way, the lessor will receive the benefit of the lessor's bargain.

"A substantial minimum" cannot be precisely defined...and factual information on this issue must be examined before a covenant will be implied.... By evaluating the facts surrounding the formulation of the contract, the courts determine if the specified sum provides the lessor with what was reasonably expected....Here, the court erred by ruling that there was an implied covenant of continued operation in

the lease prior to receiving evidence on this factual issue.[7]
The lease between ARCO and College Block was executed
approximately 17 years prior to the cessation of operations.
In the interim, great changes in property values, gasoline
prices, and the amount of sales could have occurred.   Before
finding, as a matter of law, that a covenant of continued
operation will be implied, the trier of fact must find that the
$1,000, the guaranteed minimum, was not substantial and did
not provide College Block with a fair return on its
investment.   The parties should be given an opportunity to
submit evidence as to the facts and circumstances
surrounding the contract to determine if, at the time the
contract was entered into, the guaranteed rent was
"substantial...."   We remand to the trial court so evidence
may be heard on this issue.

The judgment is reversed and the matter remanded with
directions to proceed in accordance with the views expressed
herein.   The parties are to bear their own costs on appeal.

§8.7 INTERFERENCE WITH THE TENANT'S USE AND ENJOYMENT OF THE PREMISES

§8.7.2 The Implied Warranty of Habitability

Add to End of Problem 10 on Page 498:

In Miller v. C.W. Myers Trading Post, Inc., 85 N.C.
App. 362, 370, 355 S.E.2d 189, 194 (1987) the court stated:

> The rental or lease of residential premises for a price
> that is "fair" or below fair rental value does not
> absolve the landlord of his statutory obligation to
> provide fit premises and is not a defense to plaintiffs'
> claims.   The implied warranty of habitability entitles a
> tenant in possession of leased premises to the value of
> the premises as warranted, which may be greater than
> the rent agreed upon or paid.

---

7.   The parties stipulated to the amount of damages based upon the difference
between the guaranteed monthly rentals paid by ARCO and the lease formula.
If it is appropriate to imply a covenant, the proper measure of damages is
the amount College Block would have earned had the service station been
operational and had been used in its usual and customary manner....

Add as New Case Immediately following Note 17 on Page 500:

DAVIDOW v. INWOOD NORTH PROFESSIONAL GROUP -- PHASE I
Supreme Court of Texas (1990)
747 S.W.2d 373

SPEARS, Justice.

This case presents the question of whether there is an implied warranty by a commercial landlord that the leased premises are suitable for their intended commercial purpose. Respondent Inwood North Professional Group--Phase I sued petitioner Dr. Joseph Davidow for unpaid rent on medical office space leased by Dr. Davidow. The jury found that Inwood materially breached the lease agreement and that the defects rendered the office space unsuitable for use as a medical office. The trial court rendered judgment that Inwood take nothing and that Dr. Davidow recover damages for lost time and relocation expenses. The court of appeals reversed the trial court judgment and rendered judgment that Inwood recover unpaid rents for the remainder of the lease period and that Dr. Davidow take nothing... We affirm in part and reverse...in part.

Dr. Davidow entered into a five-year lease agreement with Inwood for medical office space. The lease required Dr. Davidow to pay Inwood $793.26 per month as rent. The lease also required Inwood to provide air conditioning, electricity, hot water, janitor and maintenance services, light fixtures, and security services. Shortly after moving into the office space, Dr. Davidow began experiencing problems with the building. The air conditioning did not work properly, often causing temperatures inside the office to rise above eighty-five degrees. The roof leaked whenever it rained, resulting in stained tiles and rotting, mildewed carpet. Patients were directed away from certain areas during rain so that they would not be dripped upon in the waiting room. Pests and rodents often infested the office. The hallways remained dark because hallway lights were unreplaced for months. Cleaning and maintenance were not provided. The parking lot was constantly filled with trash. Hot water was not provided, and on one occasion Dr. Davidow went without electricity for several days because Inwood failed to pay the electric bill. Several burglaries and various acts of vandalism occurred. Dr. Davidow finally moved out of the premises and discontinued rent payments approximately fourteen months before the lease expired.

Inwood sued Dr. Davidow for the unpaid rent and costs of restoration. Dr. Davidow answered by general denial and the affirmative defenses of material breach of the lease agreement, a void lease, and breach of an implied warranty that the premises were suitable for use as a medical office. The jury found that Inwood materially breached the lease, that Inwood warranted to Dr. Davidow that the lease space was suitable for a medical office, and that the lease space was not suitable for a medical office....

With one justice dissenting, the court of appeals reversed the trial court judgment and rendered judgment in favor of Inwood for unpaid rent. The court of appeals held that because Inwood's covenant to maintain and repair the premises was independent of Dr. Davidow's covenant to pay rent, Inwood's breach of its covenant did not justify Dr. Davidow's refusal to pay rent. The court of appeals also held that the implied warranty of habitability does not extend to commercial leaseholds and that Dr. Davidow's pleadings did not support an award of affirmative relief.

Inwood contends that the defense of material breach of the covenant to repair is insufficient as a matter of law to defeat a landlord's claim for unpaid rent. In Texas, the courts have held that the landlord's covenant to repair the premises and the tenant's covenant to pay rent are independent covenants.... Thus, a tenant is still under a duty to pay rent even though his landlord has breached his covenant to make repairs....

This theory of independent covenants in leases was established in early property law prior to the development of the concept of mutually dependent covenants in contract law. At common law, the lease was traditionally regarded as a conveyance of an interest in land, subject to the doctrine of caveat emptor. The landlord was required only to deliver the right of possession to the tenant; the tenant, in return, was required to pay rent to the landlord. Once the landlord delivered the right of possession, his part of the agreement was completed. The tenant's duty to pay rent continued as long as he retained possession, even if the buildings on the leasehold were destroyed or became uninhabitable. The landlord's breach of a lease covenant did not relieve the tenant of his duty to pay rent for the remainder of the term because the tenant still retained everything he was entitled to under the lease--the right of possession. All lease covenants were therefore considered independent....

In the past, this court has attempted to provide a more equitable and contemporary solution to landlord-tenant problems by easing the burden placed on tenants as a result of the independence of lease covenants and the doctrine of caveat emptor. See, e.g., Kamarath v. Bennett, 568 S.W.2d 658 (Tex.1978); Humber v. Morton, 426 S.W.2d 554 (Tex.1968). In Kamarath v. Bennett, we reexamined the realities of the landlord-tenant relationship in a modern context and concluded that the agrarian common-law concept is no longer indicative of the contemporary relationship between the tenant and landlord. The land is of minimal importance to the modern tenant; rather, the primary subject of most leases is the structure located on the land and the services which are to be provided to the tenant. The modern residential tenant seeks to lease a dwelling suitable for living purposes. The landlord usually has knowledge of any defects in the premises that may render it uninhabitable. In addition, the landlord, as permanent owner of the premises, should rightfully bear the cost of any necessary repairs. In most instances the landlord is in a much better bargaining position than the tenant. Accordingly, we held in Kamarath that the landlord impliedly warrants that the premises are habitable and fit for living. We further implicitly recognized that the residential tenant's obligation to pay rent is dependent upon the landlord's performance under his warranty of habitability. Kamarath, 568 S.W.2d at 660-61.

When a commercial tenant such as Dr. Davidow leases office space, many of the same considerations are involved. A significant number of commentators have recognized the similarities between residential and commercial tenants and concluded that residential warranties should be expanded to cover commercial property. See, e.g., Chused, Contemporary Dilemmas of the Javins Defense: A Note on the Need for Procedural Reform in Landlord-Tenant Law, 67 Geo.L.J. 1385, 1389 (1979); Greenfield & Margolies, An Implied Warranty of Fitness in Nonresidential Leases, 45 Albany L.Rev. 855 (1981); Levinson & Silver, Do Commercial Property Tenants Possess Warranties of Habitability?, 14 Real Estate L.J. 59 (1985); Note, Landlord-Tenant--Should a Warranty of Fitness be Implied in Commercial Leases?, 13 Rutgers L.J. 91 (1981); see also Restatement (Second) of Property § 5.1, reporter's note at 176 (1977).

It cannot be assumed that a commercial tenant is more knowledgeable about the quality of the structure than a residential tenant. A businessman cannot be expected to possess the expertise necessary to adequately inspect and repair the premises, and many commercial tenants lack the financial resources to hire inspectors and repairmen to assure the suitability of the premises. Note, supra, at 111. Additionally, because commercial tenants often enter into short-term leases, the tenants have limited economic incentive to make any extensive repairs to their premises. Levinson & Silver, supra, at 68. Consequently, commercial tenants generally rely on their landlords' greater abilities to inspect and repair the premises. Id.

In light of the many similarities between residential and commercial tenants and the modern trend towards increased consumer protection, a number of courts have indicated a willingness to apply residential property warranties to commercial tenancy situations.... [citations omitted]

There is no valid reason to imply a warranty of habitability in residential leases and not in commercial leases. Although minor distinctions can be drawn between residential and commercial tenants, those differences do not justify limiting the warranty to residential leaseholds. Therefore, we hold there is an implied warranty of suitability by the landlord in a commercial lease that the premises are suitable for their intended commercial purpose. This warranty means that at the inception of the lease there are no latent defects in the facilities that are vital to the use of the premises for their intended commercial purpose and that these essential facilities will remain in a suitable condition. If, however, the parties to a lease expressly agree that the tenant will repair certain defects, then the provisions of the lease will control.

We recognized in Kamarath that the primary objective underlying a residential leasing arrangement is "to furnish [the tenant] with quarters suitable for living purposes." Kamarath, 568 S.W.2d at 661. The same objective is present in a commercial setting. A commercial tenant desires to lease premises suitable for their intended commercial use. A commercial landlord impliedly represents that the premises are in fact suitable for that use and will remain in a suitable condition. The tenant's obligation to pay rent and the landlord's implied warranty of suitability are therefore mutually dependent.

The existence of a breach of the implied warranty of suitability in commercial leases is usually a fact question to be determined from the particular circumstances of each case. Among the factors to be considered when determining whether there has been a breach of this warranty are: the nature of the defect; its effect on the tenant's use of the premises; the length of time the defect persisted; the age of the structure; the amount of the rent; the area in which the premises are located; whether the tenant waived the defects; and whether the defect resulted from any unusual or abnormal use by the tenant.   Kamarath, 568 S.W.2d at 661.

The jury found that Inwood leased the space to Dr. Davidow for use as a medical office and that Inwood knew of the intended use.   The evidence and jury findings further indicate that Dr. Davidow was unable to use the space for the intended purpose because acts and omissions by Inwood rendered the space unsuitable for use as a medical office. The jury findings establish that Inwood breached the implied warranty of suitability.   Dr. Davidow was therefore justified in abandoning the premises and discontinuing his rent payments.

[In this section the court discusses Dr. Davidow's contention that he is entitled to certain affirmative relieve.

NOTES AND QUESTIONS

1. In light of the court's definition of the warranty, how important is it for the tenant to communicate her intended use to the landlord? How is the warranty affected if the tenant subsequently changes the use of the premises?

2. Assuming it is important to communicate tenant's intended use to the landlord, how specific must that communication be? For example, Dr. Davidow's needs vary considerably depending upon whether he was a general practitioner or a radiologist.

3. Do you agree that there is little difference between the commercial tenant and the residential tenant, as the court suggests? If not, why not?

4. To what extent is the warranty waivable?

§8.9 RETALIATORY EVICTION

Add after Problem 3 on Page 521:

May a commercial tenant claim retaliatory eviction? Ontell v. Capitol Hill E.W., Ltd., 527 A.2d 1292 (D.C. App. 1987).

§8.10 TRANSFERS OF A LEASEHOLD INTEREST

Add as New Principal Case Immediately before Notes and Questions on Page 549:

KENDALL v. ERNEST PESTANA, INC.
Supreme Court of California, 1985
40 Cal.3d 488, 220 Cal.Rptr. 818, 709 P.2d 837

BROUSSARD, Justice.

This case concerns the effect of a provision in a commercial lease[1] that the lessee may not assign the lease or sublet the premises without the lessor's prior written consent. The question we address is whether, in the absence of a provision that such consent will not be unreasonably withheld, a lessor may unreasonably and arbitrarily withhold his or her consent to an assignment.[2] This is a question of first impression in this court.

...The lease at issue is for 14,400 square feet of hangar space at the San Jose Municipal Airport. The City of San Jose, as owner of the property, leased it to Irving and Janice Perlitch, who in turn assigned their interest to respondent Ernest Pestana, Inc.... Prior to assigning their interest to respondent, the Perlitches entered into a 25-year sublease with one Robert Bixler commencing on January 1, 1970. The sublease covered an original five-year term plus four 5- year options to renew. The rental rate was to be increased every 10 years in the same proportion as rents

---

1. We are presented only with a commercial lease and therefore do not address the question whether residential leases are controlled by the principles articulated in this opinion.

2. Since the present case involves an assignment rather than a sublease, we will speak primarily in terms of assignments. However, our holding applies equally to subleases. The difference between an assignment and a sublease is that an assignment transfers the lessee's entire interest in the property whereas a sublease transfers only a portion of that interest, with the original lessee retaining a right of reentry at some point during the unexpired term of the lease....

increased on the master lease from the City of San Jose. The premises were to be used by Bixler for the purpose of conducting an airplane maintenance business.

Bixler conducted such a business under the name "Flight Services" until, in 1981, he agreed to sell the business to appellants Jack Kendall, Grady O'Hara and Vicki O'Hara. The proposed sale included the business and the equipment, inventory and improvements on the property, together with the existing lease. The proposed assignees had a stronger financial statement and greater net worth than the current lessee, Bixler, and they were willing to be bound by the terms of the lease.

The lease provided that written consent of the lessor was required before the lessee could assign his interest, and that failure to obtain such consent rendered the lease voidable at the option of the lessor.[3] Accordingly, Bixler requested consent from the Perlitches' successor-in-interest, respondent Ernest Pestana, Inc. Respondent refused to consent to the assignment and maintained that it had an absolute right arbitrarily to refuse any such request. The complaint recites that respondent demanded "increased rent and other more onerous terms" as a condition of consenting to Bixler's transfer of interest.

The proposed assignees brought suit for declaratory and injunctive relief and damages seeking, inter alia, a declaration "that the refusal of ERNEST PESTANA, INC. to consent to the assignment of the lease is unreasonable and is an unlawful restraint on the freedom of alienation...." The trial court sustained a demurrer to the complaint without leave to amend and this appeal followed.

---

3. Paragraph 13 of the sublease between the Perlitches and Bixler provides: "Lessee shall not assign this lease, or any interest therein, and shall not sublet the said premises or any part thereof, or any right or privilege appurtenant thereto, or suffer any other person (the agents and servants of Lessee excepted) to occupy or use said premises, or any portion thereof, without written consent of Lessor first had and obtained, and a consent to one assignment, subletting, occupation or use by any other person, shall not be deemed to be a consent to any subsequent assignment, subletting, occupation or use by another person. Any such assignment or subletting without this consent shall be void, and shall, at the option of Lessor, terminate this lease. This lease shall not, nor shall any interest therein, be assignable, as to the interest of lessee, by operation of a law [sic], without the written consent of Lessor."

The law generally favors free alienability of property, and California follows the common law rule that a leasehold interest is freely alienable....Contractual restrictions on the alienability of leasehold interests are, however, permitted...."Such restrictions are justified as reasonable protection of the interests of the lessor as to who shall possess and manage property in which he has a reversionary interest and from which he is deriving income." (Schoshinski, American Law of Landlord and Tenant (1980) § 8:15, at pp. 578-579. See also 2 Powell on Real Property, ¶ 246[1], at p. 372.97.)

The common law's hostility toward restraints on alienation has caused such restraints on leasehold interests to be strictly construed against the lessor. (See Schoshinski, supra, § 8.16, at pp. 583-588; 2 Powell, supra, ¶ 246[1], at pp. 372.97, 372.100.) Thus, in Chapman v. Great Western Gypsum Co. (1932) 216 Cal. 420, 14 P.2d 758, where the lease contained a covenant against assignment without the consent of the lessor, this court stated: "It hardly needs citation of authority to the principle that covenants limiting the free alienation of property such as covenants against assignment are barely tolerated and must be strictly construed." (Id., at p. 426, 14 P.2d 758.)[4] This is particularly true where the restraint in question is a "forfeiture restraint," under which the lessor has the option to terminate the lease if an assignment is made without his

---

4. There are many examples of the narrow effect given to lease terms purporting to restrict assignment. Covenants against assignment without the prior consent of the lessor have been held not to affect the lessee's right to sublease (Stevinson v. Joy (1912) 164 Cal. 279, 286, 128 p. 751), to mortgage the leasehold (Chapman v. Great Western Gypsum Co., supra, 216 Cal. at pp. 426-427, 14 P.2d 758), or to assign his or her interest to a cotenant (Hoops v. Tate (1951) 104 Cal.App.2d 486, 231 P.2d 560). Such covenants also do not prevent transfer of a leasehold interest by will (Burns v. McGraw (1946) 75 Cal.App.2d 481, 171 P.2d 148), by bankruptcy (Farnum v. Hefner (1889) 79 Cal. 575, 580, 21 P. 955), by the personal representative of a deceased tenant (Joost v. Castel (1939) 33 Cal.App.2d 138, 141, 91 P.2d 172), or by transfer among partners (Safeway Stores, Inc. v. Buhlinger (1927) 85 Cal.App. 717, 718-719, 259 P. 1013), or spouses (Buck v. Cardwell (1958) 161 Cal.App.2d 830, 835, 327 P.2d 223). Covenants against assignment furthermore do not prohibit transfer of the stock of a corporate tenant (Ser-Bye Corp. v. C.P. & G. Market, Inc. (1947) 78 Cal.App.2d 915, 920-921, 179 P.2d 342), or assignment of a lease to a corporation wholly owned by the tenant (Sexton v. Nelson (1964) 228 Cal.App.2d 248, 258-259, 39 Cal.Rptr. 407).

or her consent....

Nevertheless, a majority of jurisdictions have long adhered to the rule that where a lease contains an approval clause (a clause stating that the lease cannot be assigned without the prior consent of the lessor), the lessor may arbitrarily refuse to approve a proposed assignee no matter how suitable the assignee appears to be and no matter how unreasonable the lessor's objection.... The harsh consequences of this rule have often been avoided through application of the doctrines of waiver and estoppel, under which the lessor may be found to have waived (or be estopped from asserting) the right to refuse consent to assignment....

The traditional majority rule has come under steady attack in recent years. A growing minority of jurisdictions now hold that where a lease provides for assignment only with the prior consent of the lessor, such consent may be withheld only where the lessor has a commercially reasonable objection to the assignment, even in the absence of a provision in the lease stating that consent to assignment will not be unreasonably withheld....[5]

For the reasons discussed below, we conclude that the minority rule is the preferable position. Although this is an issue of first impression in this court, several decisions of the Court of Appeal have reflected the changing trend in the law on this question. In Richard v. Degen & Brody, Inc. (1960) 181 Cal.App.2d 289, 5 Cal.Rptr. 263, the court adopted the majority rule: " '[W]here a subletting or assignment of the leased premises without the consent of the lessor is prohibited, he may withhold his assent arbitrarily and without regard to the qualifications of the proposed assignee, unless ... the lease provides that consent shall not

---

5. The minority rule has also been espoused in jurisdictions where there appears to be conflicting or uncertain authority. North Carolina: See Sanders v. Tropicana (1976) 31 N.C.App. 276, 229 S.E.2d 304 [minority rule]; L & H Inv., Ltd. v. Belvey Corp. (W.D.N.C.1978) 444 F.Supp. 1321, 1325 [minority rule, applying North Carolina law]; but see Isbey v. Crews (1981) 55 N.C.App. 47, 284 S.E.2d 534 [majority rule]. Louisiana: Gamble v. New Orleans Housing Mart, Inc. (La.App.1963) 154 So.2d 625 [minority rule]; Associates Comm. Corp. v. Bayou Management Inc. (La.App.1982) 426 So.2d 672 [minority rule]; but see Illinois Central Gulf R. Co. v. Int'l Harvester Co. (La.1979) 368 So.2d 1009, 1014-1015 [majority rule]. Massachusetts: Granite Trust Bldg. Corp. v. Great A. & P. Tea Co. (D.Mass.1940) 36 F.Supp. 77 [minority rule, applying Massachusetts law; dicta].

be arbitrarily or unreasonably withheld....' " (Id., at p. 299, 5 Cal.Rptr. 263, quoting 51 C.J.S. § 36.) Richard was not followed or cited on this point until the decision in Laguna Royale Owners Association v. Darger (1981) 119 Cal.App.3d 670, 174 Cal.Rptr. 136, which questioned the "continuing vitality" of the rule in Richard and then distinguished it on its facts. (Id., at p. 681, 174 Cal.Rptr. 136.)... The court in Laguna Royale rejected the contention that an approval clause confers an absolute right to withhold consent: "We hold that in exercising its power to approve or disapprove transfers or assignments Association must act reasonably, exercising its power in a fair and nondiscriminatory manner and withholding approval only for a reason or reasons rationally related to the protection, preservation and proper operation of the property and the purposes of Association as set forth in its governing instruments." (Id., at p. 680, 174 Cal.Rptr. 136.)

Two years later, in Cohen v. Ratinoff (1983) 147 Cal.App.3d 321, 195 Cal.Rptr. 84, the same district of the Court of Appeal that had decided Richard (the second district) directly confronted and rejected the rule of that case. The court held that "where, as here, the lease provides for assignment or subletting only with the prior consent of the lessor, a lessor may refuse consent only where he has a good faith reasonable objection to the assignment or sublease, even in the absence of a provision prohibiting the unreasonable or arbitrary withholding of consent to an assignment of a commercial lease. Examples of bases for such good faith reasonable objection would be inability to fulfill terms of the lease, financial irresponsibility or instability, suitability of premises for intended use, or intended unlawful or undesirable use of premises. No such bases were raised by the lessor." (Id., at p. 330, 195 Cal.Rptr. 84.)...

Shortly thereafter, the first district of the Court of Appeal followed suit in Schweiso v. Williams (1984) 150 Cal.App.3d 883, 198 Cal.Rptr. 238, adopting the rule set forth in Cohen. The court further noted that "denying consent solely on the basis of personal taste, convenience or sensibility or in order that the landlord may charge a higher rent than originally contracted for have been held arbitrary reasons failing the tests of good faith and reasonableness under commercial leases...." (Id., at p. 886, 198 Cal.Rptr. 238, fn. omitted.)

Before the conflict among the Courts of Appeal reached

this court for resolution, the United States Court of Appeals for the Ninth Circuit was forced to resolve the conflict in Prestin v. Mobil Oil Corp. (9th Cir. 1984) 741 F.2d 268 (applying California law). The Ninth Circuit reviewed the cases discussed above and stated: "Richard has no support in later California cases, having been rejected by the one court which has bothered to mention it [Laguna Royale].[6] We therefore find that the California Supreme Court would adopt the rule recently enunciated in Cohen v. Ratinoff, 147 Cal.App.3d at 330, 195 Cal.Rptr. 84, that a lessor ... may refuse consent to an assignment or sublease only when the lessor has a good faith reasonable objection to it." (Id., at p. 271.) We now adopt the rule tentatively ascribed to us by the Prestin court, and disapprove the holdings in Richard v. Degen & Brody, Inc., supra, 181 Cal.App.2d 289, 5 Cal.Rptr. 263 and Hamilton v. Dixon (1985) 168 Cal.App.3d 1004, 214 Cal.Rptr. 639.

III.

The impetus for change in the majority rule has come from two directions, reflecting the dual nature of a lease as a conveyance of a leasehold interest and a contract... The policy against restraints on alienation pertains to leases in their nature as conveyances. Numerous courts and commentators have recognized that "[i]n recent times the necessity of permitting reasonable alienation of commercial space has become paramount in our increasingly urban society." (Schweiso v. Williams, supra, 150 Cal.App.3d at p. 887, 198 Cal.Rptr. 238....)

Civil Code section 711 provides: "Conditions restraining alienation, when repugnant to the interest created, are void." It is well settled that this rule is not absolute in its application, but forbids only unreasonable restraints on alienation.... Reasonableness is determined by comparing the justification for a particular restraint on alienation with the quantum of restraint actually imposed by it. "[T]he greater the quantum of restraint that results from enforcement of a given clause, the greater must be the justification for that enforcement." (Wellenkamp v. Bank of America,... [21 Cal.3d 943, 949, 148 Cal. Rptr. 379, 582 P.2d 970 (1978).] In

---

6. Subsequent to the Ninth Circuit ruling, the Court of Appeal for the Fourth District, in Hamilton v. Dixon (1985) 168 Cal.App.3d 1004, 214 Cal.Rptr. 639, followed the holding of Richard and rejected that of Cohen and Schweiso.

Cohen v. Ratinoff, supra, the court examined the reasonableness of the restraint created by an approval clause in a lease: "Because the lessor has an interest in the character of the proposed commercial assignee, we cannot say that an assignment provision requiring the lessor's consent to an assignment is inherently repugnant to the leasehold interest created. We do conclude, however, that if such an assignment provision is implemented in such a manner that its underlying purpose is perverted by the arbitrary or unreasonable withholding of consent, an unreasonable restraint on alienation is established." (Id., 147 Cal.App.3d at p. 329, 195 Cal.Rptr. 84, ...)

One commentator explains as follows: "The common-law hostility to restraints on alienation had a large exception with respect to estates for years. A lessor could prohibit the lessee from transferring the estate for years to whatever extent he might desire. It was believed that the objectives served by allowing such restraints outweighed the social evils implicit in the restraints, in that they gave to the lessor a needed control over the person entrusted with the lessor's property and to whom he must look for the performance of the covenants contained in the lease. Whether this reasoning retains full validity can well be doubted. Relationships between lessor and lessee have tended to become more and more impersonal. Courts have considerably lessened the effectiveness of restraint clauses by strict construction and liberal applications of the doctrine of waiver. With the shortage of housing and, in many places, of commercial space as well, the allowance of lease clauses forbidding assignments and subleases is beginning to be curtailed by statutes." (2 Powell, supra, ¶ 246[1], at pp. 372.97-372.98, fns. omitted.)[7]

The Restatement Second of Property adopts the minority rule on the validity of approval clauses in leases: "A restraint on alienation without the consent of the landlord of a tenant's interest in leased property is valid, but the landlord's consent to an alienation by the tenant cannot be withheld unreasonably, unless a freely negotiated provision

---

7. Statutes have been enacted in at least four states prohibiting lessors from arbitrarily refusing consent to the assignment of leases. (Alaska Stat., § 34.03.060 (1975) [residential leases only]; Del.Code Ann., tit. 25, § 5512, subd. (b) (1974) [residential, commercial and farm leases]; Hawaii Rev.Stat., § 516-63 [residential leases only]; N.Y.Real Prop.Law, § 226-b (McKinney 1982) [residential leases only].

in the lease gives the landlord an absolute right to withhold consent." (Rest.2d Property, § 15.2(2) (1977), ...)[8] A comment to the section explains: "The landlord may have an understandable concern about certain personal qualities of a tenant, particularly his reputation for meeting his financial obligations. The preservation of the values that go into the personal selection of the tenant justifies upholding a provision in the lease that curtails the right of the tenant to put anyone else in his place by transferring his interest, but this justification does not go to the point of allowing the landlord arbitrarily and without reason to refuse to allow the tenant to transfer an interest in leased property." (Id., com. a.) Under the Restatement rule, the lessor's interest in the character of his or her tenant is protected by the lessor's right to object to a proposed assignee on reasonable commercial grounds. (See id., reporter's note 7 at pp. 112-113.) The lessor's interests are also protected by the fact that the original lessee remains liable to the lessor as a surety even if the lessor consents to the assignment and the assignee expressly assumes the obligations of the lease....

The second impetus for change in the majority rule comes from the nature of a lease as a contract. As the Court of Appeal observed in Cohen v. Ratinoff, supra, "[s]ince Richard v. Degan & Brody, Inc. [espousing the majority rule] was decided, ... there has been an increased recognition of and emphasis on the duty of good faith and fair dealing inherent in every contract." (Id., 147 Cal.App.3d at p. 329, 195 Cal.Rptr. 84.) Thus, "[i]n every contract there is an implied covenant that neither party shall do anything which will have the effect of destroying or injuring the right of the other party to receive the fruits of the contract...." (Universal Sales Corp. v. Cal. etc. Mfg. Co. (1942) 20 Cal.2d 751, 771, 128 P.2d 665. See also Bleecher v. Conte (1981) 29 Cal.3d 345, 350, 173 Cal.Rptr. 278, 626 P.2d 1051.) "[W]here a contract confers on one party a discretionary power affecting the rights of the other, a duty is imposed to exercise that discretion in good faith and in accordance with fair dealing." (Cal. Lettuce Growers v. Union Sugar Co. (1955) 45 Cal.2d 474, 484, 289 P.2d 785. See also, Larwin-Southern California, Inc. v.

---

8. This case does not present the question of the validity of a clause absolutely prohibiting assignment, or granting absolute discretion over assignment to the lessor. We note that under the Restatement rule such a provision would be valid if freely negotiated.

J.G.B. Inv. Co. (1979) 101 Cal.App.3d 626, 640, 162 Cal.Rptr. 52.) Here the lessor retains the discretionary power to approve or disapprove an assignee proposed by the other party to the contract; this discretionary power should therefore be exercised in accordance with commercially reasonable standards. "Where a lessee is entitled to sublet under common law, but has agreed to limit that right by first acquiring the consent of the landlord, we believe the lessee has a right to expect that consent will not be unreasonably withheld." (Fernandez v. Vazquez, supra, 397 So.2d at p. 1174; accord, Boss Barbara, Inc. v. Newbill, supra, 638 P.2d at p. 1086.)[9]

Under the minority rule, the determination whether a lessor's refusal to consent was reasonable is a question of fact. Some of the factors that the trier of fact may properly consider in applying the standards of good faith and commercial reasonableness are: financial responsibility of the proposed assignee; suitability of the use for the particular property; legality of the proposed use; need for alteration of the premises; and nature of the occupancy, i.e., office, factory, clinic, etc....

Denying consent solely on the basis of personal taste, convenience or sensibility is not commercially reasonable.... Nor is it reasonable to deny consent "in order that the landlord may charge a higher rent than originally contracted for." (Schweiso v. Williams, supra, 150 Cal.App.3d at p. 886, 198 Cal.Rptr. 238....) This is because the lessor's desire for a better bargain than contracted for has nothing to do with the permissible purposes of the restraint on alienation--to protect the lessor's interest in the preservation of the property and the performance of the lease covenants. "'[T]he clause is for the protection of the landlord in its ownership and operation of the particular property--not for its general economic protection.'" (Ringwood Associates v. Jack's of Route 23, Inc.,... [153 N.J. Super. 294, 379 A.2d 508 (1977)] quoting Krieger v. Helmsley-Spear, Inc. (1973)

---

9. Some commentators have drawn an analogy between this situation and the duties of good faith and reasonableness implied in all transactions under the Uniform Commercial Code. (U.Com.Code §§ 1-203, 2-103(b); see also U.Com.Code § 1-102, com. 1 [permitting application of the U.Com.Code to matters not expressly within its scope].) See Comment, The Approval Clause in a Lease: Toward a Standard of Reasonableness, supra, 17 U.S.F.L.Rev. 681, 695; see also Levin, Withholding Consent to Assignment: The Changing Rights of the Commercial Landlord (1980) 30 De Paul L.Rev. 109, 136.)

62 N.J. 423, 302 A.2d 129, ...)

In contrast to the policy reasons advanced in favor of the minority rule, the majority rule has traditionally been justified on three grounds. Respondent raises a fourth argument in its favor as well. None of these do we find compelling.

First, it is said that a lease is a conveyance of an interest in real property, and that the lessor, having exercised a personal choice in the selection of a tenant and provided that no substitute shall be acceptable without prior consent, is under no obligation to look to anyone but the lessee for the rent. (Gruman v. Investors Diversified Services, ... 247 Minn. 502, 78 N.W.2d 377, 380; see also, Funk v. Funk, ... 102 Idaho 521, 633 P.2d 586, 591 (Bakes, C.J., dis.).) This argument is based on traditional rules of conveyancing and on concepts of freedom of ownership and control over one's property.. ..

A lessor's freedom at common law to look to no one but the lessee for the rent has, however, been undermined by the adoption in California of a rule that lessors--like all other contracting parties--have a duty to mitigate damages upon the lessee's abandonment of the property by seeking a substitute lessee. (See Civ.Code, § 1951.2.) Furthermore, the values that go into the personal selection of a lessee are preserved under the minority rule in the lessor's right to refuse consent to assignment on any commercially reasonable grounds. Such grounds include not only the obvious objections to an assignee's financial stability or proposed use of the premises, but a variety of other commercially reasonable objections as well. (See, e.g., Arrington v. Walter E. Heller Int'l Corp. (1975) 30 Ill.App.3d 631, 333 N.E.2d 50 [desire to have only one "lead tenant" in order to preserve "image of the building" as tenant's international headquarters]; Warmack v. Merchants Nat'l Bank of Fort Smith (Ark.1981) 612 S.W.2d 733 [desire for good "tenant mix" in shopping center]; List v. Dahnke (Col.App.1981) 638 P.2d 824 [lessor's refusal to consent to assignment of lease by one restaurateur to another was reasonable where lessor believed proposed specialty restaurant would not succeed at that location].) The lessor's interests are further protected by the fact that the original lessee remains a guarantor of the performance of the assignee. (See ante, p. 825 of 220 Cal.Rptr., p. 844 of 709 P.2d.)

The second justification advanced in support of the

majority rule is that an approval clause is an unambiguous reservation of absolute discretion in the lessor over assignments of the lease. The lessee could have bargained for the addition of a reasonableness clause to the lease (i.e., "consent to assignment will not be unreasonably withheld"). The lessee having failed to do so, the law should not rewrite the parties' contract for them. (See Gruman v. Investors Diversified Services, supra, 78 N.W.2d at pp. 381-382; Funk v. Funk, supra, 633 P.2d at pp. 590, 592 (Bakes, C.J., dis.).)

Numerous authorities have taken a different view of the meaning and effect of an approval clause in a lease, indicating that the clause is not "clear and unambiguous," as respondent suggests. As early as 1940, the court in Granite Trust Bldg. Corp. v. Great Atlantic & Pacific Tea Co., supra, 36 F.Supp. 77, examined a standard approval clause and stated: "It would seem to be the better law that when a lease restricts a lessee's rights by requiring consent before these rights can be exercised, it must have been in the contemplation of the parties that the lessor be required to give some reason for withholding consent." (Id., at p. 78, ...) The same view was expressed by commentators in the 1950's. (See Note, Landlord and Tenant--Right of Lessor to Refuse Any Settlement When Lease Prohibits Transfer Without Consent (1957) 41 Minn.L.Rev. 355, 358-359; Note, Real Property--Landlord and Tenant--Lessor's Arbitrary Withholding of Consent to Sublease (1957) 55 Mich.L.Rev. 1029, 1031; 2 Powell, supra, § 229, n. 79 (1950).) Again in 1963, the court in Gamble v. New Orleans Housing Mart, Inc. (La.App.1963) 154 So.2d 625, stated: "Here the lessee is simply not permitted to sublet without the written consent of the lessor. This does not prohibit or interdict subleasing. To the contrary, it permits subleasing provided only that the lessee first obtain the written consent of the lessor. It suggests or connotes that, when the lessee obtains a subtenant acceptable or satisfactory to the lessor, he may sublet.... Otherwise the provision simply would prohibit subleasing." (Id., at p. 627, final ....) In Shaker Bldg. Co. v. Federal Lime and Stone Co.,... 28 Ohio Misc. 246, 277 N.E.2d 584, the court expressed the same view: "While the lease before the court clearly states that no assignment may take place without prior consent, inherent, however, in that provision is the representation that an assignment is possible. This court is of the opinion that equally inherent in that provision is the representation that such prior consent will not be withheld under any and all circumstances, reasonable or unreasonable." It is not a rewriting of a contract, as respondent suggests, to recognize the obligations imposed by the duty of good faith and fair dealing, which duty is implied by law in every contract.

The third justification advanced in support of the majority rule is essentially based on the doctrine of stare decisis. It is argued that the courts should not depart from the common law majority rule because "many leases now in effect covering a substantial amount of real property and creating valuable property rights were carefully prepared by competent counsel in reliance upon the majority viewpoint." (Gruman v. Investors Diversified Services, ... 78 N.W.2d at p. 381... As pointed out above, however, the majority viewpoint has been far from universally held and has never been adopted by this court. Moreover, the trend in favor of the minority rule should come as no surprise to observers of the changing state of real property law in the 20th century. The minority rule is part of an increasing recognition of the contractual nature of leases and the implications in terms of contractual duties that flow therefrom. (See Green v. Superior Court (1974) 10 Cal.3d 616, 624, 111 Cal.Rptr. 704, 517 P.2d 1168.) We would be remiss in our duty if we declined to question a view held by the majority of jurisdictions simply because it is held by a majority. As we stated in Rodriguez v. Bethlehem Steel Corp. (1974) 12 Cal.3d 382, 115 Cal.Rptr. 765, 525 P.2d 669, the "vitality [of the common law] can flourish only so long as the courts remain alert to their obligation and opportunity to change the common law when reason and equity demand it." (Id., at p. 394, 115 Cal.Rptr. 765, 525 P.2d 669.)

A final argument in favor of the majority rule is advanced by respondent and stated as follows: "Both tradition and sound public policy dictate that the lessor has a right, under circumstances such as these, to realize the increased value of his property." Respondent essentially argues that any increase in the market value of real property during the term of a lease properly belongs to the lessor, not the lessee. We reject this assertion. One California commentator has written: "[W]hen the lessee executed the lease he acquired the contractual right for the exclusive use of the premises, and all of the benefits and detriment attendant to possession, for the term of the contract. He took the downside risk that he would be paying too much rent if there should be a depression in the rental market.... Why should he be deprived of the contractual benefits of the lease because of the fortuitous inflation in the marketplace[?] By reaping the benefits he does not deprive the landlord of anything to which the landlord was otherwise entitled. The landlord agreed to dispose of possession for the limited term and he could not reasonably anticipate any more than what was given to him by the terms of the lease. His reversionary estate will benefit from the increased value from the inflation in any event, at least upon the expiration of the lease." (Miller & Starr, Current Law of Cal. Real Estate (1977) 1984 Supp., § 27:92 at p. 321.)

Respondent here is trying to get more than it bargained for in the lease. A lessor is free to build periodic rent increases into a lease, as the lessor did here. (See ante, p. 821 of 220 Cal.Rptr., p. 840 of 709 P.2d.) Any increased value of the property beyond this "belongs" to the lessor only in the sense, as explained above, that the lessor's reversionary estate will benefit from it upon the expiration of the lease. We must therefore reject respondent's argument in this regard.[10]

A different argument in favor of the majority rule is suggested by the Court of Appeal in its opinion in this case, though the point was never raised by the parties. The Court of Appeal drew an inference from Civil Code section 1951.4 that the Legislature, when it adopted that section in 1970, considered and rejected the minority rule on approval clauses.

Section 1951.4 provides, in essence, that a lessor can avoid the statutory duty to mitigate damages (see Civ.Code, § 1951.2) by contracting to shift that duty onto the lessee. The lessor could only recover, in the event of the lessee's breach, that amount of damages which the lessor could not reasonably avoid by reletting the premises. Since the statutory scheme would be frustrated if the lessor could first contract to shift the duty of mitigation onto the lessee and then block the lessee's attempts to assign or sublease, the statute provides that where consent to assignment is required, the lease must expressly state that such consent will not be unreasonably withheld. (Civ.Code, § 1951.4, subd. (b)(3).)

---

10. Amicus Pillsbury, Madison & Sutro request that we make clear that, "whatever principle governs in the absence of express lease provisions, nothing bars the parties to commercial lease transactions from making their own arrangements respecting the allocation of appreciated rentals if there is a transfer of the leasehold." This principle we affirm; we merely hold that the clause in the instant lease established no such arrangement.

It is true that section 1951.4 impliedly recognizes that absent a "reasonableness" clause, a lessor might believe that he or she had a common law right arbitrarily to withhold consent to assignment, and thus frustrate the statutory scheme. However, implicit recognition in a statute of an existing common law rule that is not the subject of the statute does not constitute a codification of that rule, and certainly does not prevent a court from reexamining it. We cannot agree with the Court of Appeal's speculation that the Legislature, when it adopted section 1951.4 in 1970, considered and rejected the minority position on the interpretation of an approval clause in a lease.

IV.

In conclusion, both the policy against restraints on alienation and the implied contractual duty of good faith and fair dealing militate in favor of adoption of the rule that where a commercial lease provides for assignment only with the prior consent of the lessor, such consent may be withheld only where the lessor has a commercially reasonable objection to the assignee or the proposed use. Under this rule, appellants have stated a cause of action against respondent Ernest Pestana, Inc.

The order sustaining the demurrer to the complaint, which we have deemed to incorporate a judgment of dismissal,...is reversed.

[Dissent Omitted]

TRUSCHINGER v. PAK
Supreme Court of Louisiana 1987
513 So.2d 1151

DIXON, CHIEF JUSTICE.

This is a suit for damages for failure to consent to a sublease. The trial court found that the lessor, Mitchell Serio, unreasonably withheld his consent to a sublease between plaintiff Hanina Truschinger and co-defendants, Helen Pak, Buddy Pak, Mary Tsar and Mark Tsai. The court of appeal affirmed... We reverse.

This case involves a piece of property leased and subsequently subleased several times. In September, 1976, defendant-lessor Mitchell Serio leased property at 140 St.

Charles Avenue to lessee Kenneth Upton, individually and as president of Flame-N-Burger, for use as a fast food hamburger restaurant. The property was located two doors from Serio's delicatessen at 130 St. Charles Avenue. The lease was to run from October, 1976 to October, 1986, with an option to renew for a second ten year term. In addition to a monthly rent of $900, Upton paid Serio $15,000 "as consideration for obtaining the lease." The lease also contained two clauses of importance in this case: (1) if Serio sold the building, the lease would be canceled and the lessee obligated to vacate upon twelve months' notice; (2) the lessee Upton was not permitted to sublease without the written consent of the lessor, Serio.

In August, 1977, Upton sublet the property to Art Spiropoulous who ran the business as the "Coffee Cove," selling Greek and American food. In addition to being obligated to pay the monthly rent, Spiropoulous paid Upton $15,000 "as consideration for obtaining this sublease," and Spiropoulous agreed to abide by the terms in the primary lease. Serio consented in writing to that sublease.

Spiropoulous and his wife, Lynne Portlock, divorced in 1980. As part of the property settlement executed by them in 1979, Portlock assumed the obligations of the sublease.

Both sublessor Upton and lessor Serio signed an "Agreement to Add Additional Party [Portlock] to Sublease" on January 7, 1980. Lynne Portlock subsequently sublet the property to plaintiff Hanina Truschinger on July 1, 1980. Truschinger agreed to abide by the terms of the primary lease and paid Portlock $32,000 consideration "for obtaining the sublease and for the trade name `Coffee Cove.'" Truschinger, Portlock and Upton signed this sublease; Serio did not.

Although the primary lease stated that Serio's consent was necessary for subleasing, Truschinger nevertheless ran the business for three years until, planning to move to another City to help care for her sick mother, she found two couples, the Paks and Tsars, who were willing to buy the business and sublet the property. The Paks and Tsais planned to add some Oriental food items to the menu. In September, 1983, Swan Realty, through its agent, Kenneth Upton, negotiated the offer to purchase and sublease. The Paks and Tsars agreed to abide by the terms of the primary lease and to pay $80,000 as consideration for obtaining the sublease and for the trade name "Coffee Cove." Truschinger,

as part of the agreement, consented to pay the agent's
commission of 6%; Upton was to receive 3% or $2400. The
offer was conditioned upon the approval of both sublessor
Upton and lessor Serio. Upton approved; Serio did not. As
a result of Serio's failure to consent to the sublease, the
sale and sublease were never consummated.

Truschinger filed suit against Serio,[1] alleging that he
arbitrarily and capriciously withheld his consent, resulting
in $80,000 damages for the loss of the sale.

At trial on the merits, Truschinger and Serio offered
contradictory evidence on the events that occurred when
Truschinger attempted to secure Serio's consent to the
sublease. Essentially, Truschinger's testimony was that in
September, 1983, she and her sister met with Serio at his
delicatessen where he told Truschinger that he would sign
the sublease for half the purchase price of the business--
$40,000. Truschinger also testified to a second meeting,
attended by herself, her sister, Mitchell Serio, Jack Serio,
a nephew, and Nick Noriea, an attorney for Serio.
Truschinger stated that Noriea told her to give Serio $40,000
to obtain his consent.

Further, Truschinger attested to a phone conversation
between herself and Jack Serio in which the latter stated
that if Truschinger could convince the purchasers to pay
$1200 instead of $900 per month rent that Mitchell Serio
would leave her alone. Truschinger's sister corroborated the
testimony regarding the meetings.

Mitchell Serio and witnesses for the defense, Jack Serio
and attorney Nick Noriea, denied that any discussion about
money in exchange for consent ever transpired. Serio also
introduced evidence of three letters written on his behalf
by Nick Noriea. The first, dated October 11, 1983 and sent
to Truschinger's attorney and Kenneth Upton, stated that
Serio objected to any further subleasing of the property and
that Serio considered the lease violated in three respects:
(1) the Portlock-Truschinger sublease was entered into
without Serio's written consent; (2) the purpose of the
original lease had been greatly expanded; (3) the property
had been poorly maintained.

---

1. The Paks and Tsais and Kenneth Upton were also defendants in this
suit; they are no longer parties.

The second letter, dated November 1, 1983, and sent to the attorney for the Paks and Tsars, requested a menu and description of the food to be sold at the "Coffee Cove." Noriea stated in the letter that Serio was negotiating with a prospective tenant for his own delicatessen and that that potential lessee planned to run an Oriental food business there.

The third letter, dated December 12, 1983, and sent to Kenneth Upton, informed him that he was in violation of his lease in two regards: (1) the use of the property in 1983 was not in accord with the "fast food hamburger restaurant" use stated in the primary lease; (2) Upton had not obtained Serio's written consent before subletting to Truschinger. Additionally, Serio testified that he also withheld consent from the sublease at issue here because he was negotiating at that time for the sale of the building in which the "Coffee Cove" was located.

The trial court held that Serio unreasonably withheld his consent and awarded Truschinger $80,000 in damages. The court noted that the only "real and valid objection that Mr. Serio could have to the sublease would be the operation of a competing Chinese restaurant" but concluded that "this excuse was not made known to the plaintiff or Mr. Upton until sometime later and that it has been used during this trial as a tactical defense."

The Fourth Circuit Court of Appeal, Judge Ward dissenting, affirmed on the ground that the determination of what constitutes unreasonable withholding of consent is a factual one and that the trial court committed no manifest error in finding that the reasons advanced by Serio "were insufficient or not credible enough to support defendant's rejection of the proposed sublease. Truschinger v. Pak,... [503 So.2d 208, 210 (La.App. 4th Cir. 1987).] We granted writs to review the standard applied by the lower courts to Serio's refusal to consent to the sublease.

Article 2725 of the Louisiana Civil Code provides that the lessor may by contract prohibit the lessee from entering a sublease:

The lessee has the right to underlease, or even to cede his lease to another person, unless this power has been expressly interdicted.

The interdiction may be for the whole, or for a part; and

this clause is always construed strictly.'

The article is not clear as to whether a clause expressly interdicting the lessee's right to sublease is to be construed strictly for or against the lessee. However, this Court has said that '[t]he language is taken literally . from the Napoleon Code; and the interpretation which it appears to have uniformly received in France ... is that the prohibition must be construed strictly against the lessee.' Cordeviolle v. Redon, 4 La.Ann. 40 (1849)." Illinois Central Gulf Railroad Co. v. International Harvester Co., 368 So.2d 1009, 1013 (La. 1979).

A lease partly interdicts a lessee's right when it stipulates that the lessor's written consent to the sublease must be obtained. A lease also partly interdicts a lessee's right to sublease when it specifies that the written consent of the lessor may not be unreasonably withheld. When a lease contains only the stipulation that the lessor's written consent is necessary to sublease, the lessor's right to refuse will be judicially protected unless the lessor has abused that right. Illinois Central Gulf Railroad Co. v. International Harvester, supra. When a lease contains the additional proviso that the lessor's consent may not be unreasonably withheld, the lessor's right to refuse will be judicially protected unless the lessor's refusal was unreasonable. Caplan v. Latter & Blum, 468 So.2d 1188 (La. 1985).

The standard to be applied in deciding whether a lessor's refusal to consent to a sublease will be judicially protected depends on the rights that the lessee or sublessee possesses with regard to subletting. In this case, the primary lease provided that the "Lessee is not permitted to rent or sub-let ... without the written consent of the Lessor." Each subsequent sublease contained the stipulation that the sublessee was to "abide by the conditions and terms of the lease." In addition to that clause, an addendum to the sublease between Truschinger and Portlock also stipulated that if Truschinger desired to sublet, "permission must be obtained in writing from Lessor."[2] Neither the primary lease nor the subsequent subleases contained an "unreasonably withholding" clause that limited the rights of the lessor, Serio. In each lease and sublease Serio had clearly

2. This clause did not purport to give Truschinger a greater right to sublet; nor could it. Only Serio could give a lessee or sublessee a greater right than what was already stated in the primary lease.

prohibited subletting without his written consent.

Truschinger never obtained the right to sublet. Serio never lost the right to refuse to consent to a sublease by Truschinger. The only possibility is an application of the doctrine of abuse of rights. The Abuse of Rights doctrine is a civilian concept which is applied only in limited circumstances because its application renders unenforceable one's otherwise judicially protected rights. In Morse v. J. Ray McDermott & Co., 344 So.2d 1353 (La. 1977), this court recognized the Abuse of Rights doctrine. There, we held that an employer could not defeat his obligation to pay an employee the remaining portions of the employee's compensation by terminating his employment without cause. Since that case, neither this court nor the courts of appeal have applied the doctrine.

The Abuse of Rights doctrine has been applied only when one of the following conditions is met:

(1) if the predominant motive for it was to cause harm;

(2) if there was no serious or legitimate motive for refusing;

(3) if the exercise of the right to refuse is against moral rules, good faith, or elementary fairness;

(4) if the right to refuse is exercised for a purpose other than that for which it is granted.

Illinois Central Gulf Railroad Co. v. International Harvester Co., supra; Cueto-Rua, Abuse of Rights, 35 La.L.Rev. 965 (1975).

We defer to the trial court's finding that Serio informed Truschinger that he wanted one-half the purchase price (that is, $40,000), in return for his consent. Truschinger refused; Serio withheld his consent. His refusal does not rise to an abuse of rights. Serio's predominant motive was economic; it was not a wish to harm Truschinger. Serio's motive was serious and legitimate. Each lessor or sublessor in this chain received consideration for granting the lease or sublease. Each lessee or sublessee agreed to pay the consideration. The record is devoid of any evidence that such business practice is against moral rules, good faith, or elementary fairness. Serio received $15,000 when he leased to Upton. Each succeeding sublessor received a sum at least as great as that. Serio's refusal was exercised for the purpose for which it was granted--for the owner to maintain control over who leases his property.

For the foregoing reasons, the judgments of the courts below are reversed, and there is now judgment in favor of defendant, Mitchell Serio, and against plaintiff, Hanina Truschinger, dismissing plaintiff's suit at her cost.

BERKELEY DEVELOPMENT CO. v. THE GREAT ATLANTIC & PACIFIC TEA COMPANY
Superior Court of New Jersey, Law Division (1986)
214 N.J. Super. 227, 518 A.2d 790

BOYLE, J.S.C.

The issue in this case is: does a tenant-assignee, a modern chain drug store, selling general merchandise including food, have the right to enforce a covenant against competition contained in an original lease between the landlord, a shopping center owner, and the original tenant-assignor, a supermarket, where the tenant-assignor has ceased its operations within the shopping center?

This court has decided that it does not under the circumstances.

Plaintiff, Berkeley Development Co. (Berkeley), filed a complaint for declaratory judgment...against defendants, Great Atlantic & Pacific Tea Co., Inc. (A & P) and Community Distributors, Inc., t/a Drug Fair (Drug Fair). Answers were filed by A & P and Drug Fair and, thereafter, Drug Fair counterclaimed against Berkeley and cross-claimed against A & P.

Berkeley has now moved for summary judgment. Both Berkeley and Drug Fair request that this court construe the terms of a lease and an "Agreement of Sublease" and make certain determinations and declarations. Counsel for A & P has submitted a letter stating that it would take no position on the motion.

The parties have stipulated that all discovery has been concluded in this case. Since there are no disputes as to any material facts, the case is ripe for summary judgment. This court has, therefore, proceeded to render its decision....

Berkeley, the landlord, is the owner of a small shopping center commonly known as Berkeley Heights Shopping Center (shopping center). On February 1, 1965, A & P became a tenant within the shopping center at 400 Springfield Avenue, Berkeley Heights, occupying one store consisting of 11,514 square feet of retail space.[1] A & P, which intended to operate a supermarket, included within the lease agreement a covenant against competition. Addendum "F" to the lease stated as follows:

> The lessor [Berkeley] obligates itself not to lease, rent or permit to be occupied a store now owned by it or wherein it is interested for the sale of food or food products within the Shopping Center now owned by the lessor so long as lessee [A & P] handles food or food products at retail. This is not intended to exclude such stores as a restaurant, luncheonette, confectionery store, drug store or bakery. This restriction is also not intended to apply to a chain, variety or department store provided, however, that any food department operated by said chain or department store does not exceed 2,000 square feet total area.

It has been established that food or food products for retail sale were displayed in the entire retail area of the A & P store, except for a small area in which beauty aids and other non-food items were sold.

Although the initial lease term ended January 31, 1976, the lease, which provided for four renewal extensions of five years each, was duly renewed and extended and continues in full force and effect. On April 16, 1977, however, A & P informed Berkeley that it was closing the store and that it intended to lease the premises to Drug Fair. Accordingly, A & P ceased to operate its food retail store shortly thereafter.

---

1. The shopping center is located on Block 701, Lot 3 on the tax map of Berkeley Heights, consisting of approximately nine acres within which is substantial vacant land. An additional series of stores, constructed earlier, are located on Lot 2; both parcels being owned by plaintiff and which physically operate together with the stores on Lot 3 as one shopping center with a sharing of parking, particularly on Lot 3. There are a total of approximately 18 stores. Drug Fair operates a store on Lot 3. There are several stores that sell food products, including a Chinese restaurant, a health food store and a dairy food store which comprise exceptions as set forth in addendum "F" of the lease.

A document entitled "Agreement of Sublease" was entered into on May 4, 1977 between A & P as "sublessor" and Drug Fair as "sublessee." In the agreement between A & P and Drug Fair, A & P purported to sublet its lease to Drug Fair. Paragraph 26 of the lease provides in part that:

Each and every provision of this lease shall bind and shall inure for the benefit of the parties hereto, their legal representatives, heirs, successors and assigns ...

and under paragraph 5A of the "Agreement to Sublease" it was provided that:

All of the rights and obligations contained in the overlease conferred and imposed upon the Sublessor (as Tenant therein) except as modified and amended by this Sublease, are hereby conferred and imposed upon Sublessee....

Drug Fair commenced business at the premises in July 1977.

It has been contended by Drug Fair that the primary business of the store at the premises is that of a "modern chain drug store" which sells "food and foodstuffs, pharmaceuticals and general merchandise." At the same time, it has been admitted that the store devotes only 1,200 to 2,000 square feet to the sale of food or food products which accounts for only 7% of the entire retail space.

Berkeley now seeks to lease to a supermarket a store to be constructed on the premises. It contends, in sum, that the covenant against competition established in addendum "F" to the lease between Berkeley and A & P prevents Berkeley from leasing space to a supermarket elsewhere in the shopping center only as long as the lessee continued to sell food in a widely-varied supermarket operation. Since Drug Fair now occupies the premises, operating a modern chain drug store, Berkeley claims that the basis for the covenant against competition no longer exists. Berkeley insists that Drug Fair does not handle food or food products at retail to the extent sold by a supermarket and that the restrictive lease provision was clearly designed only to preclude the possibility of having two supermarkets in operation simultaneously at the shopping center.

Drug Fair, on the other hand, contends that it has the right, by virtue of its "Agreement of Sublease" with A & P, to enforce addendum "F" for its own benefit, thereby preventing Berkeley from leasing to a supermarket elsewhere in the shopping center.

It is initially necessary to decide whether the document entitled "Agreement of Sublease" is a sublease or is, in fact, an assignment. The extent of the rights that Drug Fair obtained from A & P will depend upon this determination. Before declaring whether Drug Fair can assert addendum "F" of the lease, it is necessary to determine whether Drug Fair can enforce such a restraint against Berkeley.

Assignment and subletting are naturally incident to a leasehold estate. They cannot be restricted unless by express stipulation to that effect.... Therefore, absent a negative covenant or provision, a lease is as assignable as any other contractual right.... At the same time, if a lease does not contain a provision restraining the lessee from subletting, the lessee may do so at its option, even over the landlord's objection.... In the present case, the lease between Berkeley and A & P contains no language which would prevent the lease from being either assigned or sublet to any third party.

The document entered into between A & P and Drug Fair is clearly entitled "Agreement of Sublease." Furthermore, A & P is called the "sublessor" and Drug Fair is called the "sublessee" throughout the agreement. If this court were simply to look at the form of the agreement, it would be constrained to find that the parties entered into a sublease. Consequently, the answer to the question initially posed would be clear. Drug Fair would be unable to attempt to enforce addendum "F" against Berkeley.

It is well established that a subletting creates the relationship of landlord and tenant between the sublessor and the sublessee. There is no privity of contract...or estate between the landlord and the subtenant with the lessee standing as a buffer between the landlord and the subtenant.... The sublease vests no right in the sublessee to enforce the sublessor's agreement contained in the original lease.... Therefore, the insulation that exists between the prime tenant and the subtenant prevents the subtenant from enforcing against the landlord any rights given in the prime lease to the prime tenant....

Whether an agreement is an assignment or a sublease is not, however, dependent solely upon form. Rather than

relying upon the title given to a transaction by the parties,
a court must consider the actual terms and conditions of the
agreement.... Where the whole term of the lease is
transferred by a lessee to a third party, the transfer is an
assignment, not a subletting.... The lessee cannot retain
some control or interest in the lease...and he cannot reserve
a reversionary interest in the leasehold estate.... A
reversion is an absolute right of possession in the lessee
after the expiration of the transferee's interest for a period
of time however short.... Retaining only a contingent right
or possibility of possession such as the lessee's reservation
of the power of reentry for non-payment of rent or default
does not constitute a reversion....

The agreement entered into between A & P and Drug Fair
is an assignment. Reversionary rights are not retained by A
& P and the substance of the document evidences a transfer
by A & P of all of its interest in the store for the entire
unexpired term of the lease. The entire premises at 400
Springfield Avenue, previously occupied by A & P, is now
occupied by Drug Fair. More importantly, paragraph three
of the agreement provided that the initial term would expire
on January 30, 1981 and that Drug Fair would then be
entitled to three, five-year renewal options. Under the lease
agreement between A & P and Berkeley, A & P also would
have had on January 30, 1981 the right to exercise three,
five-year renewal options. Hence, A & P transferred to Drug
Fair whatever leasehold interest it had.

Since the document is actually an assignment despite its
being labeled as a sublease, this court holds that Drug Fair
can assert whatever rights A & P would have been able to
assert with respect to the enforcement of addendum "F." In
an assignment, privity of estate is created between the
lessor and the assignee... and, as a result, the assignee
assumes the burden and accedes to the benefit of all real
covenants.... The assignee takes all that interest in the
premises which his assignor had.... Additionally, paragraph
26 of the lease specifically entitles any assignee to receive
the benefit of all of the lease provisions and addendum "F"
is a provision in the original lease....

[The court then proceeded to consider the claim that the
restriction was an unreasonable restraint of trade an
concluded that it was not.]

Thus, the motion for summary judgment is hereby granted
to plaintiff and, accordingly, Berkeley can grant a tenancy

within the shopping center to a supermarket. An order consistent with this judgment shall be submitted forthwith.

Add after Problem 3 on Page 560:

T leased property form L.   T then assigned his interest to S, the sublessee. T defaulted on his rent payment to L and as a result, S was evicted from the property.   Can S sue T for breach of the covenant of quiet enjoyment? Can S sue L? Diminich v. 2001 Enterprises, Inc., 292 S.C. 141, 355 S.E.2d 275 (1987).

§8.13   RENT CONTROL

p. 589, substitute the following for the Cotati opinion:
PENNELL v. CITY OF SAN JOSE
Supreme Court of the United States (1988)
485 U.S. 1, 108 S.Ct. 849

CHIEF JUSTICE REHNQUIST delivered the opinion of the Court.

This case involves a challenge to a rent control ordinance enacted by the City of San Jose, California, that allows a hearing officer to consider, among other factors, the "hardship to a tenant" when determining whether to approve a rent increase proposed by a landlord. Appellants Richard Pennell and the Tri-County Apartment House Owners Association sued in the Superior Court of Santa Clara County seeking a declaration that the ordinance, in particular the "tenant hardship" provisions, are "facially unconstitutional and therefore . . . illegal and void." * * *

At the heart of the Ordinance is a mechanism for determining the amount by which landlords subject to its provisions may increase the annual rent which they charge their tenants. A landlord is automatically entitled to raise the rent of a tenant in possession by as much as eight percent; if a tenant objects to an increase greater than eight percent, a hearing is required before a "Mediation Hearing Officer" to determine whether the landlord's proposed increase is "reasonable under the circumstances." The Ordinance sets forth a number of factors to be considered by the hearing officer in making this determination, including "the hardship to a tenant."   Because appellants concentrate their attack on the consideration of this factor, we set forth the relevant provision of the Ordinance in full:

   §5703.29 Hardship to Tenants. In the case of a rent increase or any portion thereof which exceeds the standard set in Section 5703.28(a) or (b), then with

respect to such excess and whether or not to allow same to be part of the increase allowed under this Chapter, the Hearing Officer shall consider the economic and financial hardship imposed on the present tenant or tenants of the unit or units to which such increases apply. If, on balance, the Hearing Officer determines that the proposed increase constitutes an unreasonably severe financial or economic hardship on a particular tenant, he may order that the excess of the increase which is subject to consideration under subparagraph (c) of Section 5703.28, or any portion thereof, be disallowed. Any tenant whose household income and monthly housing expense meets [certain income requirements] shall be deemed to be suffering under financial and economic hardship which must be weighed in the Hearing Officer's determination. The burden of proof in establishing any other economic hardship shall be on the tenant."

If either a tenant or a landlord is dissatisfied with the decision of the hearing officer, the Ordinance provides for binding arbitration. A landlord who attempts to charge or who receives rent in excess of the maximum rent established as provided in the Ordinance is subject to criminal and civil penalties. * * *

[W]e first address appellants' contention that application of the Ordinance's tenant hardship provisions violates the Fifth and Fourteenth Amendments' prohibition against taking of private property for public use without just compensation. In essence, appellants' claim is as follows: §5703.28 of the Ordinance establishes the seven factors that a Hearing Officer is to take into account in determining the reasonable rent increase. The first six of these factors are all objective, and are related either to the landlord's costs of providing an adequate rental unit, or to the condition of the rental market. Application of these six standards results in a rent that is "reasonable" by reference to what appellants' contend is the only legitimate purpose of rent control: the elimination of "excessive" rents caused by San Jose's housing shortage. When the Hearing Officer then takes into account "hardship to a tenant" pursuant to §5703.28(c)(7) and reduces the rent below the objectively "reasonable" amount established by the first six factors, this additional reduction in the rent increase constitutes a "taking." This taking is impermissible because it does not serve the purpose of eliminating excessive rents -- that objective has already been accomplished by considering the first six factors -- instead, it serves only the purpose of providing assistance to "hardship tenants." In short, appellants contend, the additional reduction of rent on grounds of hardship accomplishes a transfer of the landlord's property to individual hardship tenants; the Ordinance forces private individuals to shoulder the "public" burden of subsidizing their poor tenants' housing. * * *

We think it would be premature to consider this contention on the present record. As things stand, there simply is no evidence that the "tenant hardship clause" has in fact ever been relied upon by a Hearing Officer to reduce a rent below the figure it would have been set at on the basis of the other factors set forth in the Ordinance. In addition, there is nothing in the Ordinance requiring that a Hearing Officer in fact reduce a proposed rent increase on grounds of tenant hardship. Section 5703.29 does make it mandatory that hardship be considered -- it states that "the Hearing Officer shall consider the economic hardship imposed on the present tenant" -- but it then goes on to state that if "the proposed increase constitutes an unreasonably severe financial or economic hardship * * * he may order that the excess of the increase" be disallowed. §5703.29. Given the "essentially ad hoc, factual inquir[y]" involved in the takings analysis, Kaiser Aetna v. United States, 444 U.S. 164, 175, 100 S.Ct. 383, 390, 62 L.Ed.2d 332 (1979), we have found it particularly important in takings cases to adhere to our admonition that "the constitutionality of statutes ought not be decided except in an actual factual setting that makes such a decision necessary." * * * [T]he mere fact that a Hearing Officer is enjoined to consider hardship to the tenant in fixing a landlord's rent, without any showing in a particular case as to the consequences of that injunction in the ultimate determination of the rent, does not present a sufficiently concrete factual setting for the adjudication of the takings claim appellants raise here. * * *

Appellants also urge that the mere provision in the Ordinance that a Hearing Officer may consider the hardship of the tenant in finally fixing a reasonable rent renders the Ordinance "facially invalid" under the Due Process and Equal Protection Clauses, even though no landlord ever had its rent diminished by as much as one dollar because of the application of this provision. The standard for determining whether a state price-control regulation is constitutional under the Due Process Clause is well established: "Price control is 'unconstitutional . . . if arbitrary, discriminatory, or demonstrably irrelevant to the policy the legislature is free to adopt. . . .' " Permian Basin Area Rate Cases, 390 U.S. 747, 769-770, 88 S.Ct. 1344, 1361 (1968) (quoting Nebbia v. New York, 291 U.S. 502, 539, 54 S.Ct. 505, 517, 78 L.Ed. 940 (1934)). In other contexts we have recognized that the Government may intervene in the marketplace to regulate rates or prices that are artificially inflated as a result of the existence of a monopoly or near monopoly. . . . Accordingly, appellants do not dispute that the Ordinance's asserted purpose of "prevent[ing] excessive and unreasonable rent increases" caused by the "growing shortage of and increasing demand for housing in the City of San Jose. . . ." They do argue, however, that it is "arbitrary, discriminatory, or demonstrably irrelevant" for appellees to attempt to accomplish the additional goal of reducing the burden of housing costs on low-income tenants by requiring that "hardship to a tenant" be considered in determining the amount of excess rent increase that is "reasonable under the circumstances" pursuant to §5703.28. As appellants put it, "The objective of alleviating individual tenant hardship is . . . not a 'policy the legislature is free to adopt' in a rent control ordinance."

We reject this contention, however, because we have long recognized that a legitimate and rational goal of price or rate regulation is the protection of consumer welfare. * * * Here, the Ordinance establishes a scheme in which a Hearing Officer considers a number of factors in determining the reasonableness of a proposed rent increase which exceeds eight percent and which exceeds the amount deemed reasonable under either §§ 5703.28(a) or 5703.28(b). The first six factors of §5703.28(c) focus on the individual landlord -- the Hearing Officer examines the history of the premises, the landlord's costs, and the market for comparable housing. Section 5703.28(c)(5) also allows the landlord to bring forth any other financial evidence -- including presumably evidence regarding his own financial status -- to be taken into account by the Hearing Officer. It is in only this context that the Ordinance allows tenant hardship to be considered and, under §5703.29, "balance[d]" with the other factors set out in §5703.28(c). Within this scheme, §5703.28(c) represents a rational attempt to accommodate the conflicting interests of protecting tenants from burdensome rent increases while at the same time ensuring that landlords are guaranteed a fair return on their investment. We accordingly find that the Ordinance, which so carefully considers both the individual circumstances of the landlord and the tenant before determining whether to allow an additional increase in rent over and above certain amounts that are deemed reasonable, does not on its face violate the Fourteenth Amendment's Due Process Clause.

We also find that the Ordinance does not violate the Amendment's Equal Protection Clause. Here again, the standard is deferential; appellees need only show that the classification scheme embodied in the Ordinance is "rationally related to a legitimate state interest."   As we stated in Vance v. Bradley, 440 U.S. 93, 99 S.Ct. 939, 59 L.Ed.2d 171 (1979), "we will not overturn [a statute that does not burden a suspect class or a fundamental interest] unless the varying treatment of different groups or persons is so unrelated to the achievement of any combination of legitimate purposes that we can only conclude that the legislature's actions were irrational."   In light of our conclusion above that the Ordinance's tenant hardship provisions are designed to serve the legitimate purpose of protecting tenants, we can hardly conclude that it is irrational for the Ordinance to treat certain landlords differently on the basis of whether or not they have hardship tenants. The Ordinance distinguishes between landlords because doing so furthers the purpose of ensuring that individual tenants do not suffer "unreasonable" hardship; it would be inconsistent to state that hardship is a legitimate factor to be considered but then hold that appellees could not tailor the Ordinance so that only legitimate hardship cases are redressed.

For the foregoing reasons, we hold that it is premature to consider appellants' claim under the Takings Clause and we reject their facial challenge to the Ordinance under the Due Process and Equal Protection Clauses of the 14th Amendment. The judgment of the Supreme Court of California is accordingly

Affirmed.

JUSTICE SCALIA, with whom JUSTICE O'CONNOR joins, concurring in part and dissenting in part.

Appellants * * * contend that any application of the tenant hardship provision of the San Jose Ordinance would effect an uncompensated taking of private property because that provision does not substantially advance legitimate state interests and because it improperly imposes a public burden on individual landlords. I can understand how such a claim -- that a law applicable to the plaintiffs is, root and branch, invalid -- can be readily rejected on the merits, by merely noting that at least some of its applications may be lawful. But I do not understand how such a claim can possibly be avoided by considering it "premature." Suppose, for example, that the feature of the rental ordinance under attack was a provision allowing a Hearing Officer to consider the race of the apartment owner in deciding whether to allow a rent increase. It is inconceivable that we would say judicial challenge must await demonstration that this provision has actually been applied to the detriment of one of the plaintiffs. There is no difference, it seems to me, when the facial, root-and-branch challenge rests upon the Takings Clause rather than the Equal Protection Clause. * * *

[A] facial takings challenge is not premature even if it rests upon the ground that the ordinance deprives property owners of all economically viable use of their land -- a ground that is, as we have said, easier to establish in an "as-applied" attack. It is, if possible, even more clear that the present facial challenge is not premature, because it does not rest upon a ground that would even profit from consideration in the context of particular application. * * * Appellants contend that providing financial assistance to impecunious renters is not a state interest that can legitimately be furthered by regulating the use of property. Knowing the nature and character of the particular property in question, or the degree of its economic impairment, will in no way assist this inquiry. Such factors are as irrelevant to the present claim as we have said they are to the claim that a law effects a taking by authorizing a permanent physical invasion of property.

Today's holding has no more basis in equity than it does in precedent. Since the San Jose Ordinance does not require any specification of how much reduction in rent is attributable to each of the various factors that the Hearing Officer is allowed to take into account, it is quite possible that none of the many landlords affected by the ordinance will ever be able to meet the Court's requirement of a "showing in a particular case as to the consequences of [the hardship factor] in the ultimate determination of the rent[.]" There is no reason thus to shield alleged constitutional injustice from judicial scrutiny. I would therefore consider appellants' takings claim on the merits. * * *

Traditional land-use regulation (short of that which totally destroys the economic value of property) does not violate [the Takings clause] because there is a cause-and-effect relationship between the property use restricted by the regulation and the social evil that the regulation seeks to remedy. Since the owner's use of the property is (or, but for the regulation, would be) the source of the social problem, it cannot be said that he has been singled out unfairly. Thus, the common zoning regulations requiring subdividers to observe lot-size and set-back restrictions, and to dedicate certain areas to public streets, are in accord with our constitutional traditions because the proposed property use would otherwise be the cause of excessive congestion. The same cause-and-effect relationship is popularly thought to justify emergency price regulation: When commodities have been priced at a level that produces exorbitant returns, the owners of those commodities can be viewed as responsible for the economic hardship that occurs. Whether or not that is an accurate perception of the way a free-market economy operates, it is at least true that the owners reap unique benefits from the situation that produces the economic hardship, and in that respect singling them out to relieve it may not be regarded as "unfair." That justification might apply to the rent regulation in the present case, apart from the single feature under attack here. Appellants do not contest the validity of rent regulation in general. They acknowledge that the City may constitutionally set a "reasonable rent" according to the statutory minimum and the six other factors that must be considered by the Hearing Officer (cost of debt servicing, rental history of the unit, physical condition of the unit, changes in housing services, other financial information provided by the landlord, and market value rents for similar units). San Jose Municipal Ordinance 19696, § 5703.28(c) (1979). Appellants' only claim is that a reduction of a rent increase below what would otherwise be a "reasonable rent" under this scheme may not, consistently with the Constitution, be based on consideration of the seventh factor -- the hardship to the tenant as defined in §5703.29. I think they are right. * * *

The traditional manner in which American government has met the problem of those who cannot pay reasonable prices for privately sold necessities -- a problem caused by the society at large -- has been the distribution to such persons of funds raised from the public at large through taxes, either in cash (welfare payments) or in goods (public housing, publicly subsidized housing, and food stamps). Unless we are to abandon the guiding principle of the Takings Clause that "public burdens . . . should be borne by the public as a whole," this is the only manner that our Constitution permits. The fact that government acts through the landlord-tenant relationship does not magically transform general public welfare, which must be supported by all the public, into mere "economic regulation," which can disproportionately burden particular individuals. Here the City is not "regulating" rents in the relevant sense of preventing rents that are excessive; rather, it is using the occasion of rent regulation (accomplished by the rest of the Ordinance) to establish a welfare program privately funded by those landlords who happen to have "hardship" tenants."

The politically attractive feature of regulation is not that it permits wealth transfers to be achieved that could not be achieved otherwise; but rather that it permits them to be achieved "off budget," with relative invisibility and thus relative immunity from normal democratic processes. * * *

I would hold that the seventh factor in §5703.28(c) of the San Jose Ordinance effects a taking of property without just compensation.

* * *

BRASCHI v. STAHL ASSOCIATES COMPANY
Court of Appeals of New York (1989)
74 N.Y.2d 201, 544 N.Y.S.2d 784, 543 N.E.2d 49

(The Court's opinion is printed, *supra*, Chapter 7)

NOTES AND QUESTIONS

1. In Pinewood Estates of Michigan v. Barnegat Township Leveling Bd., 898 F.2d 347 (3d Cir. 1990) the court struck down as an unconstitutional taking a rent control ordinance that applied to mobile home lots, or "pads." The statute permanently regulated pad rents and thus permitted existing tenants, who placed their own mobile homes on the pads, to sell them, together with an assignment of the lease, at a premium price. The premium reflected the fact that the lot rents were below the market rate. The court characterized this premium as the discounted present value of rents, which under the ordinance were paid not to the land owners but rather to their tenants. This forcible transfer of a valuable property interest violated the takings clause of the fifth amendment.

Chapter 9
"PRIVATE" CONTROLS OF LAND USE: SERVITUDES

§9.2 THE CREATION OF SERVITUDES
§9.2.1 Easements by Grant, Reservation, or Other Form of Agreement

p. 622, insert the following note:
6.   In Estate of Thomson v. Wade, 69 N.Y.2d 570, 516 N.Y.S.2d 614, 615, 509 N.E.2d 309, 310 (1987) the court adhered to its earlier decisions and expressly rejected the *Willard* rule that an easement may be created in favor of a third party.   The court reasoned:

> Plaintiff invites us to abandon [the traditional] rule and adopt the minority view which would recognize an interest reserved or excepted in favor of a stranger to the deed, if such was the clearly discernible intent of the grantor (see, e.g., Willard v. First Church of Christ; Townsend v. Cable, 378 S.W.2d 806 [Ky.]; Medhus v. Dutter, 184 Mont. 437, 444, 603 P.2d 669; Restatement of Property § 472, comment [b]).   Although application of the stranger-to-the-deed rule may, at times, frustrate a grantor's intent, any such frustration can readily be avoided by the direct conveyance of an easement of record from the grantor to the third party. The overriding considerations of the "public policy favoring certainty in title to real property, both to protect bona fide purchasers and to avoid conflicts of ownership, which may engender needless litigation" persuade us to decline to depart from our settled rule. We have previously noted that in this area of law, "where it can reasonably be assumed that settled rules are necessary and necessarily relied upon, stability and adherence to precedent are generally more important than a better or even a 'correct' rule of law."

§9.2.3 Prescription, Implied Dedication, and Custom

p. 652; append the following to note 2:
Subjective intent continues to play a role in easement by prescription, even though the trend is to the contrary. See Wilfon v. Hampel Trust, 781 P.2d 769 (Nev. 1989), holding that no prescriptive easement could arise where the claimant thought he was using a roadway with the landowner's permission.
Contrast Cardenas v. Kurpjuweit, 116 Idaho 739, 742, 779 P.2d 414, 417 (1989), which rejected
the curious doctrine that a claimant's subjective state of

mind may determine whether he is entitled to a prescriptive easement. This state of mind doctrine is illogical. The 'adversity' of a claimant's use lies in its derogation from the exclusive rights of the landowner; it does not lie in the claimant's state of mind. Regardless of the motive with which a prospective claimant crosses a landowner's property, his use derogates from the landowner's rights unless the crossing is by permission, express or legally presumed. Moreover, the state of mind doctrine creates a perverse incentive to offer contrived but virtually unrebuttable testimony. A sophisticated claimant * * * would never admit having thought a road was public; he would simply testify that he used the road because he found it convenient. Accordingly, * * * the adversity of a claimant's use is determined not by his subjective belief but by the nature of the use itself. As the Washington Supreme Court has noted: "[T]here is little persuasive precedent for applying a subjective standard of adverse use in prescriptive easement cases. The gravamen of adversity in such cases is whether the user has occupied the property in a manner which is adverse to the true owner. Although subjective intent may have some relevance in an adverse possession case where the user claims title, the claim in a prescriptive easement case is merely to [a] use which could have been prevented by the rightful owner. We therefore hold that adversity is to be measured by an objective standard; that is, by the objectively observable acts of the user and the rightful owner."
Quoting Dunbar v. Heinrich, 95 Wash. 2d 20, 622 P.2d 812, 815-16 (1980). Do you agree with the court's distinction between prescriptive easements and adverse possession?

p. 652; append the following to note 5:
In United States, on Behalf of Zuni Tribe v. Platt, 730 F.Supp. 318 (D. Ariz. 1990) the court held that an Indian tribe could acquire an easement by prescription over a route used for a religious pilgrimage. Although the pilgrimage had occurred since the beginning of the twentieth century, it happened only once every four years.
Compare Town of Sparta v. Hamm, 97 N.C. App. 82, 387 S.E.2d 173 (1990), which held that a town could acquire a roadway easement by prescription based on use by mail carriers, school bus drivers and others. There was no discussion of the exclusivity requirement.

p. 653, append the following to note 8:
In McDonald v. Halvorson, 308 Or. 340, 780 P.2d 714 (1989)

the Oregon Supreme Court seemed to retreat somewhat from its ruling in State ex rel. Thornton v. Hay, 254 Or. 584, 462 P.2d 671 (1969), which applied the doctrine of "custom" to recognize public access to privately owned beach front. In *McDonald*, the court held that the doctrine of custom applied only to beach front property along the ocean, and not to a freshwater inland pool.

§9.3 SCOPE
p. 661, insert the following notes:
5. In Alabama Power Co. v. Drummond, 559 So.2d 158 (Ala. 1990) the Alabama Supreme Court upheld a lower court order that permitted a homeowner to continue to maintain a house that encroached on the flood easement of an electric utility. The court noted that although an easement is a property interest and ordinarily all encroachments should be enjoined, in this case the cost of removing the house was far greater than the damage to the easement.

6. In Frenning v. Dow, 544 A.2d 145 (R.I. 1988), the court acknowledged the common law rule extinguishing an easement appurtenant when it was used to service the nondominant estate. But then, stating that the law abhors such forfeitures, the court ordered the easement owner to come up with a plan, capable of being supervised by the owner of the servient estate, for using the easement -- apparently to service both dominant and nondominant estate -- that would not increase the authorized burden on the easement. The court likened this obligation to judicially administered school desegregation, where the court would supervise a plan put forward by the defendant.

§9.4 TRANSFER OF OBLIGATIONS AND BENEFITS
§9.4.4 Implied Servitudes
p. 707, insert the following note at the end of §9.4.4:

Note:
Implied Servitudes in the New Restatement

The Restatement (Third) Property (tent. draft no. 1, 1989) treats implied servitudes and irrevocable licenses (see casebook, pp. 609-618) as siblings. What the two share in common is that both follow upon negotiations sufficient to create some kind of expectancy interest in land, but neither manifests sufficient formality to comply with the requirements of the Statute of Frauds for creating an interest in land. The Restatement draft begins with the proposition that an easement may be created by a contract as well as a conveyance (§2.1).   It then provides:

§2.8   Failure to Comply with the Statute of Frauds
If a contract or conveyance intended to create a servitude does not comply with the Statute of Frauds, the burden of the servitude is not enforceable and the benefit is terminable at will, unless there is an applicable exemption, or unless the transaction falls within the exception set forth in §2.9, or §129 of the Restatement, Second, of Contracts.

§2.9   Exception to the Statute of Frauds
The consequences of failure to comply with the Statute of Frauds, set out in §2.8, do not apply if the beneficiary of the servitude, in reasonable reliance on the existence of the servitude, has so changed position that injustice can be avoided only by giving effect to the parties' intent to create a servitude.

§2.10   Creation by Estoppel
If injustice can be avoided only by establishment of a servitude, the owner or occupier of land is estopped to deny the existence of a servitude burdening the land when:

(1) the owner or occupier permitted another to use that land under circumstances in which it was reasonable to foresee that the user would substantially change position believing that the permission would not be revoked, and the user did substantially change position in reasonable reliance on that belief; or

(2) the owner or occupier represented that the land was burdened by a servitude under circumstances in which it was reasonable to foresee that the person to whom the representation was made would substantially change position on the basis of that representation, and the person did substantially change position in reasonable reliance on that representation.

§2.14   Servitudes Implied From General Plan
Unless the facts or circumstances indicate a contrary intent, conveyance of land pursuant to a general plan of development implies the creation of servitudes as follows:

(a) Implied Benefits: Each lot included within the general plan is the implied beneficiary of all express and implied servitudes imposed to carry out the general plan.

(b) Implied Burdens:
    (1) Language of condition that creates a restriction
or other obligation to implement the general plan
creates an implied servitude imposing the same
restriction or other obligation.
    (2) A conveyance by a developer that imposes a
servitude on the land conveyed to implement a general
plan creates an implied reciprocal servitude burdening
all the developer's remaining land included in the
general plan, if injustice can be avoided only by
implying the reciprocal servitude.

§9.5 EASEMENTS, COVENANTS AND EQUITABLE SERVITUDES: WHAT IS THE DIFFERENCE AND WHEN DOES IT MATTER

p. 718: insert the following after the second paragraph:
    The proposed Restatement (Third) Property (tent. draft
no. 1, 1989) goes very far in unifying the law of servitudes
-- certainly beyond commonly given descriptions of the law,
although perhaps not very much beyond the actual outcomes
of cases.   For one thing, the Restatement would abolish the
horizontal privity requirement:

§2.4 No Horizontal Privity Required
    No Privity relationship between the parties is necessary
to create a servitude.

The Reporter's Comment then adds:
    In American law, the horizontal privity requirement
serves no function beyond insuring that most covenants
intended to run with the land will be created in
conveyances.   Formal creation of covenants is desirable
because it tends to assure that they will be recorded.
However, the horizontal privity requirement is no longer
needed for this purpose.   In modern law, the Statute of
Frauds and recording acts perform that function.
    Application of the horizontal privity requirement
prevents enforcement at law of covenants entered into
between neighbors and between other parties who do not
transfer or share some other interest in the land.   The
rule can easily be circumvented by conveyance to a
strawperson who imposes the covenant in the
reconveyance.   Since the rule serves no necessary
purpose and simply acts as a trap for the poorly
represented, it has been abandoned.

In defending a more general approach of seeking unification in the law of servitudes, the introduction to the tentative draft, p. xxv, concludes:

The differences between equitable servitudes and real covenants that arguably persisted in 1944 [at the time of the first Restatement] have since disappeared. Any remains of the horizontal privity doctrine are purely vestigial and the English prohibition on enforcing affirmative covenants in equity has been clearly repudiated by American courts. For all practical purposes, the courts have eliminated the differences between the two branches of covenants . . . . That has permitted the reclassification in the Restatement Third of equitable servitudes as covenants, and elimination of the subset of covenants enforceable in equity, recognized by the 1944 Restatement.

Chapter 10
"PRIVATE" CONTROLS OF LAND USE:
THE LAW OF NUISANCE

§10.1 INTRODUCTION

p. 744, insert the following after the second paragraph:

Although this chapter is concerned principally with the law of private nuisance, public nuisance law continues to have considerable vitality. As a general rule, only the government may sue to enjoin a public nuisance, on the theory that such injuries accrue to the public generally, and not to individual members as individuals. An individual could claim relief only if he or she could show some "particularized" injury. But having made that showing, the injured plaintiff need not be the owner of an interest in land. See, for example, Leo v. General Electric Co., 538 N.Y.S.2d 844, 145 A.D.2d 291 (1989), which permitted fishermen to sue a water polluter on a public nuisance theory after the fish taken from the water were declared unfit for human consumption. In this case the fishermen were "peculiarly aggrieved" and could sue for both damages and injunction.

Perhaps the most interesting collection of cases recently applying public nuisance doctrine are a series of actions brought by the National Organization for Women (NOW) against people interfering with women seeking abortions or other medical services delivered at facilities that also perform abortions. See, for example, NOW v. Operation Rescue, 726 F.Supp. 1483 (E.D.Va. 1989) (applying Virginia law), finding a privately actionable public nuisance in Operation Rescue's picketing of NOW-operated abortion clinics in such a fashion as to impede the entry of women seeking abortions. Accord NOW v. Operation Rescue, 726 F.Supp. 300 (D.D.C. 1989) (applying District of Columbia law); Town of West Hartford v. Operation Rescue, 726 F.Supp. 371 (D. Conn. 1989) (applying Connecticut law). And see National Organization for Women v. Terry, Operation Rescue, 886 F.2d 1339, 1362 (2d Cir. 1989 (applying New York law), where the court noted:

> [D]efendants state that reliance on the public nuisance doctrine is misplaced because a women's right to obtain an abortion is not a right common to all members of the community. Rather, they assert, it is a wholly private right and interference with it is not actionable as a public nuisance. They claim that the City has not alleged interference with rights common to the community at large. The right shown to be disrupted is not, as defendants suggest, merely the right to obtain an abortion. The City intervened to vindicate the more

general right of City residents to obtain medical services
-- a right common to all residents of New York. Women
go to the clinics for a panoply of medical, prenatal and
counseling services. Abortion may be the principal focus
of defendants' efforts, but their tactics interfere with a
broader spectrum of rights. The demonstrations simply
pose a special threat to women seeking to obtain abortions
because of delays and cancellations caused by the
blockades. Moreover, as the district court noted,
defendants' chosen tactic of en masse demonstrations has
obstructed vehicular and pedestrian traffic in New York's
already burdened streets.

The court also rejected the defense that application of the
law of public nuisance under these circumstances would
violate the defendant's first amendment rights.

§10.4. SOCIAL COST, TRANSACTIONS COSTS, AND THE LAW OF NUISANCE

p. 789, insert the following note after the first full paragraph:

Private Bargaining v. Legislation to Regulate Pollution

One argument in favor of private bargaining as an
alternative to various forms of regulation, such as zoning,
air and water quality controls, or transportation safety
regulation, begins with the observation that Coasian markets
produce efficient results. Regulation created by legislation
can hardly do better, and will generally do much worse.
See generally Richard A. Posner, Economic Analysis of Law
247-364 (3d ed. 1986).

One problem of legislation is that invariably legislators
end up not only looking for the optimal regulatory
framework, they also redistribute wealth. Wealth distribution
games may be inherently unstable. Suppose that $100 is to
be divided among A, B & C by majority vote: an agreement
by any two will be decisive. A proposes that A and B each
take $50 and C take nothing, and the proposal wins when A
and B vote for it. But then C will propose to A that A
receive $51 and C $49, and A will be better off; C and A
will agree; and so on. This is a division game that has no
"core," or equilibrium outcome, and it produces chaos. In
the words of Kenneth J. Arrow, one of the founders of this
"chaos" theory of legislative decision making, "for any
allocation which gives some individual, say 1, a positive
amount, there is another, which gives 1 nothing and divides
up his share in the first allocation among all the others; the
second is preferred to the first by all but one individual."
1 Kenneth J. Arrow, Social Choice and Justice, Collected

Papers of Kenneth J. Arrow 87 (1983).

But are Coasian markets, aided by private tort law such as nuisance, any more reliable? The likely answer is no. Consider the problem of air quality controls that affect many people. Suppose operation of a cement factory is worth $100 to its owners, and imposes $7 in losses on each of ten homeowners. The factory's operation is actionable by any one of the ten homeowners. Now the factory must bargain with the homeowners and obtain a release from all of them, and will be willing to pay them off to make continued operation of the factory possible. There is a $30 surplus to be divided. Presumably the factory and each homeowner will attempt to capture as large a portion of that surplus as possible.

If the factory negotiates with each homeowner separately, there will be holdout problems. It can afford to pay some homeowners, say, $12, but only if it pays others less. There is no obvious reason why the wrangling could not go on indefinitely. Alternatively, the factory might place, say, $90 in an escrow account, and tell the ten homeowners to divide it among themselves. Then the problem has become identical to the legislative wealth transfer problem described above, with the added complication that each homeowner might also threaten to walk away, making the entire pot worthless. No homeowner will accept less than $7, but if the pot were divided equally each would get $9. Homeowners 1 through 8 might agree with each other that they will let homeowners 9 and 10 have only $7.50 each, and keep the remaining $75.00 for themselves, giving them around $9.35 each. But homeowners 9 and 10 might then respond by (1) refusing to bargain at all; or (2) offering owners 1 through 6 a deal that will make them a little better off than under the previous deal, but give homeowners 7 and 8 only slightly more than $7, etc., etc. In short, the chaos problem shows up in exactly the same fashion as it does in the legislative situation. If endless negotiating ("cycling") is indeed costless -- and the Coase Theorem assumes costless markets -- the parties would engage in endless bargaining for division of the proceeds in a Coasian economic market just as much as in the legislative market. See Hovenkamp, Arrow's Theorem: Ordinalism and Republican Government, 75 Iowa L. Rev. 949 (1990).

Chapter 11
TAKINGS, DELIBERATE AND INADVERTENT

§11.1 EMINENT DOMAIN
  §11.1.2 "Just Compensation"

page 818, insert the following after note 4:

LEECO GAS & OIL COMPANY
v. COUNTY OF NUECES
Supreme Court of Texas (1987)
736 S.W.2d 629

GONZALEZ, JUSTICE.
This is a condemnation suit. The issue is whether Nueces
County, as grantee in a deed, may condemn a possibility of
reverter on land given to the County and pay mere nominal
damages to the owner of the reversionary interest. The trial
court answered this issue in the affirmative and the court of
appeals affirmed the judgment of the trial court. We reverse
and remand.

In 1960, Leeco gift deeded fifty acres of land on Padre
Island to Nueces County for use as a park. Leeco retained
a reversionary interest in the deed whereby the County
would keep the property "so long as a public park is
constructed and actively maintained" by the County on the
property. The County dedicated and maintained a park on
the property. However, in 1983, the County began
condemnation proceedings against Leeco's interest. The
commissioners awarded Leeco $10,000 for its reversionary
interest. Leeco appealed to the county court at law where
the trial judge granted a partial summary judgment against
Leeco resolving all issues except damages. In a separate trial
to determine compensation for Leeco, experts testified that
the land was worth between $3,000,000 and $5,000,000. The
trial court awarded Leeco $10 in nominal damages.

The Texas Constitution provides that "[n]o person's
property shall be taken . . . for . . . public use without
adequate compensation being made, unless by the consent of
such person. . . ." Tex. Const. art. I, §17.

Generally, under the Restatement of Property, a mere
possibility of reverter has no ascertainable value when the
event upon which the possessory estate in fee simple
defeasible is to end is not probable within a reasonably short
period of time. See generally Restatement of Property §53
comment b (1936). In affirming the $10 award of nominal
damages, the court of appeals relied on City of Houston v.
McCarthy, 464 S.W.2d 381 (Tex.Civ.App. -- Houston [1st

Dist.] 1971, writ ref'd n.r.e.). In *McCarthy*, the court found that when at the time of condemnation the property was being used as permitted under the deed and there was no evidence that the restrictive covenant would ever be broken, the value of the possibility of reverter was so speculative as to be nominal only. The court of appeals then held that there was no evidence in this case that the County intended to violate the deed restrictions so long as Leeco retained the possibility of reverter and no evidence that the conditions were breached. This evidence is not determinative of the issue.

Here, one county official testified that there were "various ideas and proposals and schemes" about putting income producing activities on the land. The same official further stated that "it would be in the County's best interest" to own the park outright so that it "may in the future consider plans that are inconsistent with the present deed restrictions." Furthermore, in the County's Original Statement in Condemnation, the County pleaded that its plans for future development of the Park included "uses which could be construed to cause Plaintiff's determinable fee estate, to terminate and cease." The County further alleged that the "present use and operation of the Park" placed an "undue burden upon Plaintiff in its future development of the Park." Thus, this is not a case of condemning a "remote" possibility of reverter, but rather an attempt by the County to remove the "burden" of the reversionary interest by condemning the interest and paying nominal damages. * * *

There is a constitutional requirement that if the County is to condemn land, it must adequately compensate the landowner for the property interest taken. Ten dollars in compensation for a multi-million dollar piece of property is not adequate as a matter of law. To allow a governmental entity, as grantee in a gift deed, to condemn the grantor's reversionary interest by paying only nominal damages would have a negative impact on gifts of real property to charities and governmental entities. It would discourage these types of gifts in the future. This is not in the best interests of the citizens of this State.

We hold that when a governmental entity is the grantee in a gift deed in which the grantor retains a reversionary interest, if that same governmental entity condemns the reversionary interest, it must pay as compensation the amount by which the value of the unrestricted fee exceeds the value of the restricted fee.

We reverse the judgment of the court of appeals and remand this cause to the trial court to determine the amount by which the value of the unrestricted fee exceeds the value of the restricted fee.

NOTES AND QUESTIONS

1.   Note the narrowness of the Texas Supreme Court's holding: it appears to apply only when the condemnor is the previous donee of the possessory interest. But is the principle any different when both the possessory interest and the future interest are held by private persons? Suppose I own a fee simple determinable subject to a condition that no commercial uses be made of the property. The land is worth $10,000 subject to the restriction, but $100,000 if the restriction is removed. What is the value of the possibility of reverter? Why shouldn't its owner be entitled to this amount in an eminent domain proceeding?

Finally, note that the condemnor in this case already owned the fee simple determinable and was condemning only the possibility of reverter. The fact that such an interest is worth condemning effectively undermines any claim that the interest is worthless, does it not?

§11.2   INVERSE CONDEMNATION

page 839, insert the following before PruneYard case

KEYSTONE BITUMINOUS COAL ASSN. v.DeBENEDICTIS
Supreme Court of the United States (1987)
480 U.S. 470

JUSTICE STEVENS delivered the opinion of the Court.
In Pennsylvania Coal Co. v. Mahon, 260 U.S. 393, 43 S.Ct. 158 (1922), the Court reviewed the constitutionality of a Pennsylvania statute that admittedly destroyed "previously existing rights of property and contract." Writing for the Court, Justice Holmes explained:
> Government hardly could go on if to some extent values incident to property could not be diminished without paying for every such change in the general law. As long recognized, some values are enjoyed under an implied limitation and must yield to the police power. But obviously the implied limitation must have its limits, or the contract and due process clauses are gone. One fact for consideration in determining such limits is the extent of the diminution. When it reaches a certain magnitude, in most if not in all cases there must be an exercise of

eminent domain and compensation to sustain the act.   So
the question depends upon the particular facts.

In that case the "particular facts" led the Court to hold
that the Pennsylvania Legislature had gone beyond its
constitutional powers when it enacted a statute prohibiting
the mining of anthracite coal in a manner that would cause
the subsidence of land on which certain structures were
located.   Now, 65 years later, we address a different set of
"particular facts," involving the Pennsylvania Legislature's
1966 conclusion that the Commonwealth's existing mine
subsidence legislation had failed to protect the public interest
in safety, land conservation, preservation of affected
municipalities' tax bases, and land development in the
Commonwealth.   Based on detailed findings, the legislature
enacted the Bituminous Mine Subsidence and Land
Conservation Act (the "Subsidence Act" or the "Act").
Petitioners contend, relying heavily on our decision in
Pennsylvania Coal, that § 4 and § 6 of the Subsidence Act
and certain implementing regulations violate the Takings
Clause. * * *

I

Coal mine subsidence is the lowering of strata overlying
a coal mine, including the land surface, caused by the
extraction of underground coal.   This lowering of the strata
can have devastating effects.   It often causes substantial
damage to foundations, walls, other structural members, and
the integrity of houses and buildings.   Subsidence frequently
causes sinkholes or troughs in land which make the land
difficult or impossible to develop.   Its effect on farming has
been well documented -- many subsided areas cannot be
plowed or properly prepared.   Subsidence can also cause the
loss of groundwater and surface ponds.   In short, it
presents the type of environmental concern that has been the
focus of so much federal, state, and local regulation in
recent decades. * * *

Pennsylvania's Subsidence Act authorizes the Pennsylvania
Department of Environmental Resources (DER) to implement
and enforce a comprehensive program to prevent or minimize
subsidence and to regulate its consequences.   Section 4 of
the Subsidence Act prohibits mining that causes subsidence
damage to three categories of structures that were in place
on April 17, 1966: public buildings and noncommercial
buildings generally used by the public; dwellings used for
human habitation; and cemeteries.   Since 1966 the DER has
applied a formula that generally requires 50% of the coal
beneath structures protected by § 4 to be kept in place as
a means of providing surface support. Section 6 of the
Subsidence Act authorizes the DER to revoke a mining permit

if the removal of coal causes damage to a structure or area
protected by § 4 and the operator has not within six months
either repaired the damage, satisfied any claim arising
therefrom, or deposited a sum equal to the reasonable cost
of repair with the DER as security.* * * *

III

Petitioners assert that disposition of their takings claim
calls for no more than a straightforward application of the
Court's decision in Pennsylvania Coal Co. v. Mahon.
Although there are some obvious similarities between the
cases, we agree with the Court of Appeals and the District
Court that the similarities are far less significant than the
differences, and that *Pennsylvania Coal* does not control this
case.

In *Pennsylvania Coal*, the Pennsylvania Coal Company had
served notice on Mr. and Mrs. Mahon that the company's
mining operations beneath their premises would soon reach a
point that would cause subsidence to the surface. The
Mahons filed a bill in equity seeking to enjoin the coal
company from removing any coal that would cause "the
caving in, collapse or subsidence" of their dwelling. The
bill acknowledged that the Mahons owned only "the surface
or right of soil" in the lot, and that the Coal Company had
reserved the right to remove the coal without any liability to
the owner of the surface estate. Nonetheless, the Mahons
asserted that Pennsylvania's then recently enacted Kohler Act
of 1921, which prohibited mining that caused subsidence
under certain structures, entitled them to an injunction. *
* * *

Over Justice Brandeis' dissent, this Court accepted the
company's argument. In his opinion for the Court, Justice
Holmes first characteristically decided the specific case at
hand in a single, terse paragraph:

This is the case of a single private house. No doubt
there is a public interest even in this, as there is in
every purchase and sale and in all that happens within
the commonwealth. Some existing rights may be modified
even in such a case. But usually in ordinary private
affairs the public interest does not warrant much of this
kind of interference. A source of damage to such a
house is not a public nuisance even if similar damage is
inflicted on others in different places. The damage is not
common or public. The extent of the public interest is
shown by the statute to be limited, since the statute
ordinarily does not apply to land when the surface is
owned by the owner of the coal. Furthermore, it is not
justified as a protection of personal safety. That could
be provided for by notice. Indeed the very foundation

of this bill is that the defendant gave timely notice of its intent to mine under the house. On the other hand the extent of the taking is great. It purports to abolish what is recognized in Pennsylvania as an estate in land -- a very valuable estate -- and what is declared by the Court below to be a contract hitherto binding the plaintiffs. If we were called upon to deal with the plaintiffs' position alone, we should think it clear that the statute does not disclose a public interest sufficient to warrant so extensive a destruction of the defendant's constitutionally protected rights."

Then -- uncharacteristically -- Justice Holmes provided the parties with an advisory opinion discussing "the general validity of the Act." In the advisory portion of the Court's opinion, Justice Holmes rested on two propositions, both critical to the Court's decision. First, because it served only private interests, not health or safety, the Kohler Act could not be "sustained as an exercise of the police power." Second, the statute made it "commercially impracticable" to mine "certain coal" in the areas affected by the Kohler Act.

The holdings and assumptions of the Court in *Pennsylvania Coal* provide obvious and necessary reasons for distinguishing *Pennsylvania Coal* from the case before us today. The two factors that the Court considered relevant, have become integral parts of our takings analysis. We have held that land use regulation can effect a taking if it "does not substantially advance legitimate state interests, . . . or denies an owner economically viable use of his land." Agins v. Tiburon, 447 U.S. 255, 260, 100 S.Ct. 2138, 2141 (1980); Penn Central Transportation Co. v. New York City. Application of these tests to petitioners' challenge demonstrates that they have not satisfied their burden of showing that the Subsidence Act constitutes a taking. First, unlike the Kohler Act, the character of the governmental action involved here leans heavily against finding a taking; the Commonwealth of Pennsylvania has acted to arrest what it perceives to be a significant threat to the common welfare. Second, there is no record in this case to support a finding, similar to the one the Court made in *Pennsylvania Coal*, that the Subsidence Act makes it impossible for petitioners to profitably engage in their business, or that there has been undue interference with their investment-backed expectations.

The Public Purpose

Unlike the Kohler Act, which was passed upon in *Pennsylvania Coal*, the Subsidence Act does not merely involve a balancing of the private economic interests of coal companies against the private interests of the surface owners. The Pennsylvania Legislature specifically found that important public interests are served by enforcing a policy that is designed to minimize subsidence in certain areas. Section 2 of the Subsidence Act provides:

This act shall be deemed to be an exercise of the police powers of the Commonwealth for the protection of the health, safety and general welfare of the people of the Commonwealth, by providing for the conservation of surface land areas which may be affected in the mining of bituminous coal by methods other than 'open pit' or 'strip' mining, to aid in the protection of the safety of the public, to enhance the value of such lands for taxation, to aid in the preservation of surface water drainage and public water supplies and generally to improve the use and enjoyment of such lands and to maintain primary jurisdiction over surface coal mining in Pennsylvania."

The District Court and the Court of Appeals were both convinced that the legislative purposes set forth in the statute were genuine, substantial, and legitimate, and we have no reason to conclude otherwise. * * *

Petitioners argue that at least § 6, which requires coal companies to repair subsidence damage or pay damages to those who suffer subsidence damage, is unnecessary because the Commonwealth administers an insurance program that adequately reimburses surface owners for the cost of repairing their property. But this argument rests on the mistaken premise that the statute was motivated by a desire to protect private parties. In fact, however, the public purpose that motivated the enactment of the legislation is served by preventing the damage from occurring in the first place -- in the words of the statute -- "by providing for the conservation of surface land areas." The requirement that the mine operator assume the financial responsibility for the repair of damaged structures deters the operator from causing the damage at all -- the Commonwealth's main goal -- whereas an insurance program would merely reimburse the surface owner after the damage occurs.

Thus, the Subsidence Act differs from the Kohler Act in critical and dispositive respects. With regard to the Kohler Act, the Court believed that the Commonwealth had acted only to ensure against damage to some private landowners' homes. Justice Holmes stated that if the private individuals needed support for their structures, they should not have "take[n] the risk of acquiring only surface rights." Here, by contrast, the Commonwealth is acting to protect the public interest in health, the environment, and the fiscal integrity of the area. That private individuals erred in taking a risk cannot estop the State from exercising its police power to abate activity akin to a public nuisance. The Subsidence Act is a prime example that "circumstances may so change in time . . . as to clothe with such a [public] interest what at other times . . . would be a matter of purely private concern." Block v. Hirsh, 256 U.S. 135, 155, 41 S.Ct. 458, 459 (1921).

In *Pennsylvania Coal* the Court recognized that the nature of the State's interest in the regulation is a critical factor in determining whether a taking has occurred, and thus whether compensation is required. The Court distinguished the case before it from a case it had decided eight years earlier, Plymouth Coal Co. v. Pennsylvania, 232 U.S. 531, 34 S.Ct. 359 (1914). There, "it was held competent for the legislature to require a pillar of coal to be left along the line of adjoining property." Justice Holmes explained that unlike the Kohler Act, the statute challenged in *Plymouth Coal* dealt with "a requirement for the safety of the employees invited into the mine, and secured an average reciprocity of advantage that has been recognized as a justification of various laws." * *

Diminution of Value and Investment-Backed Expectations

The second factor that distinguishes this case from *Pennsylvania Coal* is the finding in that case that the Kohler Act made mining of "certain coal" commercially impracticable. In this case, by contrast, petitioners have not shown any deprivation significant enough to satisfy the heavy burden placed upon one alleging a regulatory taking. For this reason, their takings claim must fail.

In addressing petitioners' claim we must not disregard the posture in which this case comes before us. The District Court granted summary judgment to respondents only on the facial challenge to the Subsidence Act. The court explained that "[b]ecause plaintiffs have not alleged any injury due to the enforcement of the statute, there is as yet no concrete controversy regarding the application of the specific provisions and regulations. Thus, the only question before this court is whether the mere enactment of the statutes and regulations constitutes a taking." * * *

The posture of the case is critical because we have recognized an important distinction between a claim that the mere enactment of a statute constitutes a taking and a claim that the particular impact of government action on a specific piece of property requires the payment of just compensation. * * *

Just last Term, we reaffirmed that 'this court has generally "been unable to develop any 'set formula' for determining when 'justice and fairness' require that economic injuries caused by public action be compensated by the government, rather than remain disproportionately concentrated on a few persons." Rather, it has examined the "taking" question by engaging in essentially ad hoc, factual inquiries that have identified several factors -- such as the economic impact of the regulation, its interference with reasonable investment backed expectations, and the character of the government action -- that have particular significance.' Kaiser Aetna v. United States, 444 U.S. 164, 175, 100 S.Ct. 383, 390 (1979). * * *

Petitioners thus face an uphill battle in making a facial attack on the Act as a taking.

The hill is made especially steep because petitioners have not claimed, at this stage, that the Act makes it commercially impracticable for them to continue mining their bituminous coal interests in western Pennsylvania. Indeed, petitioners have not even pointed to a single mine that can no longer be mined for profit. The only evidence available on the effect that the Subsidence Act has had on petitioners' mining operations comes from petitioners' answers to respondents' interrogatories. Petitioners described the effect that the Subsidence Act had from 1966-1982 on 13 mines that the various companies operate, and claimed that they have been required to leave a bit less than 27 million tons of coal in place to support § 4 areas. The total coal in those 13 mines amounts to over 1.46 billion tons. Thus § 4 requires them to leave less than 2% of their coal in place. But, as we have indicated, nowhere near all of the underground coal is extractable, even aside from the Subsidence Act. The categories of coal that must be left for § 4 purposes and other purposes are not necessarily distinct sets, and there is no information in the record as to how much coal is actually left in the ground solely because of § 4. We do know, however, that petitioners have never claimed that their mining operations, or even any specific mines, have been unprofitable since the Subsidence Act was passed. Nor is there evidence that mining in any specific location affected by the 50% rule has been unprofitable.

Instead, petitioners have sought to narrowly define certain segments of their property and assert that, when so defined, the Subsidence Act denies them economically viable use. They advance two alternative ways of carving their property in order to reach this conclusion. First, they focus on the specific tons of coal that they must leave in the ground under the Subsidence Act, and argue that the Commonwealth has effectively appropriated this coal since it has no other useful purpose if not mined. Second, they contend that the Commonwealth has taken their separate legal interest in property -- the "support estate."* * *

The Coal in Place

The parties have stipulated that enforcement of the DER's 50% rule will require petitioners to leave approximately 27 million tons of coal in place. Because they own that coal but cannot mine it, they contend that Pennsylvania has appropriated it for the public purposes described in the Subsidence Act.

This argument fails for the reason explained in *Penn Central* and *Andrus*. The 27 million tons of coal do not constitute a separate segment of property for takings law purposes. Many zoning ordinances place limits on the property owner's right to make profitable use of some segments of his property. A requirement that a building occupy no more than a specified percentage of the lot on which it is located could be characterized as a taking of the vacant area as readily as the requirement that coal pillars be left in place. Similarly, under petitioners' theory one could always argue that a set-back ordinance requiring that no structure be built within a certain distance from the property line constitutes a taking because the footage represents a distinct segment of property for takings law purposes. * * * There is no basis for treating the less than 2% of petitioners' coal as a separate parcel of property. * * *

The Support Estate

Pennsylvania property law is apparently unique in regarding the support estate as a separate interest in land that can be conveyed apart from either the mineral estate or the surface estate. Petitioners therefore argue that even if comparable legislation in another State would not constitute a taking, the Subsidence Act has that consequence because it entirely destroys the value of their unique support estate. It is clear, however, that our takings jurisprudence forecloses reliance on such legalistic distinctions within a bundle of property rights. For example, in *Penn Central*, the Court rejected the argument that the "air rights" above the terminal constituted a separate segment of property for Takings Clause purposes. * * *

* * * [I]n practical terms, the support estate has value only insofar as it protects or enhances the value of the estate with which it is associated. Its value is merely a part of the entire bundle of rights possessed by the owner of either the coal or the surface. Because petitioners retain the right to mine virtually all of the coal in their mineral estates, the burden the Act places on the support estate

does not constitute a taking. Petitioners may continue to mine coal profitably even if they may not destroy or damage surface structures at will in the process.

But even if we were to accept petitioners' invitation to view the support estate as a distinct segment of property for "takings" purposes, they have not satisfied their heavy burden of sustaining a facial challenge to the Act. Petitioners have acquired or retained the support estate for a great deal of land, only part of which is protected under the Subsidence Act, which, of course, deals with subsidence in the immediate vicinity of certain structures, bodies of water, and cemeteries. The record is devoid of any evidence on what percentage of the purchased support estates, either in the aggregate or with respect to any individual estate, has been affected by the Act. Under these circumstances, petitioners' facial attack under the Takings Clause must surely fail.

[The dissenting opinion of CHIEF JUSTICE REHNQUIST, joined by JUSTICES POWELL, O'CONNOR, AND SCALIA, is omitted.]

NOTES AND QUESTIONS

1. Pennsylvania law on the existence of a separate "third" estate, or support estate, had not changed significantly since the *Pennsylvania Coal* decision in 1922. Did not the Subsidence Act in *Keystone*, just as the Kohler Act in *Pennsylvania Coal*, take the entire support estate? If so, why was there no taking? The Circuit Court described the support estate as "only one 'strand' in the plaintiff's 'bundle' of property rights . . . ." But in this case the strand was an entire estate. Suppose I own a fee simple absolute in my home -- an estate of potentially infinite duration -- and the government insists on occupying it rent-free for one month. The sovereign has then taken a one-month leasehold estate, which can be an insignificantly small percentage of a fee simple absolute. But is there any doubt that a taking has occurred?

Has *Keystone* changed in some important way the importance of state law determinations of property rights? The Court describes the support estate as a "legalistic distinction," and holds that federal takings jurisprudence does not rely on them. Does this mean that the structure of state property law is now irrelevant in takings cases? Chief Justice Rehnquist's dissent objected to this innovation, noting that previously the Court had "evaluated takings claims by reference to the units of property defined by state law."

2.   Can a state legislature avoid a taking merely by
articulating a public health or safety purpose for its statute?
When the court evaluates economic regulations under the
equal protection clause it generally defers to a legislative
conclusion that a statute is justified and requires little more
than some rational basis for it.   Even under *Keystone*,
however, the Supreme Court continues to second guess
legislatures in takings cases.   It is apt to look for itself to
see whether the statute really is justified by some public
need.   Can you explain this distinction?   See the discussion
in the *Nollan* decision, reprinted below.

As the *Keystone* decision notes, Justice Holmes began the
Pennsylvania Coal opinion by noting that "[t]his is the case
of a single private house" -- thus suggesting that there was
no "public interest" in the Kohler Act.   Was this just
rhetoric -- or did Holmes really believe that?   *Keystone*
notes one important difference between the Kohler Act and
the Subsidence Act: under the former, one who owned both
the surface and the mineral estates could mine without
concern about subsidence -- that is, if there was any
"public" interest in subsidence, it disappeared as soon as
one was seeking to undermine only his own property.   From
this the *Keystone* majority concludes that Holmes was correct:
there was no "public interest" being protected by the Kohler
Act.   Its apparent purpose was to shift the bargaining power
of the surface and mineral owners, but if the surface owner
gave permission, the miner was free to cause subsidence.
On the other hand, under the Subsidence Act even someone
who owns both mineral and surface estates may not mine so
as to cause subsidence without getting permission from the
state.

The "public interest" present in *Keystone* but allegedly
absent in *Pennsylvania Coal* thus appears to be some interest
that the bargaining parties themselves will not protect.   What
might such an interest be?   Could it be environmental?   A
surface that is not pockmarked by sinkholes caused by coal
mining may have a social value that is greater than the value
that a particular surface owner places on the land,
particularly if the land is not very fertile or not well suited
to development.   But if the state legislature is claiming this
value shouldn't they have to pay just compensation for it?

3.   In Hodel v. Irving, 481 U.S. 704 (1987), the Supreme
Court struck down the "escheat" provisions of federal Indian
Land Consolidation Act of 1983 as an unconstitutional taking.
Under earlier treaty arrangements, many tribal lands were
held in trust and the rentals of the lands were paid to

individual tribe members proportionate to their shares. Over several generations the number of interest holders had grown very large, and some proportional shares very small. In some cases the rentals amounted to less than one cent per individual, only a tiny fraction of the administrative cost of making the payments. In response, Congress passed a statute that provided, in part:

> No undivided fractional interest in any tract of trust or restricted land within a tribe's reservation or otherwise subjected to a tribe's jurisdiction shall descend by intestacy or devise but shall escheat to that tribe if such interest represents 2 per centum or less of the total acreage in such tract and has earned to its owner less than $100 in the preceding year before it is due to escheat." Indian Land Consolidation Act, Pub. L. No. 97-459, §207, 96 Stat. 2515, 2519.

The statute made no provision for payment of compensation to such owners of small fractional interests taken under this statute.

In finding an unconstitutional taking, the Court noted first that in some cases the fair market value of the escheated lands was as high as $2,700, even though the annual rentals earned on such fractional interests was less than $100 per year. Thus it was not true that the statute merely caused land with a de minimis value to escheat. The Court then noted:

> [T]he regulation here amounts to virtually the abrogation of the right to pass on a certain type of property -- the small undivided interest -- to one's heirs. In one form or another, the right to pass on property -- to one's family in particular -- has been part of the Anglo-American legal system since feudal times. The fact that it may be possible for the owners of these interests to effectively control disposition upon death through complex inter vivos transactions such as revocable trusts, is simply not an adequate substitute for the rights taken given the nature of the property. Even the United States concedes that total abrogation of the right to pass property is unprecedented and likely unconstitutional. Moreover, this statute effectively abolishes both descent and devise of these property interests even when the passing of the property to the heir might result in consolidation of property -- as for instance when the heir already owns another undivided interest in the property.

481 U.S. at 716, 107 S.Ct. at 2083.

4.   New York City's Landmarks Preservation ordinance, at issue in the *Penn Central* case (casebook, p. 820), returned

to the courts in St. Bartholomew's Church v. City of New York, 914 F.2d 348 (2d Cir. 1990). That decision, which involves both the Takings Clause and the Religion Clauses of the Constitution, is reprinted below in Chapter 12.

page 852, insert the following after note 7:

NOLLAN v. CALIFORNIA COASTAL COMMISSION
Supreme Court of the United States (1987)
483 U.S. 825

JUSTICE SCALIA delivered the opinion of the Court.

James and Marilyn Nollan appeal from a decision of the California Court of Appeal ruling that the California Coastal Commission could condition its grant of permission to rebuild their house on their transfer to the public of an easement across their beachfront property. The California Court rejected their claim that imposition of that condition violates the Takings Clause of the Fifth Amendment, as incorporated against the States by the Fourteenth Amendment. We noted probable jurisdiction.

I

The Nollans own a beachfront lot in Ventura County, California. A quarter-mile north of their property is Faria County Park, an oceanside public park with a public beach and recreation area. Another public beach area, known locally as "the Cove," lies 1,800 feet south of their lot. A concrete seawall approximately eight feet high separates the beach portion of the Nollans' property from the rest of the lot. The historic mean high tide line determines the lot's oceanside boundary.

The Nollans originally leased their property with an option to buy. The building on the lot was a small bungalow, totaling 504 square feet, which for a time they rented to summer vacationers. After years of rental use, however, the building had fallen into disrepair, and could no longer be rented out. The Nollans' option to purchase was conditioned on their promise to demolish the bungalow and replace it. In order to do so, under California Public Resources Code §§ 30106, 30212, and 30600 (West 1986), they were required to obtain a coastal development permit from the California Coastal Commission. On February 25, 1982, they submitted a permit application to the Commission in which they proposed to demolish the existing structure and replace it with a three-bedroom house in keeping with the rest of the neighborhood.

The Nollans were informed that their application had been placed on the administrative calendar, and that the Commission staff had recommended that the permit be granted subject to the condition that they allow the public an easement to pass across a portion of their property bounded by the mean high tide line on one side, and their seawall on the other side. This would make it easier for the public to get to Faria County Park and the Cove. The Nollans protested imposition of the condition, but the Commission overruled their objections and granted the permit subject to their recordation of a deed restriction granting the easement. * * *

[The Commission] found that the new house would increase blockage of the view of the ocean, thus contributing to the development of "a 'wall' of residential structures" that would prevent the public "psychologically . . . from realizing a stretch of coastline exists nearby that they have every right to visit." The new house would also increase private use of the shorefront. These effects of construction of the house, along with other area development, would cumulatively "burden the public's ability to traverse to and along the shorefront." Therefore the Commission could properly require the Nollans to offset that burden by providing additional lateral access to the public beaches in the form of an easement across their property. * * *

II

Had California simply required the Nollans to make an easement across their beachfront available to the public on a permanent basis in order to increase public access to the beach, rather than conditioning their permit to rebuild their house on their agreeing to do so, we have no doubt there would have been a taking. To say that the appropriation of a public easement across a landowner's premises does not constitute the taking of a property interest but rather, (as Justice Brennan contends) "a mere restriction on its use," is to use words in a manner that deprives them of all their ordinary meaning. Indeed, one of the principal uses of the eminent domain power is to assure that the government be able to require conveyance of just such interests, so long as it pays for them. * * * In *Loretto [v. Teleprompter Manhattan CATV Corp.]* we observed that where governmental action results in "[a] permanent physical occupation" of the property, by the government itself or by others, "our cases uniformly have found a taking to the extent of the occupation, without regard to whether the action achieves an important public benefit or has only minimal economic impact on the owner." We think a "permanent physical occupation" has occurred, for purposes of that rule, where individuals are given a permanent and continuous right to pass to and fro, so that the real property may continuously be traversed, even though no particular individual is permitted to station himself permanently upon the premises.

Given, then, that requiring uncompensated conveyance of the easement outright would violate the Fourteenth Amendment, the question becomes whether requiring it to be conveyed as a condition for issuing a land use permit alters the outcome. * * *

The Commission argues that a permit condition that serves the same legitimate police-power purpose as a refusal to issue the permit should not be found to be a taking if the refusal to issue the permit would not constitute a taking. We agree. Thus, if the Commission attached to the permit some condition that would have protected the public's ability to see the beach notwithstanding construction of the new house -- for example, a height limitation, a width restriction, or a ban on fences -- so long as the Commission could have exercised its police power (as we have assumed it could) to forbid construction of the house altogether, imposition of the condition would also be constitutional. Moreover (and here we come closer to the facts of the present case), the condition would be constitutional even if it consisted of the requirement that the Nollans provide a viewing spot on their property for passersby with whose sighting of the ocean their new house would interfere. Although such a requirement, constituting a permanent grant of continuous access to the property, would have to be considered a taking if it were not attached to a development permit, the Commission's assumed power to forbid construction of the house in order to protect the public's view of the beach must surely include the power to condition construction upon some concession by the owner, even a concession of property rights, that serves the same end. If a prohibition designed to accomplish that purpose would be a legitimate exercise of the police power rather than a taking, it would be strange to conclude that providing the owner an alternative to that prohibition which accomplishes the same purpose is not.

The evident constitutional propriety disappears, however, if the condition substituted for the prohibition utterly fails to further the end advanced as the justification for the prohibition. When that essential nexus is eliminated, the situation becomes the same as if California law forbade shouting fire in a crowded theater, but granted dispensations to those willing to contribute $100 to the state treasury. While a ban on shouting fire can be a core exercise of the State's police power to protect the public safety, and can thus meet even our stringent standards for regulation of speech, adding the unrelated condition alters the purpose to one which, while it may be legitimate, is inadequate to sustain the ban. Therefore, even though, in a sense, requiring a $100 tax contribution in order to shout fire is a lesser restriction on speech than an outright ban, it would not pass constitutional muster. Similarly here, the lack of nexus between the condition and the original purpose of the building restriction converts that purpose to something other than what it was. The purpose then becomes, quite simply, the obtaining of an easement to serve some valid governmental purpose, but without payment of compensation.

Reversed.

JUSTICE BRENNAN, with whom JUSTICE MARSHALL joins, dissenting.

* * * The Coastal Commission, if it had so chosen, could have denied the Nollans' request for a development permit, since the property would have remained economically viable without the requested new development. Instead, the State sought to accommodate the Nollans' desire for new development, on the condition that the development not diminish the overall amount of public access to the coastline. Appellants' proposed development would reduce public access by restricting visual access to the beach, by contributing to an increased need for community facilities, and by moving private development closer to public beach property. The Commission sought to offset this diminution in access, and thereby preserve the overall balance of access, by requesting a deed restriction that would ensure "lateral" access: the right of the public to pass and repass along the dry sand parallel to the shoreline in order to reach the tidelands and the ocean. In the expert opinion of the Coastal Commission, development conditioned on such a restriction would fairly attend to both public and private interests.

The Court finds fault with this measure because it regards the condition as insufficiently tailored to address the precise type of reduction in access produced by the new development. The Nollans' development blocks visual access, the Court tells us, while the Commission seeks to preserve lateral access along the coastline. Thus, it concludes, the State acted irrationally. Such a narrow conception of rationality, however, has long since been discredited as a judicial arrogation of legislative authority. * * *

B

Even if we accept the Court's unusual demand for a

precise match between the condition imposed and the specific type of burden on access created by the appellants, the State's action easily satisfies this requirement. First, the lateral access condition serves to dissipate the impression that the beach that lies behind the wall of homes along the shore is for private use only. It requires no exceptional imaginative powers to find plausible the Commission's point that the average person passing along the road in front of a phalanx of imposing permanent residences, including the appellants' new home, is likely to conclude that this particular portion of the shore is not open to the public. If, however, that person can see that numerous people are passing and repassing along the dry sand, this conveys the message that the beach is in fact open for use by the public. Furthermore, those persons who go down to the public beach a quarter-mile away will be able to look down the coastline and see that persons have continuous access to the tidelands, and will observe signs that proclaim the public's right of access over the dry sand. The burden produced by the diminution in visual access -- the impression that the beach is not open to the public -- is thus directly alleviated by the provision for public access over the dry sand. The Court therefore has an unrealistically limited conception of what measures could reasonably be chosen to mitigate the burden produced by a diminution of visual access.

The second flaw in the Court's analysis of the fit between burden and exaction is more fundamental. The Court assumes that the only burden with which the Coastal Commission was concerned was blockage of visual access to the beach. This is incorrect. The Commission specifically stated in its report in support of the permit condition that "[t]he Commission finds that the applicants' proposed development would present an increase in view blockage, an increase in private use of the shorefront, and that this impact would burden the public's ability to traverse to and along the shorefront." It declared that the possibility that "the public may get the impression that the beachfront is no longer available for public use" would be "due to the encroaching nature of private use immediately adjacent to the public use, as well as the visual 'block' of increased residential build-out impacting the visual quality of the beachfront."

The record prepared by the Commission is replete with references to the threat to public access along the coastline resulting from the seaward encroachment of private development along a beach whose mean high tide line is constantly shifting. As the Commission observed in its report, "The Faria Beach shoreline fluctuates during the year depending on the seasons and accompanying storms, and the public is not always able to traverse the shoreline below the mean high tide line." As a result, the boundary between publicly owned tidelands and privately owned beach is not a stable one, and "[t]he existing seawall is located very near to the mean high water line." When the beach is at its largest, the seawall is about 10 feet from the mean high tide mark; "[d]uring the period of the year when the beach suffers erosion, the mean high water line appears to be located either on or beyond the existing seawall." Expansion of private development on appellants' lot toward the seawall would thus "increase private use immediately adjacent to public tidelands, which has the potential of causing adverse impacts on the public's ability to traverse the shoreline." As the Commission explained:

> The placement of more private use adjacent to public tidelands has the potential of creating conflicts between the applicants and the public. The results of new private use encroachment into boundary/buffer areas between private and public property can create situations in which landowners intimidate the public and seek to prevent them from using public tidelands because of disputes between the two parties over where the exact boundary between private and public ownership is located. If the applicants' project would result in further seaward encroachment of private use into an area of clouded title, new private use in the subject encroachment area could result in use conflict between private and public entities on the subject shorefront."

* * * The Court is therefore simply wrong that there is no reasonable relationship between the permit condition and the specific type of burden on public access created by the appellants' proposed development. Even were the Court desirous of assuming the added responsibility of closely monitoring the regulation of development along the California coast, this record reveals rational public action by any conceivable standard.

II

* * * Examination of the economic impact of the Commission's action reinforces the conclusion that no taking has occurred. Allowing appellants to intensify development along the coast in exchange for ensuring public access to the ocean is a classic instance of government action that produces a "reciprocity of advantage." *Pennsylvania Coal, supra*, 260 U.S., at 415, 43 S.Ct., at 160. Appellants have been allowed to replace a one-story 521-square-foot beach

home with a two-story 1,674-square-foot residence and an attached two-car garage, resulting in development covering 2,464 square feet of the lot. Such development obviously significantly increases the value of appellants' property; appellants make no contention that this increase is offset by any diminution in value resulting from the deed restriction, much less that the restriction made the property less valuable than it would have been without the new construction. Furthermore, appellants gain an additional benefit from the Commission's permit condition program. They are able to walk along the beach beyond the confines of their own property only because the Commission has required deed restrictions as a condition of approving other new beach developments. Thus, appellants benefit both as private landowners and as members of the public from the fact that new development permit requests are conditioned on preservation of public access.

JUSTICE BLACKMUN, dissenting.

I do not understand the Court's opinion in this case to implicate in any way the Public Trust doctrine. The Court certainly had no reason to address the issue, for the Court of Appeal of California did not rest its decision on Art. X, § 4, of the California Constitution. Nor did the parties base their arguments before this Court on the doctrine.

NOTES AND QUESTIONS

1. Ever since the decision in Lochner v. New York, 198 U.S. 45 (1905) was repudiated in 1937, the Supreme Court has stated that it would defer to legislative findings of facts pertaining to the public interest. Does *Nollan* undermine that tradition, or does the tradition simply not apply in takings cases? Does the Court accept the fact findings of the California Coastal Commission, or does it merely declare them to be wrong? If the latter, where did the Supreme Court obtain its facts?

2. Justice Blackmun's dissent suggests that the Supreme Court's decision does not "implicate in any way the public trust doctrine." 483 U.S. at 864, 107 S.Ct. at 3162. That doctrine, which provides for uncompensated public access to privately owned resources considered to be in a "public trust," is discussed more fully in the casebook, §11.3 at 863-872. In this case, however, the California Constitution had provided since 1879 that tidal lands were subject to public access. After you have read Matthews v. Bay Head

Improvement Ass'n, the public trust case printed in your casebook at 863, consider whether it might be overruled by *Nollan*.

3.   Some cities, such as San Francisco, have required those seeking to build high rise commercial buildings in the downtown area to provide, generally at below cost, a specified number of units of low income housing in other parts of the city. This requirement is stated as a condition for the granting of a high rise construction permit. Does the requirement constitute a taking? Would your analysis be different if the person seeking the permit had a particular site in mind, and that site contained a low income apartment house which would be destroyed if the permit were granted? See Building Indus. Assn. v. City of Oxnard, 218 Cal. App.3d 1572, 267 Cal. Rptr. 769 (1990) (upholding ordinance requiring developers to pay fee to offset construction of public facilities); San Selmo Assoc. v. City of Seattle, 108 Wash.2d 20, 735 P.2d 673 (1987) (striking down ordinance requiring those seeking to demolish low income housing in order to build nonresidential uses to pay tax into city housing fund or else construct alternative low income housing). See also Symposium, Exactions: A Controversial New Source for Municipal Funds, 50 L. & Contemp. Probs. 1 (1987).

4.   Suppose the California Coastal Commission simply charged all persons seeking to develop property a high license fee -- say, $1000 -- and then used the proceeds to acquire public access by eminent domain from a few of the developers. Could a developer forced to pay the fee successfully claim a taking had occurred? Suppose the license fee was extracted only from those whose property was on the Pacific coastline?

5.   In United States v. Riverside Bayview Homes, Inc., 474 U.S. 121, 106 S. Ct. 455 (1985), the Supreme Court held that a statute should not be declared unconstitutional on its face or interpreted very narrowly in order to avoid a taking, when the possibility remains open that the sovereign will pay just compensation when a taking is found. In other cases:

> A requirement that a person obtain a permit before engaging in a certain use of his or her property does not itself 'take' the property in any sense: after all, the very existence of a permit system implies that permission may be granted, leaving the landowner free to use the property as desired. Moreover, even if the permit is

denied, there may be other viable uses available to the owner. Only when a permit is denied and the effect of the denial is to prevent 'economically viable' use of the land in question can it be said that a taking has occurred." 474 U.S. at 126, 106 S.Ct. at 459.

At issue in *Riverside* was the scope of the Clean Water Act, 33 U.S.C.A. § 1251 et seq, which forbad people from depositing fill dirt in privately owned wetlands adjacent to navigable waters unless they obtained a permit. But federal sovereignty extends only to navigable "waters." "Lands," no matter how wet, are not "waters." The Court of Appeals for the Sixth Circuit had interpreted the statute narrowly to apply only to lands that were under water for a large part of the year, holding that a broader interpretation would amount to a federal taking of private property. 729 F.2d 391 (6th Cir. 1984). In reversing, the Court held that "so long as compensation is available for those whose property is in fact taken, the governmental action is not unconstitutional." 474 U.S. at 128, 106 S.Ct. at 459.

6. In Hernando County v. Budget Inns, 555 So.2d 1319 (Fla. App. 1990), the court found that a county's requirement that a developer dedicate land for a public frontage road as a condition of development constituted a taking, since the county could not show that the development created a need for the frontage road.

Jones Ins. Trust v. City of Fort Smith, 731 F.Supp. 912 (W.D.Ark. 1990) applied *Nollan* to condemn a city's refusal to permit the plaintiff to add a convenience store to his gasoline station unless he dedicated an easement to the city for purposes of widening the street. The court rejected the city's argument that the business would increase traffic along the street, and that this fact satisfied *Nollan*'s requirement of a reasonable relationship between any increased public burden caused by the landowner's request and the government's demand. The court reasoned:

[T]he condition which the City wishes to impose on the granting of the building permit in this case would be constitutional if the "condition at issue . . . is reasonably related to the public need or burden that [the plaintiff's new construction] creates or to which it contributes." In this case, the court believes that the *Nollan* ruling requires the City to show that plaintiff's planned expansion of its business will create additional burdens on the present public right-of-way along Phoenix Avenue. In other words, Nollan teaches that the City may constitutionally "tax" plaintiff to recoup the costs of the negative externalities that its increased business activities cause: Without a showing of such externalities, the condition which the City attaches to building permits is simple extortion. Perhaps it is not necessary for the City to show an exact, mathematical, one-to-one correspondence between increased burden and tax, though it is plain that any clearly disproportionate tax would run afoul of the Fifth Amendment.

At a hearing held by the court to determine the relevant factual issue, plaintiff produced an expert civil engineer who testified that the additional burden on Phoenix Avenue created by plaintiff's planned expansion would be *de minimis* at most. One of the trustees of the plaintiff testified that he certainly hoped that the plaintiff's business would increase as a result of the expansion; but that increase, of course, would not have to translate into an increase of traffic on Phoenix Avenue. Indeed, there was testimony from which a reasonable fact-finder could conclude that the very purpose of convenience stores is to capture business from people who already regularly travel the routes on which such stores are situated, either to or from work or on other routinized business. It is true that increased traffic into and out of plaintiff's property will tend to increase congestion there, thus slowing traffic and perhaps contributing to the risk of accidents. But there was a showing that there were other convenience stores on Phoenix Avenue and near plaintiff's projected one, and so a reasonable fact-finder could conclude that whatever congestion or risk might be created by plaintiff's expansion would not be new but rather represents a redistribution of those costs from one locus on Phoenix Avenue to another.

For its part, the City produced credible testimony from its planners that convenience stores ordinarily had a certain and specific number of cars associated with them over a fixed period of time. The court does not doubt these data. But what the City could not show was what incremental traffic change, if any, could reasonably be expected from plaintiff's change in land use. 731 F.Supp. at 914.

Likewise, in Seawall Assoc. v. City of New York, 74 N.Y.2d 92, 544 N.Y.S.2d 542, 542 N.E.2d 1059 (1989), the court found that a moratorium on demolition of single room occupancy housing and requirement that owners restore such housing to habitable conditions, subject to rent control, constituted a taking; *Nollan* forbad such "forced occupation by strangers."

7. In Clem v. Christole, Inc., 548 N.E.2d 1180 (Ind. App. 1990), the court held that a zoning ordinance forcing a neighborhood to accommodate a group home for developmentally disabled contrary to private restrictive covenants amounted to a taking of the restrictive covenants without just compensation. The court found that the building of a group home in violation of the restrictions was a "forced physical occupation" in the neighborhood, and thus unconstitutional under *Nollan*. A dissenter objected that it was far-fetched to characterize the building of a group home in the *neighborhood* as a forced physical invasion. After all, the home was placed on property that was purchased by its users. The statute permitting the group home could only be analyzed as a regulatory taking. Under that analysis, there was no taking because the plaintiffs' property was as useful as it had been before, and there was little evidence of diminution in value. 548 N.E.2d at 1188-91 (Miller, J., dissenting). In Minder v. Martin Luther Home Foundation, 558 N.E.2d 833 (Ind. App. 1990), the court agreed with the *Clem* dissenter and found no taking on similar facts. Which decision is correct? To be sure, one stick in the bundle of property rights is the right to exclude the world. A covenant for the benefit of Blackacre excluding group homes from Whiteacre gives Blackacre's owner a right to "exclude" group homes from Whiteacre. But is this the kind of exclusion that the traditional concept of property encompasses? Would someone building a group home on Whiteacre, after purchasing it, be guilty of a common law trespass on Blackacre?

p. 853, the following case should be read with or substituted for the Martin *decision*:

FIRST ENGLISH EVANGELICAL LUTHERAN CHURCH
v. COUNTY OF LOS ANGELES
Supreme Court of the United States (1987)
482 U.S. 304

CHIEF JUSTICE REHNQUIST delivered the opinion of the Court.

In this case the California Court of Appeal held that a landowner who claims that his property has been "taken" by a land-use regulation may not recover damages for the time before it is finally determined that the regulation constitutes a "taking" of his property. We disagree, and conclude that in these circumstances the Fifth and Fourteenth Amendments to the United States Constitution would require compensation for that period.

In 1957, appellant First English Evangelical Lutheran Church purchased a 21-acre parcel of land in a canyon along the banks of the Middle Fork of Mill Creek in the Angeles National Forest.   The Middle Fork is the natural drainage channel for a watershed area owned by the National Forest Service.   Twelve of the acres owned by the church are flat land, and contained a dining hall, two bunkhouses, a caretaker's lodge, an outdoor chapel, and a footbridge across the creek.   The church operated on the site a campground, known as "Lutherglen," as a retreat center and a recreational area for handicapped children.

In July 1977, a forest fire denuded the hills upstream from Lutherglen, destroying approximately 3,860 acres of the watershed area and creating a serious flood hazard.   Such flooding occurred on February 9 and 10, 1978, when a storm dropped 11 inches of rain in the watershed.   The runoff from the storm overflowed the banks of the Mill Creek, flooding Lutherglen and destroying its buildings.

In response to the flooding of the canyon, appellee County of Los Angeles adopted Interim Ordinance No. 11,855 in January 1979.   The ordinance provided that "[a] person shall not construct, reconstruct, place or enlarge any building or structure, any portion of which is, or will be, located within the outer boundary lines of the interim flood protection area located in Mill Creek Canyon. . . ."   The ordinance was effective immediately because the county determined that it was "required for the immediate preservation of the public health and safety. . . ."   The interim flood protection area described by the ordinance included the flat areas on either side of Mill Creek on which Lutherglen had stood.

The church filed a complaint in the Superior Court of California a little more than a month after the ordinance was adopted.   * * *   As a part of this claim, appellant * * * alleged that "Ordinance No. 11,855 denies [appellant] all use of Lutherglen."   * * * *   The defendants moved to strike the portions of the complaint alleging that the county's ordinance denied all use of Lutherglen, on the view that the California Supreme Court's decision in Agins v. Tiburon, 24 Cal.3d 266, 157 Cal.Rptr. 372, 598 P.2d 25 (1979), aff'd on other grounds, 447 U.S. 255, 100 S.Ct. 2138 (1980), rendered the allegation "entirely immaterial and irrelevant [, with] no bearing upon any conceivable cause of action herein." * * *

In Agins v. Tiburon, *supra*, the Supreme Court of California decided that a landowner may not maintain an inverse condemnation suit in the courts of that State based upon a "regulatory" taking. In the court's view, maintenance of such a suit would allow a landowner to force the legislature to exercise its power of eminent domain. Under this decision, then, compensation is not required until the challenged regulation or ordinance has been held excessive in an action for declaratory relief or a writ of mandamus and the government has nevertheless decided to continue the regulation in effect. Based on this decision, the trial court in the present case granted the motion to strike the allegation that the church had been denied all use of Lutherglen. It explained that "a careful re-reading of the *Agins* case persuades the Court that when an ordinance, even a non-zoning ordinance, deprives a person of the total use of his lands, his challenge to the ordinance is by way of declaratory relief or possibly mandamus." Because the appellant alleged a regulatory taking and sought only damages, the allegation that the ordinance denied all use of Lutherglen was deemed irrelevant.

On appeal, the California Court of Appeal * * * affirmed the trial court's decision to strike the allegations concerning appellee's ordinance. The Supreme Court of California denied review. * * *

I

Concerns with finality left us unable to reach the remedial question in the earlier cases where we have been asked to consider the rule of *Agins*. * * * * In each of these cases, we concluded either that regulations considered to be in issue by the state court did not effect a taking, Agins v. Tiburon, *supra*, 24 Cal.3d, at 263, 157 Cal.Rptr. 372, 598 P.2d 25, or that the factual disputes yet to be resolved by state authorities might still lead to the conclusion that no taking had occurred. *MacDonald, Sommer & Frates; Williamson County; San Diego Gas & Electric Co.* Consideration of the remedial question in those circumstances, we concluded, would be premature.

The posture of the present case is quite different. Appellant's complaint alleged that "Ordinance No. 11,855 denies [it] all use of Lutherglen," and sought damages for this deprivation. In affirming the decision to strike this allegation, the Court of Appeal assumed that the complaint sought "damages for the uncompensated taking of all use of Lutherglen by County Ordinance No. 11,855." * * * It relied on the California Supreme Court's *Agins* decision for the conclusion that "the remedy for a taking [is limited] to nonmonetary relief. . . ." The disposition of the case on these grounds isolates the remedial question for our consideration. The rejection of appellant's allegations did not rest on the view that they were false. * * * Nor did the court rely on the theory that regulatory measures such as Ordinance No. 11,855 may never constitute a taking in the constitutional sense. Instead, the claims were deemed irrelevant solely because of the California Supreme Court's decision in *Agins* that damages are unavailable to redress a "temporary" regulatory taking. The California Court of Appeal has thus held that regardless of the correctness of appellants' claim that the challenged ordinance denies it "all use of Lutherglen" appellant may not recover damages until the ordinance is finally declared unconstitutional, and then only for any period after that declaration for which the county seeks to enforce it. The constitutional question pretermitted in our earlier cases is therefore squarely presented here. * * *

II

Consideration of the compensation question must begin with direct reference to the language of the Fifth Amendment, which provides in relevant part that "private property [shall not] be taken for public use, without just compensation." As its language indicates, and as the Court has frequently noted, this provision does not prohibit the taking of private property, but instead places a condition on the exercise of that power. * * * This basic understanding of the Amendment makes clear that it is designed not to limit the governmental interference with property rights per se, but rather to secure compensation in the event of otherwise proper interference amounting to a taking. Thus, government action that works a taking of property rights necessarily implicates the "constitutional obligation to pay just compensation."

We have recognized that a landowner is entitled to bring an action in inverse condemnation as a result of " 'the self-executing character of the constitutional provision with respect to compensation. . . .' " United States v. Clarke, 445 U.S. 253, 257, 100 S.Ct. 1127, 1130 (1980), quoting 6 P. Nichols, Eminent Domain §25.41 (3d rev. ed. 1972). As noted in Justice Brennan's dissent in San Diego Gas & Electric Co., 450 U.S., at 654-655, 101 S.Ct., at 1305, it has been established at least since Jacobs v. United States, 290 U.S. 13, 54 S.Ct. 26 (1933), that claims for just compensation are grounded in the Constitution itself:

> The suits were based on the right to recover just compensation for property taken by the United States for public use in the exercise of its power of eminent domain. That right was guaranteed by the Constitution. The fact that condemnation proceedings were not instituted and that the right was asserted in suits by the owners did not change the essential nature of the claim. The form

of the remedy did not qualify the right. It rested upon the Fifth Amendment. Statutory recognition was not necessary. A promise to pay was not necessary. Such a promise was implied because of the duty imposed by the Amendment. The suits were thus founded upon the Constitution of the United States."

* * * * The Supreme Court of California justified its conclusion at length in the *Agins* opinion, concluding that:

In combination, the need for preserving a degree of freedom in the land-use planning function, and the inhibiting financial force which inheres in the inverse condemnation remedy, persuade us that on balance mandamus or declaratory relief rather than inverse condemnation is the appropriate relief under the circumstances.

We, of course, are not unmindful of these considerations, but they must be evaluated in the light of the command of the Just Compensation Clause of the Fifth Amendment. The Court has recognized in more than one case that the government may elect to abandon its intrusion or discontinue regulations. * * * Similarly, a governmental body may acquiesce in a judicial declaration that one of its ordinances has affected an unconstitutional taking of property; the landowner has no right under the Just Compensation Clause to insist that a "temporary" taking be deemed a permanent taking. But we have not resolved whether abandonment by the government requires payment of compensation for the period of time during which regulations deny a landowner all use of his land.

* * * "[T]emporary" takings which, as here, deny a landowner all use of his property, are not different in kind from permanent takings, for which the Constitution clearly requires compensation. * * * It is axiomatic that the Fifth Amendment's just compensation provision is "designed to bar Government from forcing some people alone to bear public burdens which, in all fairness and justice, should be borne by the public as a whole." Armstrong v. United States, 364 U.S., at 49, 80 S.Ct., at 1569. *See also* Penn Central Transportation Co. v. New York City, 438 U.S., at 123-125, 98 S.Ct., at 2658- 2659; Monongahela Navigation Co. v. United States, 148 U.S., at 325, 13 S.Ct., at 625. In the present case the interim ordinance was adopted by the County of Los Angeles in January 1979, and became effective immediately. Appellant filed suit within a month after the effective date of the ordinance and yet when the Supreme Court of California denied a hearing in the case on October 17, 1985, the merits of appellant's claim had yet to be determined. The United States has been required to pay

compensation for leasehold interests of shorter duration than
this.   The value of a leasehold interest in property for a
period of years may be substantial, and the burden on the
property owner in extinguishing such an interest for a
period of years may be great indeed.   Where this burden
results from governmental action that amounted to a taking,
the Just Compensation Clause of the Fifth Amendment
requires that the government pay the landowner for the
value of the use of the land during this period.

Invalidation of the ordinance or its successor ordinance
after this period of time, though converting the taking into
a "temporary" one, is not a sufficient remedy to meet the
demands of the Just Compensation Clause. * * *

Nothing we say today is intended to abrogate the
principle that the decision to exercise the power of eminent
domain is a legislative function, " 'for Congress and
Congress alone to determine.' " Hawaii Housing Authority v.
Midkiff, 467 U.S. 229, 240, 104 S.Ct. 2321, 2329 (1984),
quoting Berman v. Parker, 348 U.S. 26, 33, 75 S.Ct. 98,
103 (1954).   Once a court determines that a taking has
occurred, the government retains the whole range of options
already available -- amendment of the regulation, withdrawal
of the invalidated regulation, or exercise of eminent domain.
Thus we do not, as the Solicitor General suggests, "permit
a court, at the behest of a private person, to require the
. . . Government to exercise the power of eminent domain.
. . ."   We merely hold that where the government's
activities have already worked a taking of all use of
property, no subsequent action by the government can
relieve it of the duty to provide compensation for the period
during which the taking was effective.

We also point out that the allegation of the complaint
which we treat as true for purposes of our decision was that
the ordinance in question denied appellant all use of its
property.   We limit our holding to the facts presented, and
of course do not deal with the quite different questions that
would arise in the case of normal delays in obtaining building
permits, changes in zoning ordinances, variances, and the
like which are not before us.   We realize that even our
present holding will undoubtedly lessen to some extent the
freedom and flexibility of land-use planners and governing
bodies of municipal corporations when enacting land-use
regulations.   But such consequences necessarily flow from
any decision upholding a claim of constitutional right; many
of the provisions of the Constitution are designed to limit the
flexibility and freedom of governmental authorities and the
Just Compensation Clause of the Fifth Amendment is one of
them.   As Justice Holmes aptly noted more than 50 years

ago, "a strong public desire to improve the public condition is not enough to warrant achieving the desire by a shorter cut than the constitutional way of paying for the change." Pennsylvania Coal Co. v. Mahon, 260 U.S., at 416, 43 S.Ct., at 160.

Here we must assume that the Los Angeles County ordinances have denied appellant all use of its property for a considerable period of years, and we hold that invalidation of the ordinance without payment of fair value for the use of the property during this period of time would be a constitutionally insufficient remedy. The judgment of the California Court of Appeal is therefore reversed, and the case is remanded for further proceedings not inconsistent with this opinion.

It is so ordered.

JUSTICE STEVENS, with whom JUSTICE BLACKMUN and JUSTICE O'CONNOR join as to Parts I and III, dissenting.

There is, of course, a possibility that land-use planning, like other forms of regulation, will unfairly deprive a citizen of the right to develop his property at the time and in the manner that will best serve his economic interests. The "regulatory taking" doctrine announced in *Pennsylvania Coal* places a limit on the permissible scope of land-use restrictions. In my opinion, however, it is the Due Process Clause rather than that doctrine that protects the property owner from improperly motivated, unfairly conducted, or unnecessarily protracted governmental decision making. Violation of the procedural safeguards mandated by the Due Process Clause will give rise to actions for damages under 42 U.S.C. § 1983, but I am not persuaded that delays in the development of property that are occasioned by fairly conducted administrative or judicial proceedings are compensable, except perhaps in the most unusual circumstances. On the contrary, I am convinced that the public interest in having important governmental decisions made in an orderly, fully informed way amply justifies the temporary burden on the citizen that is the inevitable by-product of democratic government.

As I recently wrote:

The Due Process Clause of the Fourteenth Amendment requires a State to employ fair procedures in the administration and enforcement of all kinds of regulations. It does not, however, impose the utopian requirement that enforcement action may not impose any cost upon the citizen unless the government's position is completely vindicated. We must presume that regulatory bodies such as zoning boards, school boards, and health boards, generally make a good-faith effort to advance the public interest when they are performing their official duties, but we must also recognize that they will often become involved in controversies that they will ultimately lose. Even though these controversies are costly and temporarily harmful to the private citizen, as long as fair procedures are followed, I do not believe there is any basis in the Constitution for characterizing the inevitable by-product of every such dispute as a 'taking' of private property." *Williamson, supra*, 473 U.S., at 205, 105 S.Ct., at 3127 (opinion concurring in judgment).

The policy implications of today's decision are obvious and, I fear, far reaching. Cautious local officials and land-use planners may avoid taking any action that might later be challenged and thus give rise to a damage action. Much important regulation will never be enacted, even perhaps in the health and safety area. Were this result mandated by the Constitution, these serious implications would have to be ignored. But the loose cannon the Court fires today is not only unattached to the Constitution, but it also takes aim at a long line of precedents in the regulatory takings area. It would be the better part of valor simply to decide the case at hand instead of igniting the kind of litigation explosion that this decision will undoubtedly touch off.

I respectfully dissent.

NOTES AND QUESTIONS

1. On remand, the state court found that no taking had occurred. 210 Cal. App. 3d 1353, 258 Cal. Rptr. 893 (1989).

2. The 300 members of the National Association of County Planning Directors were presented with this hypothetical:
A municipality, concerned that a water-filled gravel pit might prove a dangerous attraction to children attending schools in the vicinity, enacts an ordinance requiring the owner to fill in the pit and to construct a high fence around the site. The effect is to shut down a functioning quarry that opened more than thirty years ago when the area was still rural. Can the town use its land use regulatory powers to shut down the quarry, in effect destroying the landowner's business, without violating the takings clause?
Forty-eight of the planners said they would risk adopting the ordinance provided that the risk was only invalidation,

should it prove unconstitutional. But if the risk was a damage award to the landowner only twenty-four were willing to adopt it. What does this say about the impact that *First English* might have on land use planning by municipalities or counties? See Sallet, The Problem of Municipal Liability for Zoning and Land Use Regulation, 31 Cath. U. L. Rev. 465, 478 (1982). See Goldblatt v. Town of Hempstead, 369 U.S. 590 (1962), which refused to find a taking on somewhat similar facts.

3. Consider the Pennsylvania subsidence legislation whose constitutionality was upheld in the *Keystone* decision, reprinted *supra.* That was a five-four decision, with Chief Justice Rehnquist, Justices O'Connor and Scalia, and former Justice Powell dissenting. At the time of this writing, Justice Powell has been replaced by Justice Kennedy and Justice Brennan has been replaced by Justice Souter. Is the *Keystone* decision sufficiently "secure" that other states can pass similar legislation with confidence? Suppose that in two years the court overrules itself and declares the Pennsylvania legislation unconstitutional. Should the state have to pay damages to landowners for injuries they suffered while the statute was being enforced? The *First English Evangelical* decision places the risk of uncertainty about takings law on the regulatory authority, and that risk is greatly increased when the Supreme Court is badly fractured and inconsistent.

4. How expensive can the loss from a temporary taking be? Consider the damages analysis in Wheeler v. City of Pleasant Grove, 896 F.2d 1347 (11th Cir. 1990), which found that a municipality's refusal to permit development of an apartment building was an unconstitutional taking. The unconstitutional denial applied to a relatively small apartment building and for the relatively short period of fourteen months. The court predicated damages on the difference in rate of return on the land with the right to develop and its return while the right was denied, for as many months as the unconstitutional regulation was in force:

> [T]he landowner should be awarded the market rate of return computed over the period of the temporary taking on the difference between the property's fair market value without the regulatory restriction and its fair market value with the restriction. The complex which appellants had the right to construct had an undisputed appraised fair market value of $2.3 million in 1978. After the City prohibited appellants from constructing apartments, appellants retained only the land, appraised at $200,000.

Experts at the damages hearing testified that the loan-to-value ratio was seventy-five percent in 1978, so that appellants would have held a twenty-five percent equity interest. The investment on which appellants could have expected a return, then, was twenty-five percent of the project's value, or $575,000. After the City withdrew the permit, appellants held a twenty-five percent equity in the land, a value of $50,000. The difference in fair market value lost as a result of the regulatory restrictions was $525,000. The City withdrew appellants' building permit on September 6, 1978. The district court enjoined the City from enforcing Ordinance No. 216 against appellants on November 9, 1979. The period of temporary taking spans fourteen months and three days. According to the experts, the market rate of return for that period was 9.77 percent. When we compute the return on $525,000 over fourteen months at 9.77 percent, we arrive at a figure of $59,841.23. This is the correct amount of damages sustained by appellants.

896 F.2d at 1351-1352.

Isn't the court assuming that the plaintiff's money earned nothing during the period that development was prohibited? Suppose the government unconstitutionally delays the starting date of my project by one year. The investment in the project is $1,000,000 and the court predicts it would have earned a 12% return. But during the one year delay my $1,000,000 is in the bank earning 9%. Is my injury $120,000 or $30,000?

5.   A municipality or other governmental entity might still be able to take advantage of the federal Declaratory Judgment Act, 28 U.S.C.A. § 2201, to get a determination of a statute's constitutionality before it is enforced. Such an action binds only those who are properly served and made parties, but this would be quite possible where the number of affected persons is small. For example, if a municipality passed an historic preservation ordinance declaring ten buildings to be landmarks, and restricting their modification, it might bring a declaratory judgment action against the ten owners and obtain a judgment that application of the act is not a taking. A zoning statute affecting, say, 10,000 homeowners would be far less suitable for such an action, particularly if it required evidence about the nature of the losses imposed upon each owner by the zoning act. Administration of declaratory judgment actions is complex, and not all "potential" controversies are suitable for them, even if the number of parties is relatively small. See 10A C. Wright, A. Miller & M. Kane, Federal Practice and

Procedure § 2757 (2d ed. 1983).

6.   The United States Department of Agriculture imposes a quarantine on turkeys to control an outbreak of lethal avian influenza. One farmer's quarantined flock is later found to be healthy, but was sold during the quarantine period for 23% of its value if healthy. Has a compensable taking occurred? See Yancey v. United States, 915 F.2d 1534 (Fed. Cir. 1990).

7.   A particularly thoughtful commentary on the *Nollan*, *First English*, *Irving* and *Keystone* cases is Michelman, Takings, 1987, 88 Colum. L. Rev. 1600 (1988).

NOTE
Takings and Public Choice

During the Warren era the Supreme Court articulated the view that the law forbidding uncompensated takings was designed to protect isolated minorities who might not be well represented in the political process from unfair treatment by a legislative majority. For example, in Armstrong v. United States, 364 U.S. 40, 49, 80 S.Ct. 1563, 1569 (1960) the Supreme Court suggested that the takings clause was "designed to bar Government from forcing some people alone to bear public burdens which, in all fairness and justice, should be borne by the public as a whole." See also Richard Ely, *Democracy and Distrust* (1980); Michelman, "Property, Utility and Fairness: Comments on the Ethical Foundations of 'Just Compensation' Law," 80 Harv. L. Rev. 1165, 1218-1224 (1967).

Under this theory a court might consider whether the group victimized by a statute challenged under the takings clause (such as the owners of landmarked buildings or of underground coal mines) were relatively unique, isolated, and not well represented in the political process. If so, they might be branded as the victims of an unconstitutional attempt to transfer wealth away from them for the benefit of the public at large, or at least of some larger and more powerful interest group. This view of takings jurisprudence followed closely after the Warren's Court development of the Equal Protection clause to protect "discreet and insular" minorities from unjust discrimination at the hands of the majority. The purpose of the taking clause is to "spread the cost of operating the governmental apparatus throughout the society rather than imposing it upon some small segment of it." Sax, "Takings and the Police Power," 74 Yale L.J. 36, 75 (1964).

But the intellectual landscape has changed a good deal since the 1960's. Today a much more frequently heard theory is that small, homogenous interest groups are actually much more effective at carrying their message to legislatures than larger, more diffuse groups. In particular, the larger groups are plagued by "free rider" problems; each member of the larger group knows that there are plenty of others who are able to lobby the legislature, and so the tendency to shirk is very high. Further, the larger group tends to be less homogenous and may have more poorly articulated goals. This scholarship, which goes under the name of "Public Choice" theory, argues that the small, homogenous special interest groups will often succeed in obtaining the legislation they want at the expense of the public in general. The Public Choice classic is James Buchanan & Gordon Tullock, *The Calculus of Consent* (1962).

The implications of Public Choice for takings law are quite different from the implications of the older, liberal view. Under the public choice approach, the court would look for instances of legislative "capture" by homogeneous special interest groups. However, if the beneficiaries of legislation are diffuse, while the victims are discrete and homogeneous, then no taking should be found. Thus in *Keystone Bituminous Coal* there should *not* be a taking "because the burdened class [coal mining companies] is far more compact than the beneficiaries of the regulation." See Daniel A. Farber & Philip P. Frickey, *Law and Public Choice* 72 (1991). In short, the same facts that tend to prove a taking under the liberal theory, tend to disprove it under the public choice theory.

Which theory is the better fit between the takings clause and the legislation to which it applies? Suppose a city council representing 10,000 people passes an ordinance preventing any development on the land of a half dozen adjoining property owners, in order to protect the view from a public park across those property owners' land. Would the liberal view (taking) or the Public Choice view (no taking) be more sensible? Suppose the only three apartment building owners in a town lobbied for and obtained an ordinance preventing any further apartment buildings from being built. Would the liberal view (no taking) or the Public Choice view (taking) be more sensible? Do all forms of legislation fall into one category or another? Would a court be able to distinguish one kind of "legislative failure" from the other?

Chapter 12
"PUBLIC" CONTROLS OF LAND USE:
AN INTRODUCTION TO
ZONING AND LAND USE PLANNING

§12.2 LEGITIMATE PURPOSES (AND EFFECTS) OF ZONING LAW

p. 893, insert the following after the Schad *opinion:*

ST. BARTHOLOMEW'S CHURCH v.
CITY OF NEW YORK
United States Court of Appeals
Second Circuit (1990)
914 F.2d 348

WINTER, CIRCUIT JUDGE.

This appeal poses the question of whether a church may be prevented by New York City's Landmarks Law * * * from replacing a church-owned building with an office tower. The question implicates both First and Fifth Amendment issues. * * *

St. Bartholomew's Church is a Protestant Episcopal Church organized in 1835 under the laws of the State of New York as a not-for-profit religious corporation. The main house of worship ("the Church building") stands on the east side of Park Avenue, between 50th and 51st Streets, in New York City. * * *

Adjacent to the Church building, at the northeast corner of Park Avenue and 50th Street, is a terraced, seven-story building known as the Community House. It is the replacement of this building with an office tower that is at issue in the instant matter. Completed in 1928 by associates of Goodhue, the Community House complements the Church building in scale, materials and decoration. Together with the Church building, the Community House houses a variety of social and religious activities in which the Church is engaged. It contains a sixty-student preschool, a large theater, athletic facilities (including a pool, gymnasium, squash court, and weight and locker rooms), as well as several meeting rooms and offices for fellowship and counseling programs. A community ministry program, which provides food, clothing, and shelter to indigent persons, is operated mainly from the Church building. Meals are prepared in a small pantry on the first floor and served in the mortuary chapel. Ten homeless persons are housed nightly in the narthex.

In 1967, finding that "St. Bartholomew's Church and

Community House have a special character, special historical
and aesthetic interest and value as part of the development,
heritage and cultural aspects of New York City," the
Landmarks Preservation Commission of the City of New York
(the "Commission") designated both buildings as "landmarks"
pursuant to the Landmarks Law. This designation prohibits
the alteration or demolition of the buildings without approval
by the Commission. The Church did not object to the
landmarking of its property. In December 1983, pursuant to
what is now New York City Administrative Code Section
25-307, the Church applied to the Commission for a
"certificate of appropriateness" permitting it to replace the
Community House with a fifty-nine story office tower. This
request was denied as an inappropriate alteration. In
December 1984, the Church filed a second application,
scaling down the proposed tower to forty-seven stories. This
application was also denied.

The Church thereafter filed a third application under a
different procedure. Pursuant to Sections 207-4.0 and
207-8.0 of the New York City Administrative Code, commonly
known as the "hardship exception," it sought a certificate of
appropriateness for the forty-seven story tower on the
ground of the Community House's present inadequacy for
church purposes. The Church's application was the subject
of a series of public hearings before the Commission in late
1985 and early 1986. At those hearings, the Commission
gathered evidence from various interested parties, including
expert testimony and written reports regarding the adequacy
of the Community House for the Church's charitable
programs, the necessity and cost of structural and
mechanical repairs for the Church building and Community
House, and the Church's financial condition. Following the
public hearings, the Commission convened in Executive
Session, open to the public, on several occasions in
February 1986. At these meetings the Commission discussed
the Church's application, accepted further submissions from
interested parties, and took testimony and reports from its
own pro bono experts. On February 24, the Commission
voted to deny the application because the Church had failed
to prove the necessary hardship. Several months later the
Commission issued a lengthy written determination detailing
the reasons for its denial. * * *

The [Church sued, setting] forth a host of constitutional
claims. It alleged that the Landmarks Law, facially and as
applied to the Church, violates * * * the free exercise
clause of the First Amendment by excessively burdening the
practice of religion. * * * It also alleged that the
Landmarks Law violates the equal protection and due process

clauses of the Fourteenth Amendment because it applies different standards to charitable and commercial institutions respectively and constitutes a taking of property without just compensation. * * *

1. The Free Exercise Claim

* * * [T]he Church contends that by denying its application to erect a commercial office tower on its property, the City of New York and the Landmarks Commission (collectively, "the City") have impaired the Church's ability to carry on and expand the ministerial and charitable activities that are central to its religious mission. It argues that the Community House is no longer a sufficient facility for its activities, and that the Church's financial base has eroded. The construction of an office tower similar to those that now surround St. Bartholomew's in midtown Manhattan, the Church asserts, is a means to provide better space for some of the Church's programs and income to support and expand its various ministerial and community activities. The Church thus argues that even if the proposed office tower will not house all of the Church's programs, the revenue generated by renting commercial office space will enable the Church to move some of its programs -- such as sheltering the homeless -- off-site. The Church concludes that the Landmarks Law unconstitutionally denies it the opportunity to exploit this means of carrying out its religious mission. * * *

As the Court recently stated in Employment Division v. Smith, 110 S.Ct. 1595 (1990), the free exercise clause prohibits above all " 'governmental regulation of religious beliefs as such.' " * * * No one seriously contends that the Landmarks Law interferes with substantive religious views. However, apart from impinging on religious beliefs, governmental regulation may affect conduct or behavior associated with those beliefs. Supreme Court decisions indicate that while the government may not coerce an individual to adopt a certain belief or punish him for his religious views, it may restrict certain activities associated with the practice of religion pursuant to its general regulatory powers. For example, in Smith the Court held that the free exercise clause did not prohibit the State of Oregon from applying its drug laws to the religious use of peyote.

The synthesis of this case law has been stated as follows: "[T]he right of free exercise does not relieve an individual of the obligation to comply with a 'valid and neutral law of general applicability on the ground that the law proscribes (or prescribes) conduct that his religion prescribes (or proscribes).'" *Smith*, 110 S.Ct. at 1600. The critical distinction is thus between a neutral, generally applicable law that happens to bear on religiously motivated action, and a regulation that restricts certain conduct because it is religiously oriented. The Landmarks Law is a facially neutral regulation of general applicability within the meaning of Supreme Court decisions. It thus applies to "[a]ny improvement, any part of which is thirty years old or older, which has a special character or special historical or aesthetic interest or value."

It is true that the Landmarks Law affects many religious buildings. The Church thus asserts that of the six hundred landmarked sites, over fifteen percent are religious properties and over five percent are Episcopal churches. Nevertheless, we do not understand those facts to demonstrate a lack of neutrality or general applicability. Because of the importance of religion, and of particular churches, in our social and cultural history, and because many churches are designed to be architecturally attractive, many religious structures are likely to fall within the neutral criteria -- having "special character or special historical or aesthetic interest or value" -- set forth by the Landmarks Law. This, however, is not evidence of an intent to discriminate against, or impinge on, religious belief in the designation of landmark sites.

The Church's brief cites commentators, including a former chair of the Commission, who are highly critical of the Landmarks Law on grounds that it accords great discretion to the Commission and that persons who have interests other than the preservation of historic sites or aesthetic structures may influence Commission decisions.[1] Nevertheless, absent proof of the discriminatory exercise of discretion, there is no constitutional relevance to these observations. Zoning similarly regulates land use but it is hardly a process in which the exercise of discretion is constrained by scientific principles or unaffected by selfish or political interests, yet it passes constitutional muster.

The Church argues that landmarking and zoning differ in that landmarking targets only individual parcels while zoning affects larger segments. However, the Landmarks Law permits the designation of historic districts, while all zoning

---

1. The Landmarks Law made a cameo appearance in a recent best-selling novel as a vehicle for political retaliation against a clerical official seeking to develop Church property. See T. Wolfe, Bonfire of the Vanities 569 (1987) ("Mort? You know that church, St. Timothy's? ... Right ... LANDMARK THE SON OF A BITCH!").

laws provide for variances for individual sites. Even if the two forms of regulation bear the different characteristics asserted by the Church, those differences are of no consequence in light of Penn Central Transportation Company v. New York City, 438 U.S. 104, 98 S.Ct. 2646, 57 L.Ed.2d 631 (1978). There, the Court stated: [L]andmark laws are not like discriminatory, or 'reverse spot,' zoning: that is, a land-use decision which arbitrarily singles out a particular parcel for different, less favorable treatment than the neighboring ones. In contrast to discriminatory zoning, which is the antithesis of land-use control as part of some comprehensive plan, the New York City law embodies a comprehensive plan to preserve structures of historic or aesthetic interest whenever they might be found in the city. . . .

It is obvious that the Landmarks Law has drastically restricted the Church's ability to raise revenues to carry out its various charitable and ministerial programs. In this particular case, the revenues involved are very large because the Community House is on land that would be extremely valuable if put to commercial uses. Nevertheless, we understand Supreme Court decisions to indicate that neutral regulations that diminish the income of a religious organization do not implicate the free exercise clause. * * * The central question in identifying an unconstitutional burden is whether the claimant has been denied the ability to practice his religion or coerced in the nature of those practices. In Lyng v. Northwest Cemetery Protective Ass'n, 485 U.S. 439, 108 S.Ct. 1319, 1326 (1988), the Court explained,

> It is true that . . . indirect coercion or penalties on the free exercise of religion, not just outright prohibitions, are subject to scrutiny under the First Amendment. . . . This does not and cannot imply that incidental effects of government programs, which may make it more difficult to practice certain religions but which have no tendency to coerce individuals into acting contrary to their religious beliefs, require government to bring forward a compelling justification for its otherwise lawful actions. The crucial word in the constitutional text is "prohibit" . . .

* * * * In sum, the Landmarks Law is a valid, neutral regulation of general applicability, and as explained below, we agree with the district court that the Church has failed to prove that it cannot continue its religious practice in its existing facilities.

2. The Takings Claim

In *Penn Central*, the Supreme Court held that the

application of New York City's Landmarks Law to Grand
Central Terminal did not effect an unconstitutional taking. *
* * Central to the Court's holding were the facts that the
regulation did not interfere with the historical use of the
property and that that use continued to be economically
viable. * * *

Applying the *Penn Central* standard to property used for
charitable purposes, the constitutional question is whether
the land-use regulation impairs the continued operation of the
property in its originally expected use. We conclude that the
Landmarks Law does not effect an unconstitutional taking
because the Church can continue its existing charitable and
religious activities in its current facilities. Although the
regulation may "freeze" the Church's property in its existing
use and prevent the Church from expanding or altering its
activities, *Penn Central* explicitly permits this. In that case,
the Landmarks Law diminished the opportunity for Penn
Central to earn what might have been substantial amounts by
preventing it from building a skyscraper atop the Terminal.
Here it prevents a similar development by the Church -- one
that, in contrast to the proposal to build an office tower
over Grand Central Terminal, would involve the razing of a
landmarked building -- at least so long as the Church is
able to continue its present activities in the existing
buildings. In both cases, the deprivation of commercial value
is palpable, but as we understand *Penn Central*, it does not
constitute a taking so long as continued use for present
activities is viable.

The Church offers several arguments to distinguish *Penn
Central*, but we find them unavailing. First, it argues that
while *Penn Central* stipulated that it was able to earn a
"reasonable return" on the Terminal even under the
regulation, see 438 U.S. at 129, 98 S.Ct. at 2662, in this
case, the use of the Community House for commercial
purposes would yield an estimated return of only six
percent. Even if true, this fact is irrelevant. "Reasonable
return" analysis was appropriate to determine the viability of
the existing commercial use of the Terminal but has no
bearing on the instant matter because the existing use of the
Community House is for charitable rather than commercial
purposes. So long as the Church can continue to use its
property in the way that it has been using it -- to house its
charitable and religious activity -- there is no
unconstitutional taking.

Second, the Church notes that it presented a second
proposal for a smaller building to the Commission, but *Penn
Central* did not. This hardly makes any difference. Just as
the Commission in *Penn Central* remained open to a building

addition that " 'would harmonize in scale, material and character,' " 438 U.S. at 137, 98 S.Ct. at 2666 (quoting record on appeal), with the Terminal, it invited appellant to propose an addition to the Community House in the instant matter. Finally, we reject as unsupported appellant's argument that in *Penn Central* the property owner continued to enjoy valuable, transferrable rights to develop the airspace above the Terminal, while the Church's development rights have little value.[2]

* * *

NOTES AND QUESTIONS

1. In Employment Division v. Smith, 110 S.Ct. 1595 (1990), the Supreme Court upheld a state drug statute that was applied so as to forbid the smoking of an hallucinogenic drug in a religious ceremony. The Supreme Court held that the Free Exercise Clause does not permit someone to violate a "valid and neutral law of general applicability." But does the court leap too quickly to the conclusion that New York's landmark preservation law is such a law of "general applicability?" After all, the statute designates only 600 buildings as historical landmarks out of the tens of thousands of buildings within the statute's jurisdiction.

p. 894, *append the following to note 5:*
The Sixth Circuit affirmed the *Haskell* decision, finding that the township had intentionally acted so as to interfere with the plaintiff physician's exercise of a constitutionally protected right. Haskell v. Washington Tp., 864 F.2d 1266 (6th Cir. 1988). See Note, Exclusionary Zoning of Abortion Facilities, 32 Wash. U.J. Urb. & Contemp. L. 361 (1987).

§12.2.2 *Exclusion by Zoning: Federal Law*

p. 929, *insert the following after third full paragraph:*
In Huntington Branch, NAACP v. Town of Huntington, 844 F.2d 926 (2d Cir.), aff'd per curiam, 488 U.S. 15 (1988) the court held that a municipality violated the Fair Housing Act by limiting multifamily housing to a designated "urban renewal" area and denying a permit to someone wishing to build multifamily housing outside that area. The Supreme Court's per curiam affirmance approved the lower court's

---

2. The lower court had found the transferable development rights to be valuable, and the Second Circuit accepted that finding -- ed.

decision, but did not necessarily approve the disparate impact test that the lower court employed.

§12.3 SETTLED EXPECTATIONS AND THE ZONING PROCESS

§12.3.1 The Comprehensive Plan, Zoning Amendments, and "Spot" Zoning

p. 943, insert the following note:
    4.   In Kaiser Hawaii Kai Development Co. v. City of Honolulu, 70 Haw. 480, 777 P.2d 244 (1989), the Hawaii Supreme Court condemned a procedure using an initiative, or public vote, to downzone property.   The court concluded that "[z]oning by initiative is inconsistent with the goal of long range comprehensive planning."   It continued:

Zoning is intended to be accomplished in accordance with a comprehensive plan and should reflect both present and prospective needs of the community.   Among other things, the social, economic, and physical characteristics of the community should be considered.   The achievement of these goals might well be jeopardized by piecemeal attacks on the zoning ordinances if referenda were permissible for review of any amendment.   Sporadic attacks on a municipality's comprehensive plan would tend to fragment zoning without any overriding concept.   That concept should not be discarded because planning boards and governing bodies may not always have acted in the best interest of the public and may not, in every case, have demonstrated the expertise which they might be expected to develop. * * *

A single decision by electors in a referendum could well destroy the very purpose of zoning where such decision was in conflict with the general scheme fixing the uses of property in designated areas. * * *   It would permit the electors by referendum to change, delay, and defeat the real purposes of the comprehensive zoning ordinance by creating the chaotic situation such ordinance was designed to prevent.

777 P.2d at 247. By contrast, Silverman v. Barry, 845 F.2d 1072 (D.C. Cir. 1988), upheld an ordinance permitting an apartment building to be converted into condominiums only with the consent of a majority of the tenants.   The court held that this did not unconstitutionally delegate a legislative function to a small group of interested voters.   Query: Is a requirement of a vote of the general public, as in *Eastlake*, more or less threatening of property rights than a requirement of a vote of a small number of interested voters, such as the tenants of a particular building seeking to go

condo? In Hornstein v. Barry, 560 A.2d 530 (D.C. App. 1990), the court agreed with the D.C. Circuit that the ordinance's delegation of authority was constitutional, but remanded for a finding whether its application in this case might constitute an unconstitutional taking.

§12.5 GROWTH CONTROLS

p. 978, insert the following note:
6. In Lockary v. Kayfetz, 917 F.2d 1150 (9th Cir. 1990), the public utility district enacted a moratorium on new water hookups within the district. Several landowners challenged the moratorium as a regulatory taking and as violating their equal protection and procedural and substantive due process rights. The district court granted summary judgment for the district on all claims. The Ninth Circuit affirmed with respect to the procedural due process claim, but reversed and remanded for trial with respect to the takings, equal protection and substantive due process claims.

Chapter 13
THE ANTIDISCRIMINATION PRINCIPLE
AND THE "NEW PROPERTY,"
ESPECIALLY IN HOUSING

§13.1 INTRODUCTION: THE RIGHT TO FAIR TREATMENT IN THE PROVISION OF HOUSING SERVICES

§13.1.2   Housing Discrimination and Federal Law: The 1866 Civil Rights Act and the 1968 Fair Housing Act

p. 990, add the following after the text of the 1968 Fair Housing Act:
    In 1988 Congress passed the "Fair Housing Amendments Act of 1988," which inserted the following language in various sections:

42 U.S.C. §3602:
  (h) **"Handicap"** means, with respect to a person --
    (1) a physical or mental impairment which substantially limits one or more of such person's major life activities,
    (2) a record of having such an impairment, or
    (3) being regarded as having such an impairment, But such term does not include current, illegal use of or addiction to a controlled substance as defined in section 802 of Title 21. * * *
(k) **"Familial status"** means one or more individuals (who have not attained the age of 18 years) being domiciled with --

    (1) a parent or another person having legal custody of such individual or individuals; or
    (2) the designee of such parent or other person having such custody, with the written permission of such parent or other person.
The protections afforded against discrimination on the basis of familial status shall apply to any person who is pregnant or is in the process of securing legal custody of any individual who has not attained the age of 18 years. * * *
    Transvestism.   Section 6(b)(3) of Pub.L. 100-430 provided that: "For the purposes of this Act (see Short Title of 1988 Amendment note under section 3601 of this title) as well as chapter 16 of title 29 of the United States Code, (section 701 et seq. of Title 29, Labor), neither the term 'individual with handicaps' nor the term 'handicap' shall apply to an individual solely because that individual is a transvestite."

42 U.S.C. §3604

1. The section heading is amended by inserting "and other prohibited practices" after "rental of housing".

2. **Subsecs. (a) and (b) are amended by inserting "familial status," after "sex," wherever appearing.**

3. Subsecs. (c), (d), and (e) are each amended by inserting "handicap, familial status," after "sex," wherever appearing.

4. A subsection (f) is added reading as follows:

(1) To discriminate in the sale or rental, or to otherwise make unavailable or deny, a dwelling to any buyer or renter because of a handicap of --

"(A) that buyer or renter,

"(B) a person residing in or intending to reside in that dwelling after it is so sold, rented, or made available; or

"(C) any person associated with that buyer or renter.

(2) To discriminate against any person in the terms, conditions, or privileges of sale or rental of a dwelling, or in the provision of services or facilities in connection with such dwelling, because of a handicap of --

(A) that person; or

(B) a person residing in or intending to reside in that dwelling after it is so sold, rented, or made available; or

(C) any person associated with that person.

(3) For purposes of this subsection, discrimination includes--

(A) a refusal to permit, at the expense of the handicapped person, reasonable modifications of existing premises occupied or to be occupied by such person if such modifications may be necessary to afford such person full enjoyment of the premises except that, in the case of a rental, the landlord may where it is reasonable to do so condition permission for a modification on the renter agreeing to restore the interior of the premises to the condition that existed before the modification, reasonable wear and tear excepted;

(B) a refusal to make reasonable accommodations in rules, policies, practices, or services, when such accommodations may be necessary to afford such person equal opportunity to use and enjoy a dwelling; or

(C) in connection with the design and construction of covered multifamily dwellings for first occupancy after the date that is 30 months after September 13, 1988, a failure to design and construct those dwellings in such a manner that --

(i) the public use and common use portions of such dwellings are readily accessible to and usable by handicapped persons;

(ii) all the doors designed to allow passage into and within all premises within such dwellings are sufficiently wide to allow passage by handicapped persons in wheelchairs; and

(iii) all premises within such dwellings contain the following features of adaptive design:

(I) an accessible route into and through the dwelling;

(II) light switches, electrical outlets, thermostats, and other environmental controls in accessible locations;

(III) reinforcements in bathroom walls to allow later installation of grab bars; and

(IV) usable kitchens and bathrooms such that an individual in a wheelchair can maneuver about the space.

(4) Compliance with the appropriate requirements of the American National Standard for buildings and facilities providing accessibility and usability for physically handicapped people (commonly cited as 'ANSI A117.1') suffices to satisfy the requirements of paragraph (3)(C)(iii).

*****

"(7) As used in this subsection, the term 'covered multifamily dwellings' means --

(A) buildings consisting of 4 or more units if such buildings have one or more elevators.

(8) Nothing in this subchapter shall be construed to invalidate or limit any law of a State or political subdivision of a State, or other jurisdiction in which this subchapter shall be effective, that requires dwellings to be designed and constructed in a manner that affords handicapped persons greater access than is required by this subchapter.

(9) Nothing in this subsection requires that a dwelling be made available to an individual whose tenancy would constitute a direct treat to the health or safety of other individuals or whose tenancy would result in substantial physical damage to the property of others."

p. 992, *insert the following notes:*

9. In Association of Relatives and Friends of AIDS Patients v. Regulations and Permits Administration, 740 F.Supp. 95, 103 (D. Puerto Rico 1990), the court held that

a public agency's denial of a special use permit to operate a hospice for AIDS patients violated the "handicap" provisions of the 1988 Fair Housing Act amendments. It rejected an argument that §3604(f)(9) of the Amendments, which create an exception for facilities that might pose a threat to the community, exempted the agency's decision. There was "absolutely no evidence" that the housing of ten AIDS patients in a neighborhood posed a health threat to the community, although there was evidence of unfounded neighborhood fears. See also Baxter v. City of Belleville, Ill., 720 F.Supp. 720 (S.D.Ill. 1989) (city's refusal to rezone property for a group residence for AIDS patients might violate the 1988 Fair Housing Act Amendments).

10. In Doe v. City of Butler, 892 F.2d 315, 323 (3d Cir. 1989), the court held that a zoning ordinance that limited group homes to six persons did not violate the gender discrimination provision of the Fair Housing Act when applied to a home for women who had been physically abused by their husbands. The court noted that the provision was "nondiscriminatory" in that it applied equally to group homes for men, such as recovering male alcoholics. Further, it could find no intent to discriminate against women. However, the court remanded the case for a determination whether the limitation violated the "familial status" provision of the 1988 Fair Housing Act Amendments. The plaintiffs alleged that the six-person limitation made it impossible to permit battered women to bring their children with them to the group home. In Familystyle of St. Paul v. City of St. Paul, 923 F.2d 94 (8th Cir. 1991) the court held that a city ordinance spreading out the distribution of group homes for the mentally handicapped did not violate the Fair Housing Act.

p. 1005, insert the following after note 4:
UNITED STATES v. STARRETT CITY ASSOCIATES
United States Court of Appeals,
Second Circuit (1988)
840 F.2d 1096
cert. denied, 488 U.S. 946

Miner, Circuit Judge.
Appellants . . . own and operate "Starrett City," the largest housing development in the nation, consisting of 46 high-rise buildings containing 5,881 apartments in Brooklyn, New York * * * *
Starrett has sought to maintain a racial distribution by apartment of 64% white, 22% black and 8% hispanic. * * *

Starrett claims that these racial quotas are necessary to prevent the loss of white tenants, which would transform Starrett City into a predominantly minority complex. Starrett points to the difficulty it has had in attracting an integrated applicant pool from the time Starrett City opened, despite extensive advertising and promotional efforts. Because of these purported difficulties, Starrett adopted a tenanting procedure to promote and maintain the desired racial balance. This procedure has resulted in relatively stable percentages of whites and minorities living at Starrett City between 1975 and the present. * * *

The government commenced the present action against Starrett in June 1984. * * * The complaint alleged that Starrett, through its tenanting policies, discriminated in violation of the Fair Housing Act. Specifically, the government maintained that Starrett violated the Act by making apartments unavailable to blacks solely because of race, 42 U.S.C. §3604(a); by forcing black applicants to wait significantly longer for apartments than whites solely because of race, id. §3604(b); by enforcing a policy that prefers white applicants while limiting the numbers of minority applicants accepted, id. §3604(c); and by representing in an acknowledgement letter that no apartments are available for rental when in fact units are available, id. §3604(d).

Starrett maintained that the tenanting procedures "were adopted * * * solely to achieve and maintain integration and were not motivated by racial animus." To support their position, appellants submitted the written testimony of three housing experts. They described the "white flight" and "tipping" phenomena, in which white residents migrate out of a community as the community becomes poor and the minority population increases, resulting in the transition to a predominantly minority community. Acknowledging that " 'the tipping point for a particular housing development, depending as it does on numerous factors and the uncertainties of human behavior, is difficult to predict with precision,' " one expert stated that the point at which tipping occurs has been estimated at from 1% to 60% minority population, but that the consensus ranged between 10% and 20%. Another expert, who had prepared a report in 1980 on integration at Starrett City for the New York State Division of Housing and Community Renewal, estimated the complex's tipping point at approximately 40% black on a population basis. A third expert, who had been involved in integrated housing ventures since the 1950's, found that a 2:1 white-minority ratio produced successful integration.

The court, however, accepted the government's

contention that Starrett's practices of making apartments unavailable for blacks, while reserving them for whites, and conditioning rental to minorities based on a "tipping formula" derived only from race or national origin are clear violations of the Fair Housing Act. The district court found that apartment opportunities for blacks and hispanics were far fewer "than would be expected if race and national origin were not taken into account," while opportunities for whites were substantially greater than what their application rates projected. Minority applicants waited up to ten times longer than the average white applicant before they were offered an apartment. * * *

The court concluded that Starrett's obligation was "simply and solely to comply with the Fair Housing Act" by treating "black and other minority applicants . . . on the same basis as whites in seeking available housing at Starrett City." * * * Accordingly, Judge Neaher granted summary judgment for the government, enjoining Starrett from discriminating against applicants on the basis of race and "[r]equiring [them] to adopt written, objective, uniform, nondiscriminatory tenant selection standards and procedures" subject to the court's approval. * * *

[P]rograms designed to maintain integration by limiting minority participation, such as ceiling quotas * * * are of doubtful validity. * * * First, Starrett City's practices have only the goal of integration maintenance. The quotas already have been in effect for ten years. Appellants predict that their race-conscious tenanting practices must continue for at least fifteen more years, but fail to explain adequately how that approximation was reached. In any event, these practices are far from temporary. Since the goal of integration maintenance is purportedly threatened by the potential for "white flight" on a continuing basis, no definite termination date for Starrett's quotas is perceivable. Second, appellants do not assert, and there is no evidence to show, the existence of prior racial discrimination or discriminatory imbalance adversely affecting whites within Starrett City or appellants' other complexes. On the contrary, Starrett City was initiated as an integrated complex, and Starrett's avowed purpose for employing race-based tenanting practices is to maintain that initial integration.

Finally, Starrett's quotas do not provide minorities with access to Starrett City, but rather act as a ceiling to their access. Thus, the impact of appellants' practices falls squarely on minorities, for whom Title VIII was intended to open up housing opportunities. Starrett claims that its use of quotas serves to keep the numbers of minorities entering Starrett City low enough to avoid setting off a wave of "white flight."

Although the "white flight" phenomenon may be a factor "take[n] into account in the integration equation," Parent Ass'n of Andrew Jackson High School v. Ambach, 598 F.2d 705, 720 (2d Cir.1979), it cannot serve to justify attempts to maintain integration at Starrett City through inflexible racial quotas that are neither temporary in nature nor used to remedy past racial discrimination or imbalance within the complex.

NEWMAN, CIRCUIT JUDGE (dissenting)

Congress enacted the Fair Housing Act to prohibit racial segregation in housing. Starrett City is one of the most successful examples in the nation of racial integration in housing. I respectfully dissent because I do not believe that Congress intended the Fair Housing Act to prohibit the maintenance of racial integration in private housing. * * *

Though the terms of the statute literally encompass the defendants' actions, the statute was never intended to apply to such actions. This statute was intended to bar perpetuation of segregation. To apply it to bar maintenance of integration is precisely contrary to the congressional policy "to provide, within constitutional limitations, for fair housing throughout the United States." 42 U.S.C. § 3601.

Title VIII bars discriminatory housing practices in order to end segregated housing. Starrett City is not promoting segregated housing. On the contrary, it is maintaining integrated housing. It is surely not within the spirit of the Fair Housing Act to enlist the Act to bar integrated housing. Nor is there any indication that application of the statute toward such a perverse end was within the intent of those who enacted the statute. It is true that there are some statements in the legislative history that broadly condemn discrimination for "any" reason. Senator Mondale, the principal sponsor of Title VIII, said that "we do not see any good reason or justification, in the first place, for permitting discrimination in the sale or rental of housing." 114 Cong.Rec. 5642 (1968). But his context, like that in which the entire debate occurred, concerned maintenance of segregation, not integration. His point was that there was no reason for discriminating against a Black who wished to live in a previously all-White housing project. He explicitly decried the prospect that "we are going to live separately in white ghettos and Negro ghettos." The purpose of Title VIII, he said, was to replace the ghettos "by truly integrated and balanced living patterns." As he pointed out, "[O]ne of the biggest problems we face is the lack of experience in actually living next to Negroes." Starrett City is committed to the proposition that Blacks and Whites shall live next to each other. A law enacted to enhance the opportunity for people of all races to live next to each other should not be interpreted to prevent a landlord from maintaining one of the most successful integrated housing projects in America.

None of the legislators who enacted Title VIII ever expressed a view on whether they wished to prevent the maintenance of racially balanced housing. Most of those who passed this statute in 1968 probably could not even contemplate a private real estate owner who would deliberately set out to achieve a racially balanced tenant population. Had they thought of such an eventuality, there is not the slightest reason to believe that they would have raised their legislative hands against it.

* * *

WOODS V. BEAVERS
United States Court of Appeals,
Sixth Circuit (1991)
922 F.2d 842 (unpublished)

PER CURIAM.

Plaintiffs-appellees Jeffrey and Joyce Woods are an interracially married couple. He is white, and she is black. They allege that they were denied rental housing by the defendants-appellants, Alfred and Annie Beavers. The Woods won a jury verdict of $11,500 in compensatory damages and $23,500 in punitive damages. The Beavers appealed alleging that several errors were committed by the district court. Because we find no reversible error, we affirm the district court.

From the evidence, the jury could have found the following facts to be true. The Woods moved to Toledo, Ohio from Texas in November, 1988. The couple immediately began searching for a rental house in which to live. Mr. Woods responded to a classified ad that Annie and Alfred Beavers had placed. Arrangements were made for Alfred Beavers to show the house to Mr. and Mrs. Woods. After the inspection, the Woods returned to the Beavers' residence to finalize the rental arrangements. This was the first time that Annie Beavers had seen Joyce Woods. Annie Beavers became flustered when confronted with the interracial couple. Annie Beavers, however, accepted their $100 deposit and indicated that the Woods owed a balance of $800 for a security deposit and rent. A moving-in date of December 3, 1988 was established.

The Beavers did not show up or provide the key on

December 3. Jeffrey Woods then called the Beavers'
residence, and Annie Beavers answered. She said "please
hold," and left the telephone. She never came back.
Jeffrey Woods went to the Beavers' residence. As he
approached the front door, the door closed and no one
responded when he knocked.

The Woods filed suit pursuant to the Fair Housing Act,
42 U.S.C. §3601 and the Civil Rights Acts of 1866 and 1870,
42 U.S.C. §§ 1981 and 1982. * * *

II.

The Beavers maintain that the jury instructions in this
case were incorrect. * * * The jury instructions, in part,
stated with respect to damages:

> Third, the value of the loss of the plaintiffs' right not to
> be discriminated against. In the eyes of the law, this
> right is so valuable that damages are presumed from the
> wrongful deprivation of it without evidence of actual loss
> of money, property, or any other valuable thing, and the
> amount of damages is a question peculiarly appropriate for
> the determination of a jury because each member of you
> has personal knowledge of the value of the right.
>
> I call particularly to your attention the instruction just
> given that civil rights are so valuable that actual
> damages, not nominal damages such as one cent or one
> dollar, that is, actual compensatory damages are presumed
> from the wrongful deprivation of civil rights. What the
> instruction just given means is that if you find that the
> plaintiffs were wrongfully deprived of their rights not be
> discriminated against in the rental of property, you must
> compensate them for that loss in an amount which you
> consider to be the value you would place on your own
> rights the amount that you would consider necessary to
> make each of you whole if you were deprived of your
> right not to be discriminated against in this particular
> respect.

The Beavers maintain that the court's instructions on
damages violate the principles set forth in Memphis
Community School District v. Stachura, 477 U.S. 299 (1986).
Stachura involved a 42 U.S.C. § 1983 claim for violation of
plaintiff's constitutional rights. In *Stachura*, the trial court
gave the following instruction:

> If you find that the Plaintiff has been deprived of a
> Constitutional right, you may award damages to
> compensate him for the deprivation. ... The precise
> value you place upon any Constitutional right which you
> find denied to plaintiff is within your discretion. You

may wish to consider the importance of the right in our system of government, the role which the right has played in the history of our republic, [and] the significance of the right in the context of the activities which the Plaintiff was engaged in at the time of the violation of the right.

The *Stachura* jury instruction was incorrect, according to the Supreme Court, because no "actual injury" was required by the charge. The Court felt that the instructions "permitted the jury to award damages based on its own unguided estimation of the value of such rights." The Supreme Court, however, did state in *Stachura* "[w]hen a plaintiff seeks compensation for an injury that is likely to have occurred but difficult to establish, some form of presumed damages may possibly be appropriate." Presumed damages must be tied to a compensatory purpose for harms that are "impossible to measure." In *Stachura*, for example, the Court referred to a line of cases that allowed a recovery of presumed damages for an "inability to vote in a particular election...."

Under the Fair Housing Act, providing false information on the availability of rental units because of a party's race violates the statute and creates a cause of action. Havens Realty Corp. v. Coleman, 455 U.S. 363 (1982). A person who has suffered from a discriminatory act in violation of the Act "has suffered injury in precisely the form the statute was intended to guard against, ..." Id. at 373. No physical or mental injuries need be shown under the Act to justify a recovery.[1] Under the facts of this case, an actual injury occurred merely by committing discriminatory acts in violation of the Fair Housing Act. Furthermore, a discriminatory act in violation of the Fair Housing Act is a type of injury that is likely to have occurred but "impossible to measure." Under these circumstances, the jury instructions cannot be characterized as plain error.

DAVID A. NELSON, CIRCUIT JUDGE, CONCURRING.

I write separately to note my belief that the trial court's charge to the jury contained a fairly significant error.

The court told the members of the jury that if the

---

1. *Havens Realty Corp.* involved certain volunteers, called testers, who sought out information concerning rental housing to insure that no racial steering was occurring. "That the tester may have approached the real estate agent fully expecting that he would receive false information, and without any intention of buying or renting a home, does not negate the simple fact of injury within the meaning of [the Fair Housing Act]."

plaintiffs had suffered a loss of their civil rights, "you must compensate them for that loss in an amount which you consider to be the value you would place on your own rights [--] the amount that you would consider necessary to make each of you whole if you were deprived of your right not to be discriminated against in this particular respect."

It is widely believed to be improper for lawyers to invite juries to apply this sort of "golden rule" approach to the calculation of damages--and if it is wrong for lawyers to suggest such an approach, it is doubly wrong for a court to direct it.

At least two of our sister circuits have declared that "[a] 'Golden Rule' appeal in which the jury is asked to put itself in the plaintiff's position 'is universally recognized as improper because it encourages the jury to depart from neutrality and to decide the case on the basis of personal interest and bias rather than on the evidence." Spray-Rite Service Corp. v. Monsanto Co., 684 F.2d 1226, 1246 (7th Cir.1982) (quoting Ivy v. Security Barge Lines, Inc., 585 F.2d 732, 741 (5th Cir.1978), rev'd on other grounds, 606 F.2d 524 (5th Cir.1979) (en banc), cert. denied, 446 U.S. 956 (1980)).

NOTES AND QUESTIONS

1.   What is the evil that the Fair Housing Act was designed to correct: discrimination or segregation? Do you suppose it occurred to Congress that those could be conflicting, rather than harmonious, goals? Would the *Starrett* case have come out the other way if white persons rather than people of color were forced to be on the longer waiting list?

2.   One of the cases that the *Woods* concurrence cited against the "Golden Rule" damages measure (*Spray-Rite v. Monsanto*) was an antitrust case, where damages are ordinarily based on lost business profits. Is there any reason a court might wish to reject a "Golden Rule" measure in such a case, but preserve it in a case such as *Woods*?

3.   Suppose a newspaper routinely accepts display advertising for apartments or condominiums and the advertisers use only white models in the photographs in the advertising. No verbal statements in the advertisements suggests that the advertisers discriminate on the basis of race, and the advertisers in fact do not discriminate in their sales. Has the Fair Housing Act been violated? See Girardeau v. Colonial Village, 899 F.2d 24 (D.C.Cir. 1990) (use of white models to the exclusion of blacks in advertising

for housing might violate Fair Housing Act); Ragin v. New York Times Co., 726 F.Supp. 953 (S.D.N.Y.1989), aff'd mem., 922 F.2d 836 (2d Cir. 1991); Saunders v. General Services Corp., 659 F.Supp. 1042, 1058 (E.D.Va.1986). The *Ragin* court relied on a Department of Housing and Urban Development (HUD) Regulation which reads:

> Human models in photographs, drawings, or other graphic techniques may not be used to indicate exclusiveness because of race, color, religion, sex, handicap, familial status, or national origin.

24 C.F.R. §109.30(b).

4. Suppose a male landlord conditions a female tenant's lease renewal on her having sexual relations with him, or engages in a pattern of harassing women tenants. Has the landlord violated the Fair Housing Act? Has he denied someone a housing opportunity on the basis of sex? The Supreme Court has never applied the Fair Housing Act to sexual harassment; however, it has applied similar language in Title VII, which involves employment discrimination, to such situations. Meritor Savings Bank v. Vinson, 477 U.S. 57, 106 S.Ct. 2399 (1986). Taking their cue from *Meritor*, several lower courts have held that sexual harassment can violate the Fair Housing Act if it interferes with the victim's right to obtain housing, or amounts to threats or intimidation against someone in the exercise of housing privileges. See Shellhammer v. Llewallyn, 770 F.2d 167 (6th cir. 1987) (memorandum affirmance of unpublished district court opinion finding landlord's sexual harassment of tenant to violate Fair Housing Act); New York v. Merlino, 694 F. Supp. 1101 (S.D.N.Y. 1988) (real estate broker's sexual harassment of female customers is prohibited under §3617 of Fair Housing Act); Grieger v. Sheets, 689 F.Supp. 835 (N.D.Ill. 1988) (Fair Housing Act forbids sexual harassment).

5. Another case borrowing from Title VII is Pinchback v. Armistead Homes, 689 F. Supp. 541, 552-553 (D. Md. 1988), which applied labor law's "futile gesture" theory to the Fair Housing Act. If it is clear from the defendant landlord's statements that he will not rent to blacks, so that it would be a "futile gesture" for a prospective black tenant to apply, then failure to apply will not bar recovery under the Fair Housing Act.

6. In Bachman v. St. Monica's Congregation, 902 F.2d 1259 (7th Cir. 1990) the court held that a Catholic Church's policy of giving its own members preferred access to housing did not constitute discrimination on the basis of "race" even

though the policy subjected the Jewish plaintiffs to unequal treatment.   To be sure, concluded the court, the action probably constituted discrimination on the basis of religion under the terms of the Fair Housing Act, but the Act contains a provision permitting a religious organization to "limit * * * the sale * * * of dwellings which it owns or operates for other than a commercial purpose to persons of the same religion," and to "giv[e] preference to such persons."   42 U.S.C. §3607.   Although the older Civil Rights statutes, 42 U.S.C. §§ 1981 & 1982, contained no such defense, they applied only to discrimination on the basis of race.   And

> while for this purpose Jews constitute a race, it is not the case that every preference based on religion is a discrimination against a race.   Suppose a Bahai organization refused to sell property to persons not of the Bahai faith.   It would be extremely odd to describe such a policy as anti-Semitic.   The policy would cut across racial grounds, however broadly or narrowly the term "race" was construed. * * *   A preference for Bahais hurts all non-Bahais, a preference for Catholics all non-Catholics; it is not a harm to a particular group of non-Bahais, or of non-Catholics, such as Jews.   This case is therefore much like Personnel Administrator of Massachusetts v. Feeney, 442 U.S. 256, 99 S.Ct. 2282, 60 L.Ed.2d 870 (1979), where a statute that discriminated in favor of veterans was held not to be a form of sex discrimination, even though few veterans are women, just as few Catholics are of Jewish ancestry.

902 F.2d at 1261-1262.   Compare United States v. Columbus Country Club, 915 F.2d 877 (3d Cir. 1990), holding that a country club affiliated with the Catholic Church could not discriminate against non-catholics.   Although the club was affiliated with the Church, it was not itself a "religious organization," and on this point the Fair Housing Act should be narrowly construed.

Suppose a realtor advertises housing in a newspaper and, without stating an explicit religious preference, adds a Christian cross or the statement "Jesus Saves" to the advertisement.   Does the use of such symbols constitute discrimination on the basis of religious belief?   See Virginia v. Lotz Realty Co., 237 Va. 1, 376 S.E.2d 54 (1989).

§13.1.3 *Housing Discrimination and State Law*

p. 1005, substitute the following for the Marina decision:

STATE v. FRENCH
Supreme Court of Minnesota (1990)
460 N.W.2d 2

YETKA, JUSTICE.

Appellant was found guilty of discrimination by an administrative law judge to whom a complaint filed with the Department of Human Rights was referred for hearing. Appellant had refused to rent his property to one Susan Parsons because she planned to live there with her fiance. French was ordered to pay $368.50 in compensatory damages to Parsons, $400 for mental anguish and suffering, and $300 civil penalties. We reverse. * * *

French owned and occupied a two-bedroom house ("subject property") in Marshall, Minnesota, until moving to a house he purchased in the country. While attempting to sell the subject property, French rented it to both single individuals and married couples. From January to March 1988, French advertised the subject property as being available for rent. On February 22, 1988, French agreed to rent the property to Parsons and accepted a $250 check as a security deposit.

Shortly thereafter, French decided that Parsons had a romantic relationship with her fiance, Wesley Jenson, and that the two would likely engage in sexual relations outside of marriage on the subject property. On February 24, 1988, French told Parsons that he had changed his mind and would not rent the property to her because unmarried adults of the opposite sex living together were inconsistent with his religious beliefs. French is a member of the Evangelical Free Church in Marshall, and his beliefs include that an unmarried couple living together or having sexual relations outside of marriage is sinful. Despite being questioned by French, neither Parsons nor Jenson told French whether they were planning to have sexual relations on the subject property. The record is in dispute as to whether appellant had knowledge of Parsons' intended sexual activity with her fiance, but Parsons did not deny such an intent when queried by French. Even if they would not have had sexual relations on the property, French believes that living together constitutes the "appearance of evil" and would not have rented to them on that basis. French admits that if Parsons had been married to Jenson, he would not have objected renting to them. * * *

We must examine whether appellant's refusal to rent to

Parsons constituted a prima facie violation of the Human
Rights Act's prohibition of marital status discrimination. The
act provides in relevant part:
    It is an unfair discriminatory practice:
        (1) For an owner, lessee * * *
            (a) to refuse to sell, rent, or lease * * * any real
            property because of race, color, creed, religion,
            national origin, sex, marital status, status with
            regard to public assistance, disability, or familial
            status.
Minn.Stat. §363.03, subd. 2.

I. The Definition of "Marital Status"

The administrative law judge (ALJ) found that appellant
refused to rent to Parsons because she "was single and
planned to cohabit with another person of the opposite sex."
The version of the MHRA in effect at the time the alleged
discrimination occurred and when the charge was filed did
not contain a definition of the term "marital status."

It is well settled that, in the interpretation of ambiguous
statutes, this court is required to discover and effectuate
legislative intent. The term "marital status" is ambiguous
because it is susceptible to more than one meaning, namely,
a meaning which includes cohabiting couples and one which
does not. In order to show that construing "marital status"
to include unmarried cohabiting couples is inconsistent with
public policy, legislative intent, and previous decisions of
this court, it is necessary to examine the history of the
MHRA and our cases interpreting it. * * *

This court, in construing the term "marital status" has
consistently looked to the legislature's policy of discouraging
the practice of fornication and protecting the institution of
marriage. See Kraft, Inc. v. State ex rel. Wilson, 284
N.W.2d 386, 388 (Minn.1979). *Kraft* presented the question
of whether an employer's anti-nepotism policy constituted
marital status discrimination within the meaning of the MHRA.
In answering this question in the affirmative, Chief Justice
Sheran stated:
    Endorsing a narrow definition of marital status and
    uncritically upholding an employment policy such as
    respondent's could discourage similarly situated employees
    from marrying. In a locale where a predominant employer
    enforced such a policy, economic pressures might lead two
    similarly situated individuals to forsake the marital union
    and live together in violation of Minn.Stat. §609.34
    [fornication statute]. Such an employment policy would
    thus undermine the preferred status enjoyed by the
    institution of marriage.

* * * The *Kraft* court unanimously concluded that the fornication statute was a valid expression of Minnesota public policy. Moreover, the *Kraft* court did not ignore the destructive practical effect of a contrary ruling simply because there was no direct evidence of fornication. It is easy to see that, but for these important public policies, the *Kraft* decision would have been different. * * *

Kraft [as well as other cases] stand for the proposition that, absent express legislative guidance, the term "marital status" will not be construed in a manner inconsistent with this state's policy against fornication and in favor of the institution of marriage. [Recent legislative amendments in the employment discrimination act] also demonstrate that the legislature did not intend to expand the definition of "marital status" in order to penalize landlords for refusing to rent to unmarried, cohabiting couples. Minn.Stat. §363.01, subd. 40 (1988) defines "marital status" as follows:

"Marital status" means whether a person is single, married, remarried, divorced, separated, or a surviving spouse and, in employment cases, includes protection against discrimination on the basis of the identity, situation, actions, or beliefs of a spouse or former spouse.

The plain language of this new definition shows that, in non-employment cases, the legislature intended to address only the status of an individual, not an individual's relationship with a spouse, fiance, fiancee, or other domestic partner. The extremely broad language following the phrase "and, in employment cases" constitutes legislative recognition that employment cases are fundamentally different from housing cases such as the case at bar. The legislative history of this subdivision indicates that the legislature did not intend to extend the protection of the MHRA to unmarried, cohabiting couples in the area of housing. * * *

Other courts which have addressed the same issue have considered their state's policy with respect to fornication as expressed in statutory law. See Foreman v. Anchorage Equal Rights Comm'n, 779 P.2d 1199, 1201-02 (Alaska 1989); Mister v. A.R.K. Partnership, 197 Ill.App.3d 105, 113-14, 143 Ill.Dec. 166, 171, 553 N.E.2d 1152, 1157 (1990). The facts in *Mister* were virtually identical to the instant case except the record was silent as to the defendants' alleged religious beliefs. In *Mister*, the court held that the Illinois Human Rights Act's prohibition against discrimination on the basis of sex or marital status does not include a landlord's refusal to rent an apartment to unmarried persons of the opposite sex. In ascertaining legislative intent, the court observed that: Illinois law defined "marital status" as "the legal status of being married, single, separated, divorced or widowed."

Plaintiffs' interpretation of the Act would have us conclude that the legislature intended to protect from discrimination those individuals who choose to cohabit with a person of the opposite sex without entering into marriage. The fornication statute, as it existed when plaintiffs attempted to rent the apartments, evidenced this State's policy against such a practice. We believe plaintiffs' interpretation of the Act is in conflict with the longstanding policy reflected by the fornication statute. Statutory provisions relating to the same subject matter should be construed harmoniously where possible. * * *

Such a stance [by this court] expresses neither approval nor disapproval of discreet cohabitation; couples who wish to live together without being married can certainly still do so, but they must find a landlord who does not object to the arrangement. The Act's failure to protect such couples from "discrimination" merely evidences the legislature's hesitancy to require landlords to acquiesce.

II. Minnesota Constitution

Although, in arguments to this court, appellant emphasized the United States Constitution, the issue of protection of religious liberty under the Minnesota Constitution was properly preserved for appeal. * * * As we said in State v. Fuller, 374 N.W.2d 722 (Minn.1985):

It is axiomatic that a state supreme court may interpret its own constitution to offer greater protection of individual rights than does the federal constitution. Indeed, as the highest court of this state, we are "independently responsible for safeguarding the rights of [our] citizens." State courts are, and should be, the first line of defense for individual liberties within the federalist system.

The pertinent language in the Minnesota Constitution addressing religious liberty is as follows:

The right of every man to worship God according to the dictates of his own conscience shall never be infringed * * * nor shall any control of or interference with the rights of conscience be permitted, or any preference be given by law to any religious establishment or mode of worship; but the liberty of conscience hereby secured shall not be so construed as to excuse acts of licentiousness or justify practices inconsistent with the peace or safety of the state * * *.

Minn. Const. art. I, § 16 (emphasis added). The plain language of this section commands this court to weigh the competing interests at stake whenever rights of conscience are burdened. Under this section, the state may interfere with the rights of conscience only if it can show that the religious practice in question is "licentious" or "inconsistent with the peace or safety of the state."

In view of the above considerations * * * we are compelled to conclude that French must be granted an exemption from the MHRA unless the state can demonstrate compelling and overriding state interest, not only in the state's general statutory purpose, but in refusing to grant an exemption to French.

In short, we interpret the Minnesota Constitution as requiring a more stringent burden on the state in our opinion and grants far more protection of religious freedom than the broad language of the United States Constitution. Pursuant to this analysis, we conclude that the state has failed to sustain its burden in demonstrating a sufficiently compelling interest. It appears that we have now reached the stage in Minnesota constitutional law where the religious views of a probable majority of the Minnesota citizens are being alleged by a state agency to violate state law. Today we have a department of state government proposing that, while French has sincere religious beliefs and those beliefs are being infringed on by the Human Rights Act, the state, nevertheless, has an interest in promoting access to housing for cohabiting couples which overrides French's right to exercise his religion. Respondent characterizes the state's interest as "eliminating pernicious discrimination, including marital status discrimination." We are not told what is so pernicious about refusing to treat unmarried, cohabiting couples as if they were legally married. * * *

How can there be a compelling state interest in promoting fornication when there is a state statute on the books prohibiting it? See Minn.Stat. §609.34 (1988). Moreover, if the state has a duty to enforce a statute in the least restrictive way to accommodate religious beliefs, surely it is less restrictive to require Parsons to abide by the law prohibiting fornication than to compel French to cooperate in breaking it. Rather than grant French an exemption from the MHRA, the state would rather grant everyone an exemption from the fornication statute. Such a result is absurd. * * *

[A long, vehement dissent by CHIEF JUSTICE POPOVICH is omitted.]

NOTES AND QUESTIONS

1.   Contrast the approach to "family" here and in the

Braschi case reprinted *supra*, ch. seven. Suppose the
French decision had been decided under the federal Fair
Housing Act, with its 1988 Amendments to include "familial
status" as a protected classification. What outcome? Should
a landlord be able to deny a lease to a tenant on religious
or moral grounds, because the tenant is engaging in legal
activity that does no damage to the landlord's property? For
example, suppose a physician, a commercial tenant, began
performing legal abortions on the leased premises, and a
Catholic landlord objects.

§13.2 The "New Property," Especially in Housing

p. 1026, substitute the following for Question 3:

WRIGHT v. CITY OF ROANOKE
Supreme Court of the United States (1987)
479 U.S. 418

JUSTICE WHITE delivered the opinion of the Court.

Petitioners in this case, tenants living in low-income
housing projects owned by respondent, brought suit under
42 U.S.C. § 1983, alleging that respondent overbilled them
for their utilities and thereby violated the rent ceiling
imposed by the Brooke Amendment to the Housing Act of
1937, and the implementing regulations of the Department of
Housing and Urban Development (HUD). The District Court
and the Court of Appeals for the Fourth Circuit, 771 F.2d
833 (1985), concluded that petitioners did not have a cause
of action under § 1983. We granted certiorari and now
reverse.

I

Respondent is one of many public housing authorities
(PHAs) established throughout the country under the United
States Housing Act of 1937, to provide affordable housing for
low-income people. In 1969, the Housing Act was amended
in a fundamental respect: the Brooke Amendment imposed a
ceiling for rents charged to low-income people living in
public housing projects, and, as later amended, provides
that a low-income family "shall pay as rent" a specified
percentage of its income. HUD has consistently considered
"rent" to include a reasonable amount for the use of utilities,
which is defined by regulation as that amount equal to or
less than an amount determined by the PHA to be a
reasonable part of the rent paid by low-income tenants.
In their suit against respondent, petitioners alleged that

respondent had overcharged them for their utilities by failing to comply with the applicable HUD regulations in establishing the amount of utility service to which petitioners were entitled. Thus, according to petitioners, respondent imposed a surcharge for "excess" utility consumption that should have been part of petitioners' rent and deprived them of their statutory right to pay only the prescribed maximum portion of their income as rent. The District Court granted summary judgment for respondent on petitioners' § 1983 claim, holding that a private cause of action was unavailable to enforce the Brooke Amendment. The Court of Appeals for the Fourth Circuit affirmed. * * * [T]he Court of Appeals held that while the Brooke Amendment confers certain rights on tenants, these rights are enforceable only by HUD, not by the individual tenant: "the situation is very analogous to the one in which a trustee [that is, HUD], not the *cestui que* trust, must bring suit."

II

Maine v. Thiboudot, 448 U.S. 1, 100 S.Ct. 2502 (1980), held that § 1983 was available to enforce violations of federal statutes by agents of the State. Pennhurst State School and Hospital v. Halderman, 451 U.S. 1, 101 S.Ct. 1531 (1981) and Middlesex County Sewerage Authority v. National Sea Clammers Assn., 453 U.S. 1, 101 S.Ct. 2615 (1981), however, recognized two exceptions to the application of § 1983 to remedy statutory violations: where Congress has foreclosed such enforcement of the statute in the enactment itself and where the statute did not create enforceable rights, privileges, or immunities within the meaning of § 1983. In *Pennhurst*, a § 1983 action did not lie because the statutory provisions were thought to be only statements of "findings" indicating no more than a congressional preference -- at most a "nudge in the preferred directio[n]," and not intended to rise to the level of an enforceable right. In *Sea Clammers*, an intent to foreclose resort to § 1983 was found in the comprehensive remedial scheme provided by Congress, a scheme that itself provided for private actions and left no room for additional private remedies under § 1983. Similarly, Smith v. Robinson, 468 U.S. 992, 1012, 104 S.Ct. 3457, 3469 (1984), held that allowing a plaintiff to circumvent the Education of the Handicapped Act's administrative remedies would be inconsistent with Congress' carefully tailored scheme, which itself allowed private parties to seek remedies for violating federal law. Under these cases, if there is a state deprivation of a "right" secured by a federal statute, § 1983 provides a remedial cause of action unless the state actor demonstrates by express provision or

other specific evidence from the statute itself that Congress
intended to foreclose such private enforcement. "We do not
lightly conclude that Congress intended to preclude reliance
on § 1983 as a remedy" for the deprivation of a federally
secured right. * * *

We disagree with the Court of Appeals' rather summary
conclusion that the administrative scheme of enforcement
foreclosed private enforcement. * * * We are unconvinced
* * * that respondent has overcome its burden of showing
that "the remedial devices provided in [the Housing Act] are
sufficiently comprehensive * * * to demonstrate congressional
intent to preclude the remedy of suits under § 1983." They
do not show that "Congress specifically foreclosed a remedy
under § 1983." * * * Not only are the Brooke Amendment
and its legislative history devoid of any express indication
that exclusive enforcement authority was vested in HUD, but
there have also been both congressional and agency actions
indicating that enforcement authority is not centralized and
that private actions were anticipated. Neither, in our view,
are the remedial mechanisms provided sufficiently
comprehensive and effective to raise a clear inference that
Congress intended to foreclose a § 1983 cause of action for
the enforcement of tenants' rights secured by federal law.

In 1981, Congress changed the maximum percentage of
income that could be paid as "rent" from 25 percent to 30
percent. Omnibus Budget Reconciliation Act of 1981, Pub.L.
97-35, § 322, 95 Stat. 400. In making this change,
Congress gave the Secretary discretion to raise tenants' rent
incrementally over a 5-year period to ease the burden on
low-income tenants during the transition. To avoid a
potential multitude of litigation over the way in which the
Secretary implemented the phased-in rate increase, Congress
specifically made the Secretary's decisions effectuating the
phase-in immune from judicial review. At congressional
hearings in which this specific and limited exception to
judicial review was discussed, HUD representatives explained
that this exception had no effect on tenants' ability to
enforce their rights under the Housing Act in federal court
other than the limited exception concerning the phase-in. *
* *

There is other evidence clearly indicating that in HUD's
view tenants have the right to bring suit in federal court to
challenge housing authorities' calculations of utility
allowances. Among HUD's 1982 proposed regulations was §
865.476(d), 47 Fed.Reg. 35249, 35254 (1982), which would
have confined tenant utility-allowance challenges to the
procedures available in state court. The final regulation,
however, contained no such limitation and contemplated that

tenants could challenge PHA actions in federal as well as state courts. 24 CFR § 965.473(e) (1985). As the comment accompanying the final regulation explained, the proposal to limit challenges to state court actions had been abandoned. The final "provision does not preclude federal court review." * * *

In both *Sea Clammers* and Smith v. Robinson, the statutes at issue themselves provided for private judicial remedies, thereby evidencing congressional intent to supplant the § 1983 remedy. There is nothing of that kind found in the Brooke Amendment or elsewhere in the Housing Act. Indeed, the only private remedy provided for is the local grievance procedures which the Act now requires. These procedures are not open to class grievances; and even if tenants may grieve about a PHA's utility allowance schedule, * * * the existence of a state administrative remedy does not ordinarily foreclose resort to § 1983. *See* Patsy v. Board of Regents of Florida, 457 U.S. 496, 516, 102 S.Ct. 2557, 2568 (1982). * * *

Lastly, it is said that tenants may sue on their lease in state courts and enforce their Brooke Amendment rights in that litigation. Perhaps they could, but the state-court remedy is hardly a reason to bar an action under § 1983, which was adopted to provide a federal remedy for the enforcement of federal rights.

In sum, we conclude that nothing in the Housing Act or the Brooke Amendment evidences that Congress intended to preclude petitioners' § 1983 claim against respondent.

III

Although the Court of Appeals read the Brooke Amendment as extending to housing project tenants certain rights enforceable only by HUD, respondent asserts that neither the Brooke Amendment nor the interim regulations gave the tenants any specific or definable rights to utilities, that is, no enforceable rights within the meaning of § 1983. We perceive little substance in this claim. The Brooke Amendment could not be clearer: as further amended in 1981, tenants could be charged as rent no more and no less than 30 percent of their income. This was a mandatory limitation focusing on the individual family and its income. The intent to benefit tenants is undeniable. Nor is there any question that HUD interim regulations, in effect when this suit began, expressly required that a "reasonable" amount for utilities be included in rent that a PHA was allowed to charge, an interpretation to which HUD has adhered both before and after the adoption of the Brooke Amendment. HUD's view is entitled to deference as a valid interpretation of the statute,

and Congress in the course of amending that provision has
not disagreed with it.

Respondent nevertheless asserts that the provision for a
"reasonable" allowance for utilities is too vague and
amorphous to confer on tenants an enforceable "right" within
the meaning of § 1983 and that the whole matter of utility
allowances must be left to the discretion of the PHA, subject
to supervision by HUD. The regulations, however, defining
the statutory concept of "rent" as including utilities, have
the force of law, Chrysler Corp. v. Brown, 441 U.S. 281,
294-295, 99 S.Ct. 1705, 1713-1714 (1979), they specifically
set out guidelines that the PHAs were to follow in
establishing utility allowances, and they require notice to
tenants and an opportunity to comment on proposed
allowances. In our view, the benefits Congress intended to
confer on tenants are sufficiently specific and definite to
qualify as enforceable rights under *Pennhurst* and § 1983,
rights that are not, as respondent suggests, beyond the
competence of the judiciary to enforce.

The judgment of the Court of Appeals is accordingly

Reversed.

JUSTICE O'CONNOR, with whom CHIEF JUSTICE REHNQUIST, JUSTICE
POWELL, and JUSTICE SCALIA join, dissenting.

Assuming, as the Court finds, that Congress intended to
create an enforceable right to a limitation on the amount
PHAs may charge "as rent," the question remains whether
petitioners' claim to reasonable utilities comes within the
scope of the right that Congress intended to confer. On the
face of the statute, there is nothing to suggest that
Congress intended that utilities be included within the
statutory entitlement. "Rent" in ordinary usage simply
means consideration paid for the use or occupation of
property, and the statute does not suggest congressional
intent to adopt a broader construction of the term.

The legislative history of the Brooke Amendment, far from
indicating an intent to create a statutory right to utilities,
shows that Congress was presented with, and ultimately
rejected, a proposal to create an enforceable right to
"reasonable utilities." As originally reported out of the
Senate, Senator Brooke's bill enumerated a range of shelter
costs in addition to "rent" that were to be subject to the
statutory rent limit. The Senate bill provided that the term
"rental" was to include "the proportionate share attributable
to the unit of the total shelter costs to be borne by the
tenants in a low-rent housing project, including any separate

charges to a tenant for reasonable utility use and for public services and facilities." In the bill reported out of Conference, however, this reference to utilities was deleted. The Conference Report stated that the substitute bill "retain[ed] the basic concept" of the Senate bill by "generally limiting rents that may be charged to no more than 25% of [the tenant's] income," but it included no reference to the utilities charges provided for in the Senate bill. * * *

Even assuming that agency regulations of the sort at issue here could create rights enforceable in a § 1983 action, the temporary regulations involved in this case are not capable of judicial enforcement. The provisions remained subject to the exercise of wide discretion by the local housing authorities, thereby rendering it difficult or impossible to determine whether a violation occurred. Moreover, the regulations were cast as overall standards rather than as a method for determining the utilities rates for particular tenants, making it impossible to fashion appropriate relief for individual plaintiffs. * * * *

In my view, petitioners do have a remedy in seeking to secure utilities from respondent: they may sue on their leases.[1] Pursuant to its authority to ensure the lower-rental character of publicly assisted housing, HUD requires PHAs to set forth in their leases that they will "supply running water and reasonable amounts of hot water and reasonable amounts of heat at appropriate times of the year (according to local custom and usage)," and will "maintain in good and safe working order and condition electrical, plumbing, sanitary, heating, ventilating, and other facilities and appliances, including elevators, supplied or required to be supplied by the PHA." HUD has developed a standard lease reflecting these requirements, which respondent's leases

---

1. Paragraph 4 of respondent's standard lease provides:

Utilities: Management Agent agrees to furnish at no charge to the Resident the following utilities as reasonably necessary: hot and cold water, gas for cooking, and electricity for lighting and general household appliances and heat at appropriate times of the year, and also range and refrigerator. Resident will be required to pay for all excess consumption of utilities above the monthly allocated amount as developed by the Authority and determined by the individual check meter servicing the leased unit. The schedule of allocations and charges for excess consumption is posted on the bulletin board of each Housing Development office."

Record, Exh. H.

closely follow. * * * If respondent fails to fulfill these
obligations, petitioners may, like any other tenants, bring
suit for breach of contract. * * *

NOTES AND QUESTIONS

1. One important difference between the §1983 action that
the petitioners brought and the breach of contract action
that the dissent claimed was a better alternative is that a
prevailing party under § 1983 is entitled to attorney's fees.
A low income tenant might not be able to afford a breach of
contract action, but in the successful § 1983 action the
defendant would end up paying for the plaintiff's attorney.

Chapter 14
PUBLIC REGULATION OF COMMUNITY OWNERSHIP:
CONDOMINIUMS AND COOPERATIVES

§14.2   INTERNAL DISPUTES

page 1045, insert the following before the Note:

PENNEY v.
ASS'N OF APARTMENT OWNERS OF HALE KAANAPALI
Supreme Court of Hawaii (1989)
70 Haw. 469, 776 P.2d 393

WAKATSUKI, JUSTICE.

Robert C. Penney and P. Jean Penney (Plaintiffs-Appellants) are owners of an apartment in Hale Kaanapali, a condominium project which has both residential/hotel apartments and apartments used as commercial spaces. Hale Kaanapali Hotel Associates, a Hawaii Limited Partnership, (Defendant-Appellee) is the owner of an apartment designated in the Declaration of the horizontal property regime as Building F constituting a snack bar containing 625 square feet except for the two bathrooms which are common elements within the Building. When a special meeting was called for the purpose of amending the Declaration, Defendant-Appellee had approximately 72.3% of the common interest of the condominium project and controlled another 4.53% interest by proxies. The amendment proposed to change a common area of approximately 2,664 square feet which was used as the Association clubhouse area including the restrooms from a common element to a limited common element for Defendant-Appellee's exclusive use. The proposed amendment was approved by a vote of 76.83% of the interest of all the apartment owners.

Plaintiffs-Appellants contended in the circuit court that the amendment is invalid because approval of 100 percent of the ownership interest is required to change a common element to a limited common area for the exclusive use by an apartment owner. * * *

Hawaii Revised Statutes (HRS) §514A-13(b) (1985) provides:

The common interest appurtenant to each apartment as expressed in the declaration shall have a permanent character and shall not be altered without the consent of all the apartment owners affected[.]

In contrast, HRS §514A-13(d)(1) (1985) permits the board of directors of the association of apartment owners "upon the approval of the owners of seventy-five per cent of the common interests, to change the use of the common elements."

Defendant-Appellee contends that the amendment to the Declaration is merely a change in the use of the common elements, and therefore, § 514-13(d)(1) applies. This would require an approval of only 75 percent of the common interests.

The change of use of a common element (e.g., changing from shuffleboard to tennis court, or erecting a maintenance shed on what was open space), and conversion of a common element to a limited common element are significantly different. In the former, the benefit to all the apartment owners is not diminished. In the latter, however, the benefit to all the apartment owners is significantly diminished by the restricted and exclusive use of the limited common area to one or fewer than all of the apartment owners. "In effect, then, the common elements as to all other tenants have thereby been diminished." Stuewe v. Lauletta, 93 Ill.App.3d 1029, 1031, 49 Ill.Dec. 494, 496, 418 N.E.2d 138, 140 (1981).

Defendant-Appellee further contends that although there may be an alteration to the common elements, § 514A-13(b) requires unanimous consent only when the common interest is altered.

"Common interest" is defined as the percentage of undivided interest in the common elements appertaining to each apartment. HRS §514A-3 (1985). Since the percentage of undivided interest in the common elements owned by each apartment owner will remain the same, Defendant-Appellee reasons that §514-13(b) is inapplicable. We disagree.

We agree with the Florida appellate court which stated: "An undivided interest [in the common elements] is an undivided interest in the whole and when that whole changes, that interest, if not the percent, also changes." Tower House Condominium, Inc. v. Millman, 410 So.2d 926, 930 (Fla.Dist.Ct.App., 3d Dist.1981). See also Grimes v. Moreland, 41 Ohio Misc. 69, 74, 322 N.E.2d 699, 703 (1974) ("Fencing-in of one area for almost exclusive use of one unit owner will not alter the percentage interest of the other unit owners (each will still have this approximately 6% interest) but it will mean that each unit owner will have 6% of the smaller remaining common area.")

For all intents and purposes, converting a common element to a limited common element diminishes the common interest appurtenant to each apartment. Under HRS § 514A-13(b), we hold that such conversion requires the consent of all the apartment owners.

NOTES AND QUESTIONS

1. Ordinarily, the right to enforce the condominium's claims respecting injury to the common elements lies with the owners association, not with individual unit owners. However, in Cigal v. Leader Development Corporation, 408 Mass. 212, 557 N.E.2d 1119 (1990), the court held that each individual unit owner could sue the developer for defective construction of common elements where each had a purchase contract describing the developer's obligations respecting the common elements, and where the contracts varied from one purchaser to another. However, the court limited this individual right to defects in the common area that were expressly covered by the home owner's individual purchase contracts. With respect to other defects, the action lay with the owners' association. In any event, individual unit owners can sometimes use a class action to sue developers against whom they have a common claim. Villa Sierra Condominium Ass'n v. Field Corp., 787 P.2d 661 (Colo. App. 1990) permitted such an action.

Chapter 15
VOLUNTARY TRANSFERS OF
INTERESTS IN REAL PROPERTY:
THE LAND SALE CONTRACT

p. 1080 substitute the following for Kramer v. Mobley:

BEARD v. S/E JOINT VENTURE
Court of Appeals of Maryland (1990)
321 Md. 126, 581 A.2d 1275

RODOWSKY, JUDGE.

This case involves the measure of damages for the breach by vendors of a contract to construct a residence and then to convey the improved realty. The real estate market for the subject property was escalating during the potentially relevant period. * * * We shall hold that the purchasers' damages are not limited to certain out-of-pocket losses, as held by the courts below, but that the purchasers may also recover damages for loss of the benefit of their bargain. * * *

The purchasers are the petitioners, DeLawrence and Lillian M. Beard (the Beards), who were plaintiffs in the circuit court. The vendors, respondents here and defendants in the circuit court, are Diana C. Etheridge (Etheridge) and Gene Stull (Stull), joint venturers in S/E Joint Venture. Etheridge is a licensed real estate agent and Stull is a home builder. S/E Joint Venture had acquired an unimproved lot in Piney Glen Farms subdivision in the Potomac section of Montgomery County for the purpose of building a home for speculation.

Protracted negotiations between the Beards and S/E Joint Venture led to a contract formed on March 17, 1986, under which S/E Joint Venture would construct a house on the lot and convey the improved premises to the Beards for $785,000. The contract in part provided "that the PURCHASER is purchasing a completed dwelling [and] that the SELLER is not acting as a contractor for the PURCHASER in the construction of the dwelling[.]" The contract recited that "the approximate date of completion of the improvements now scheduled by the SELLER is November 30, 1986." For a period of ninety days the contract was contingent on the sale of two residences, one the then residence of the Beards and the other that of Mrs. Beard's mother, who also was to occupy the home to be built.

Matters did not proceed smoothly. On March 16, 1987, the vendors, through counsel, terminated the contract.

The letter declaring the contract terminated invoked a provision under which "the SELLER shall have the right to return the PURCHASER'S deposit and to declare this Contract null and void if, in the SELLER'S sole discretion, it determines that . . . performance within 365 days from the date hereof will not be possible."

In May 1987 the Beards filed a * * * complaint against respondents. * * *

In a written opinion the circuit judge found, on conflicting evidence, that the vendors had breached the contract by the purported termination of March 16, 1987. The trial judge concluded "that it is implicit that before the right of termination can be exercised the defendants must have acted in good faith to try to complete construction of the house within the stated time period; this, in the court's judgment, they did not do." The circuit court found that Stull "knew some two months after the inception of the contract that he would be unable to meet the time deadline." This was found to be "significant because defendants were aware that the plaintiffs and [Mrs. Beard's mother] had to sell their homes in order to meet their financial commitment[.]" The trial court also found undue delay in the performance of plumbing work, which "had a ripple effect on the subsequent course of construction." * * *

Itemizing claimed damages in their post trial memorandum, the Beards included $100,000 for "loss of bargain." Factually, the $100,000 figure is said to represent the excess of the value of the property, with the home completed in accordance with the contract, as of March 16, 1987, over the contract price. * * *

Legally to support their loss of the bargain claim, the plaintiffs relied on Horner v. Beasley, 105 Md. 193, 65 A. 820 (1907). *Horner* was a purchaser's action against a vendor for breach of a contract to convey, for $1,200, improved realty worth $1,800. * * * This Court * * * approved a jury instruction that if "the defendant acted in good faith in failing to perform the contract of sale, the plaintiff was entitled to recover only the amount of his deposit with interest and the expense if any incurred in the investigation of the title; but if they found that the defendant did not act in good faith then in addition to the amounts aforesaid the plaintiff could recover the excess, if any, of the market value of the property, at the time of the sale, over the contract price."

The Beards, also citing Charles County Broadcasting Co. v. Meares, 270 Md. 321, 311 A.2d 27 (1973), argued that, because the respondents were able to perform, their breach was in "bad faith," so that benefit of the bargain damages

should be awarded. The trial court did not accept this
contention, explaining that it did "not award any damages
for loss of the benefit of the bargain[,] finding no evidence
of bad faith in the sense that the termination was activated
by malice, fraud or the like." * * *

Damages for breach of a contract ordinarily are that sum
which would place the plaintiff in as good a position as that
in which the plaintiff would have been, had the contract
been performed. These expectation interest damages embrace
both losses incurred and gains prevented. See Restatement
(Second) of Contracts §347 (1981); Restatement, Contracts
§329 (1932). Here the circuit court undertook to apply an
exception to the ordinary rule. The exception traces to
Flureau v. Thornhill, 2 W. Black. 1078, 96 Eng.Rep. 635
(K.B.1776). In England, and in the diminishing number of
American states that recognize *Flureau*, the exception applies
only where, due to no fault on the part of the seller, there
is an inability to convey good title. In the case at hand
respondents' breach had nothing to do with title to the
property. Further, under the trial court's findings, the
inability timely to deliver a completed house, which motivated
the wrongful termination of March 16, 1987, is not a "good
faith" failure to perform within the meaning of the *Flureau*
exception. In any event, "good faith," per the *Flureau*
rule, is not so all inclusive as to embrace any breach which
was not "activated by malice, fraud or the like," as the trial
judge said. Thus, the trial court applied an erroneous legal
standard when it refused to consider benefit of the bargain
damages.

In *Flureau*, the plaintiff had purchased at auction a
property that paid an advantageous rent in relation to the
purchase price. The seller, however, could not produce
good title. In the ensuing suit the court's instructions
limited the jury to awarding the return of the deposit paid,
plus interest; but the jury allowed an additional twenty
pounds. A new trial was ordered. The report of the
judgment of De Grey, C.J., reads in full: "I think the
verdict wrong in point of law. Upon a contract for a
purchase, if the title proves bad, and the vendor is (without
fraud) incapable of making a good one, I do not think that
the purchaser can be entitled to any damages for the fancied
goodness of the bargain, which he supposes he has lost."
Flureau, 2 W. Black 1078, 96 Eng.Rep. 635. * * *

It has been recognized in England that the *Flureau*
exception was an "anomalous rule" brought about by the
difficulties in that country, as late as 1899 (if not later),
"in shewing a good title to real property" and that the
exception "ought not be extended to cases in which the

reasons on which it is based do not apply." Day v. Singleton, [1899] 2 Ch. 320, 329 (C.A.).[1]

Although English courts have struggled over the scope of the *Flureau* exception, the English cases considering *Flureau* have all concerned some aspect of title. See Hopkins v. Grazebrook, 6 B. & C. 31 (K.B.1826) (vendor who knows he has no title, but expects to be able to procure it prior to sale cannot rely on *Flureau* exception); Engell v. Fitch, [1869] L.R. 4 Q.B. 659 (Ex.Ch.) (*Flureau* limitation on damages not available where failure to convey results from vendor's refusal to oust a tenant); Bain v. Fothergill, [1874] L.R. 7 H.L. 158 (1873-74) (*Flureau* applies when inability to convey interest in mining royalty results from inability to get permission from lessor); Day v. Singleton, [1899] 2 Ch. 320 (C.A.) (*Flureau* limitation on damages unavailable in sale of leasehold, where vendor fails to use best efforts to obtain lessor's consent to sale); In re Daniel, [1917] 2 Ch. 405 (*Flureau* not applicable where difficulty in conveyance results from inability to obtain partial release of mortgage); Braybrooks v. Whaley, [1919] 1 K.B. 435 (*Flureau* not applicable where failure to convey relates to noncompliance with Emergency Powers Act, rather than title defect).

More recently, *Flureau* has been given a very narrow reading in England. In Malhotra v. Choudhury, [1979] 1 All E.R. 186 (C.A.), a partner in a medical practice, Malhotra, conveyed the medical office to the junior partner, Choudhury, and the latter's wife. The partnership agreement provided that, if Choudhury left the practice, Malhotra would have the option to buy back the property at fair market value. The next year Malhotra gave notice of dissolution of the partnership, exercised the option, and later brought an action for specific performance, which was denied. Two years later Malhotra sought damages. The trial court found that Choudhury could not convey good title because of his wife's refusal to join and, applying *Flureau*,

---

1. The difficulties included the absence of a land register. The deeds evidencing the chain of title were delivered by the solicitor for the vendor to the solicitor for the purchaser. "Neither possession of the land nor possession of the deeds was a sufficient guarantee of a good title. Deeds might be suppressed intentionally, or as the result of mistake or accident." 15 W. Holdsworth, A History of English Law 173 (A. Goodhart & H. Hanbury ed. 1965) (footnote omitted). In Donovan v. Bachstadt, 91 N.J. 434, 441, 453 A.2d 160, 164 (1982), the court attributes to Lord Westbury, a mid-nineteenth century Lord Chancellor, the description of a bundle of documents evidencing title as "difficult to read, disgusting to touch, and impossible to understand."

limited the recovery to reliance damages. The Court of Appeal reversed, holding that the *Flureau* rule was an exception to be applied only where the vendor showed best efforts to make a good title. The court reasoned that the origin of the exception virtually required that bad faith be defined as a failure to make best efforts, with no requirement for fraud, and that failure of the vendor to demonstrate good faith precluded the *Flureau* exception.

With respect to this country, Professor Corbin summarizes: "A great many courts in the United States have not been inclined to follow the English courts or to differentiate land contracts from other contracts. The rule they adopt is that, if the seller fails to convey the title that he contracted to convey, the buyer has a right to damages measured by the value of the land at the time it should have been conveyed, less the contract price as yet unpaid." 5 A. Corbin, Corbin on Contracts § 1098, at 525 (1964) (footnote omitted). "Some of the courts, however, have recognized the English rule...." Id. at 525-28 (footnote omitted). But even among American courts applying *Flureau*, "[i]f the seller in fact has title and refuses to perform his contract without excuse, the buyer has a right to damages." * * *

The first mention of *Flureau* in the reports of this Court is in Baltimore Permanent Bldg. & Land Soc'y v. Smith, 54 Md. 187 (1880). The land was Solomon's Island, described in the contract as about "sixty-five acres." The vendor's retained land, however, surveyed at thirty-six acres. In the purchaser's damage action the trial court instructed that return of the deposit plus interest and expenses of title examination could be awarded together with benefit of the bargain damages. This Court reversed and remanded for a new trial. The "different rule" in England under *Flureau* was noted. Id. at 206. This Court traced the rule through commentators and noted that it had been followed in a great number of cases in England. Citing 2 Addison on Contracts § 529, the rule limiting recovery to reliance damages was said to apply where the vendor had " 'reasonable ground for believing that he was the owner of the property, and had the right to sell at the time he agreed to sell, but is prevented by an unexpected defect of title....' " Id. at 207. * * *

Respondents have no basis for invoking the *Flureau* exception because they do not even assert that inability to convey title produced their breach of the contract to convey. * * *

Thus, the trial court erred in failing to consider breach of the bargain damages.

Chapter 16
VOLUNTARY TRANSFERS OF
INTERESTS IN REAL PROPERTY:
CONVEYANCING BY DEED

§16.3 DESCRIPTIONS

§16.3.4   Problems Involving Deed Descriptions

page 1129, insert the following after note 6:

SUN VALLEY SHAMROCK RESOURCES, INC. v.
TRAVELERS LEASING CORPORATION
Supreme Court of Idaho (1990)
118 Idaho 116, 794 P.2d 1389

BOYLE, JUSTICE.
   * * * The dispute in this case centers around the location of a parcel of real estate known as the "Bowman parcel" and whether a two-unit dwelling (hereafter "duplex") was located on this particular parcel. At issue is the interpretation of what plaintiffs-appellants, Sun Valley Shamrock Resources and Nancy Gunderson (hereafter "Shamrock") assert is an ambiguous legal description in the deed.
   The Bowman parcel was created in 1960 out of a larger parcel owned by a common grantor, R.B. Randall. Between 1960 and 1983, the Bowman parcel was transferred eight different times, including the transfer to plaintiff Shamrock in 1983. Until 1986, various surveys and appraisals placed the duplex on the Bowman parcel. The legal description consistently used in the conveyances, including the sheriff's deed, is the following:
   A portion of the SW 1/4 SE 1/4 , Section 27, described as follows: beginning at the Southeast corner of said Section 27; thence North 1322 feet; thence N. 89 47'W., 1391 feet; thence S. 50 14'W., 758.5 feet along the Northerly boundary line of Clarendon Hot Springs Road; thence N. 39 46'W., 100 feet to the real point of beginning; thence N. 39 46'W., 56 feet; thence N. 50 14'E., 100 feet; thence S. 39 46'E., 56 feet; thence S. 50 14'W., 100 feet to the real point of beginning.
   In 1985, the defendant-respondent, Travelers Leasing Corporation (hereafter "Travelers") purchased the land surrounding the Bowman parcel at a sheriff's sale. The sheriff's deed from which Travelers claim title to the adjacent property excepted five smaller parcels which were not part of the underlying foreclosure action. One of these excepted

parcels was thought to be the Bowman parcel. In 1986, Travelers hired a surveyor to locate and stake the excepted parcels. The surveyor followed the distance of 1391 feet in the second call of the description contained in the deed and rejected the other language because he could not locate the "northerly boundary line of the Clarendon Hot Springs Road" with what he felt was an appropriate degree of certainty. As a result, the surveyor determined that the duplex was located on Travelers' property and not on one of the excepted parcels. Relying upon this survey, Travelers bulldozed the duplex and burned the remnants of the building. In September 1986, this action was filed by Shamrock against Travelers seeking damages for the wrongful destruction of the duplex which was allegedly situated on the Bowman parcel and owned by Shamrock. Shamrock neither pled nor attempted to prove adverse possession or boundary by acquiescence. Instead, Shamrock claimed that the language "758.5 feet along the northerly boundary line of the Clarendon Hot Springs Road," is a reference to a landmark and is therefore a call to a "monument." Shamrock asserts that the call to a monument conflicts with the distance call of "1391 feet", and that the call to the monument should control over the conflicting course of distance call. Shamrock claims that use of the monument call is the proper interpretation of the language contained in the description and places the destroyed duplex on its property.

Travelers argues that the reference to "758.5 feet along the northerly boundary line of the Clarendon Hot Springs Road" is not a call to a monument and that there is no conflict between this call and the "1391 feet" course of distance description. Travelers contends that these calls can be read together and when done so, clearly situate the duplex on Travelers' property and not on the Bowman parcel. Accordingly, Travelers asserts it is not liable for destruction or removal of the duplex.

The trial court ruled in favor of Travelers concluding that the language contained in the deed description did not refer to a monument and held the language referring to the northerly boundary line of the Clarendon Hot Springs Road lacked the requisite visibility necessary for the designation as a call to a monument. Based on the facts and evidence presented, the trial court concluded that there was no conflict between the call to course and distance and the call to a monument. The trial court held that the property on which the duplex was located belonged to Travelers pursuant to the sheriff's deed and Travelers was not liable to Shamrock for its removal. This appeal followed. * * *

In construing a deed, physical features existing upon the

ground and referred to in the description must be considered. Monuments, natural or artificial, or lines marked on ground, control over calls for courses and distances. A fixed monument or marker is controlling over a conflicting call to course and distance, if it is of a permanent nature, and established with "reasonable certainty." Thus the determination of what is a "monument" is generally made on a case-by-case basis. Achter v. Maw, 27 Utah 2d 149, 493 P.2d 989 (1972) (monument must be a "tangible landmark," have physical properties such as "stability, permanence, and definiteness of location); Scott v. Hansen, 18 Utah 2d 303, 422 P.2d 525 (1966) (monument must be "definitely identified and located"); Lester v. Schutt, 128 Fla. 302, 174 So. 583 (1937) (requirements for establishing a monument were "permanence, identity and visibility"); Russo v. Corideo, 102 Conn. 663, 129 A. 849 (1925) (a monument must be "known and fixed").

In the present case, Shamrock offered into evidence aerial photographs of the area in the years 1957, 1964 and 1969. These photographs demonstrated that the location of the Clarendon Hot Springs Road has remained fixed over this period of time. However, in spite of the road's apparent fixed location, Shamrock's expert witnesses, all professional engineers and/or land surveyors, located the northerly boundary line of the Clarendon Hot Springs Road and the Bowman parcel in varying locations depending on the description or method utilized. One surveyor called by Shamrock interpreted the deed in the manner argued by Shamrock. However, this particular witness, Gordon Williams, acknowledged that he never actually surveyed the property and testified that his placement of the Bowman parcel and the placement of that parcel by Dennis Zimmerman, the defendant's surveyor, was determined by the manner in which each interpreted the language contained in the third call referring to "along the northerly boundary of the Clarendon Hot Springs Road." Williams admitted in this regard that there was no language contained in the deed description which directs that the course of the second call is to be followed to the point of intersection with the northerly boundary line of the Clarendon Hot Springs Road. Except for his particular use of and reliance on the language referencing the Clarendon Hot Springs Road, Williams testified that his location of the Bowman parcel would have been the same as that found by Zimmerman.

Zimmerman testified that in his opinion, reference to "along the northerly boundary line of the Clarendon Hot Springs Road" was too indefinite to be used in locating the boundaries in question. Zimmerman also testified that a monument takes precedence over a conflicting distance or course only when the call in question is to or from a monument. Under cross-examination, one of Shamrock's expert witnesses testified that the word "along" was generally understood by surveyors to mean "parallel to" when determining boundaries. Zimmerman also testified that he conducted a survey on this property in 1972 and while doing so disregarded the call "along the northerly boundary of the Clarendon Hot Springs Road" because he was unable to determine the northerly boundary of the road and because it did not call to the boundary. At that time Zimmerman also researched an adjacent piece of property known as the Abegglen parcel, which was senior to the Bowman parcel. The legal description for the Abegglen parcel was the same as the Bowman parcel except it did not contain a call referring to the Clarendon Hot Springs Road. Zimmerman concluded that the call to course and distance was more definite and concluded that the phrase "along the northerly boundary of the Clarendon Hot Springs Road" did not have significance. As a result, Zimmerman testified that he utilized the third call, "south 50 degrees 14 minutes, west 758.5 feet" in determining the boundaries of the property.

Although the location of the Clarendon Hot Springs Road has remained fixed over many years, the difficulty experienced by the several engineers and surveyors in locating the northerly boundary line of the road supports the trial court's finding and conclusion that this line lacks the degree of definiteness and visibility necessary for designation as a call to a monument. When construing a deed description, effect must be given, if possible, to all of the language contained in the description. Quality Plastics, Inc. v. Moore, 131 Ariz. 238, 640 P.2d 169 (1982). It is our holding, based upon the record before us, that the trial court did not err in concluding that the phrase "along northerly boundary line of the Clarendon Hot Springs Road" is not sufficiently definite to constitute a call to a monument.

§16.4 DELIVERY

§16.4.1 Delivery to the Grantee

p. 1136, insert the following after note 5:
ESTATE OF O'BRIEN v. ROBINSON
Washington Supreme Court, en banc (1988)
109 Wash.2d 913, 749 P.2d 154

BRACHTENBACH, JUSTICE
The issue is whether RCW §11.02.090 validates two deeds

when the trial court found that the grantor "made no delivery of the deeds prior to her death in the sense that she did not intend an immediate transfer of the property but was intending to have a testamentary disposition take effect only at her death." As a result of that finding, the trial court held that the deeds did not vest title during grantor's life nor did they satisfy the formalities of execution required by the wills statute, RCW 11.12.020; thus, the deeds were ineffective.

This case arises from the execution of two quitclaim deeds by Mary O'Brien, a widow, to her then only surviving child, defendant Peaches Robinson. Mrs. O'Brien's other child died a month before she executed the deeds. The deceased daughter was survived by three children, one of whom is the plaintiff, as personal representative of the estate of the intestate widow O'Brien. * * *

The deeds * * * were absolute on their face. They were placed in a safety deposit box which was in the joint names of the grantor-decedent and the grantee, with equal access by both. When the joint safety deposit box was closed in December 1982, the grantee took possession of the deeds in question. * * * Peaches Robinson testified that she had possession of the originals of the two deeds at issue continuously from December 1982 until they were recorded April 29, 1983.

On April 23, 1983 Mrs. O'Brien suffered a stroke. She died in July 1983. From the time she executed the deeds until her death, Mrs. O'Brien retained possession and control of the two parcels of real property.

The trial court recognized a presumption of delivery arising from the grantee's possession of the deeds, but found the presumption overcome by clear and convincing evidence. The deadman's statute prevented any testimony as to the intent or understanding of the decedent at the time the grantee obtained possession of the deeds. Two longtime friends of Mrs. O'Brien testified that Mrs. O'Brien told them she had deeded the properties to her daughter Peaches, although one, on cross examination, expressed the legal conclusion that she thought Mrs. O'Brien still owned the property until she died.

In its oral opinion the trial court commented that it was clear "and really can't be disputed" that it was Mrs. O'Brien's intent to leave the real property to her daughter upon her death, but that she could not find a present intent to pass title at the time of execution of the deeds. Thus, the trial court concluded that (1) the deeds failed as conveyances and (2) failed as testamentary instruments because they were not executed in compliance with the wills

statute.   Neither the oral opinion nor the findings of fact
and conclusions of law mention RCW §11.02.090.

RCW §11.02.090 provides in part: (1) Any of the following
provisions in [a] . . . conveyance . . . is deemed to be
nontestamentary . . . : (c) that any property which is the
subject of the instrument shall pass to a person designated
by the decedent in either the instrument or a separate
writing, including a will, executed at the same time as the
instrument or subsequently.

For our purposes the statute means that a provision (the
words of conveyance here) in a conveyance (the deeds here)
by which any property (the real estate here) which is the
subject of the instrument (the deeds here) shall pass to a
person (the defendant-grantee here) designated by the
decedent (Mrs. O'Brien) is nontestamentary.   * * *   In
(1)(a), (b) and (c) the statute describes certain provisions
which will be nontestamentary when contained in certain
types of instruments. Subsection (1) of the statute states
that any of those provisions in * * * (11) a conveyance, or
(12) "any other written instrument effective as a contract,
gift, conveyance, or trust is deemed to be nontestamentary".

It is urged and the Court of Appeals held that the word
conveyance is modified by subsequent language so that it
must be effective as a conveyance before the statute applies.
Such an interpretation renders the statute meaningless in
this context. If an instrument were effective as a conveyance
it, by definition, would have passed a present title during
the decedent's lifetime. Therefore, there would be no need
to validate the instrument as nontestamentary. If proof of
delivery of these deeds had been made, the facts here would
indicate a valid *inter vivos* passage of a future interest with
the grantor retaining a lifetime interest.   Stated differently,
RCW §11.02.090 cannot operate upon a conveyance which is
effective as a conveyance because its operation as a
conveyance would in and of itself make it nontestamentary.

We are to construe a statute in such a manner as to avoid
rendering meaningless a word or portion thereof. Nisqually
Delta Ass'n v. DuPont, 95 Wash.2d 563, 627 P.2d 956 (1981).
We conclude that a correct construction of the statute is that
subsection (1) lists 12 types of instruments to which it may
apply with the 12th and separate category being "any other
written instrument effective as a contract, gift, conveyance,
or trust", i.e., if a written instrument is effective to
accomplish one of the specified consequences, it need not be
categorized as one of the 11 preceding instruments.

In construing the statute and its effect given the facts of
this case, we must not only consider whether these particular
deeds are within the scope of the statute, we must also deal

with the well established common law rule that legal "delivery" is necessary for a deed to be operative. Delivery is a legal concept. It is an expression rooted in a symbolical manual transfer, analogous to livery of seisin. 4 H. Tiffany, Real Property § 1033 (3d ed. 1975). The rule has evolved into a determination of the intention of the grantor. Determining the intention of the grantor has led to an examination of the facts and circumstances of the particular transaction.

In requiring "delivery" in the technical, legal sense, the courts have in fact been attempting to ascertain and effectuate the intent of the grantor. To insist, in this case, upon a strict compliance with a fictional legal delivery requirement would thwart the unchallenged intent of the grantor. We would be holding that the deeds, voluntarily signed by the decedent who intended to pass the property to her only surviving child upon her death, were not "conveyances" so they fail as deeds. Since they fail as deeds and were intended to take effect at death, they are testamentary instruments which do not comply with the wills statute. This analysis would compel us to ignore the grantor's intent, and the result would be terribly illogical when the very purpose of determining delivery is to ascertain and carry out the intent of the grantor. In its oral opinion the trial court felt compelled to comment that it "really can't be disputed" that it was the decedent's intent to pass the real property to her only surviving daughter.

We hold (1) that when it is determined that the proved intent of the grantor was to pass title upon his or her death, the legal requirement of "delivery" is satisfied, and (2) that RCW §11.02.090 removes the conveyance from the requirements of the statute relating to execution of wills, RCW §11.12.020. Our result satisfies the policy underlying the legal delivery requirement. This fact, coupled with the philosophy expressed in RCW §11.02.090, leads to a just result which implements rather than frustrates the intent of the decedent. We note that the Uniform Probate Code § 1-102(b)(2), 8 U.L.A. 24 (1983) states that one of its purposes and policies is "to discover and make effective the intent of a decedent in distribution of his [her] property."

The Court of Appeals and the trial court are reversed and this matter is remanded to the trial court for further proceedings consistent with this opinion.

DORE, JUSTICE (dissenting).

The majority holds that two deeds are effective to pass property at death even though the deeds were neither valid inter vivos conveyances nor valid testamentary dispositions of property. In so holding, the majority radically alters the long-standing requirements for the effective conveyance of property by deed and misconstrues the nature and purpose of RCW §11.02.090. I dissent.

Mary O'Brien attempted to use two deeds to make a testamentary disposition of her Seattle and Camano properties to her daughter, Peaches Robinson. In Washington, a deed can operate as a "will substitute" in that a grantor by deed can retain a life estate in property with a future interest passing to the grantee upon the death of the grantor. * * * A deed, in order to be valid, must be delivered by the grantor to the grantee. Juel v. Doll, 51 Wash.2d 435, 436-37, 319 P.2d 543 (1957). To constitute a delivery "it must be clearly apparent that the grantor intended that the deed should presently pass title." *Juel*, at 437, 319 P.2d 543.

The trial court found that O'Brien "retained control, possession and use of the propert[ies] and up to the date of her death made no delivery of the propert[ies] or [of] the deed[s]." The trial court concluded that O'Brien made no delivery in the sense that "she did not intend an immediate transfer of the property but was intending to have a testamentary disposition take effect only at her death . . ." The parties in their petition for review and answer do not challenge the trial court's findings that the deeds were not delivered. Rather than accept these findings as verities, as the court is mandated to do, the majority does the reverse, and holds that the legal requirements of delivery have been satisfied. The majority reaches the incongruous conclusion that a present intent to transfer property can be found upon proof of a future intent to transfer upon the grantor's death.

The majority's analysis fails to perceive the distinction between *inter vivos* and testamentary dispositions of property. By failing to perceive this distinction, the majority has altered the rule that an undelivered deed cannot convey an interest in property. I would hold, based on the undisputed facts, that Mary O'Brien failed to execute valid deeds conveying her property to Robinson as there was no delivery of the deeds.

The majority's conclusion that the deeds meet the legal requirements of delivery should have ended the matter as a valid deed is effective to pass an interest in property at death. The majority, however, goes on to hold that these undelivered deeds effectively passed title to Robinson by operation of RCW §11.02.090. The statute provides in relevant part:

(1) Any of the following provisions in an insurance policy, contract of employment, bond, mortgage, promissory note, deposit agreement, pension plan, joint tenancy, community property agreement, trust agreement, conveyance, or any other written instrument effective as a contract, gift, conveyance, or trust is deemed to be nontestamentary, and this title [RCW Title 11] does not invalidate the instrument or any provision:

* * *

(c) that any property which is the subject of the instrument shall pass to a person designated by the decedent in either the instrument or a separate writing, including a will, executed at the same time as the instrument or subsequently.

The majority reaches the obvious conclusion that the word "conveyance" is not modified by the subsequent language "effective as a conveyance". The majority's statutory construction analysis misses the mark. The question still remains as to whether RCW §11.02.090 is intended to validate an otherwise invalid conveyance.

The statute was adopted almost verbatim from section 6 of the Uniform Probate Code. Section 6-201 "authorizes a variety of contractual arrangements which have in the past been treated as testamentary. . . . The sole purpose of this section is to eliminate the testamentary characterization from the arrangements falling within the terms of the section." Uniform Probate Code §6-201, 8 U.L.A. 534, Comment at 534-35 (1983). RCW §11.02.090, like section 6-201, characterize as nontestamentary certain provisions in written instruments that call for the transfer of property at death. By characterizing these provisions as nontestamentary, they are immune from invalidation due to noncompliance with the statute of wills.

I find nothing in RCW §11.02.090 indicating that the Legislature intended to eliminate the legal requirements governing a valid inter vivos conveyance by deed. The statute is intended to validate an instrument against testamentary attack only where the instrument has been made in the manner usual to the type of transaction involved. The rule applicable here is that enunciated by Professors Reutlinger and Oltman: "The statute [RCW §11.02.090] does not validate an otherwise-ineffective agreement, but operates only to prevent 'testamentary' invalidation of an instrument . . . ." M. Reutlinger & W. Oltman, Washington Wills and Intestate Succession 352 (1985); accord, First Nat'l Bank v. Bloom, 264 N.W.2d 208 (N.D.1978).

O'Brien's purported transfers of her property did not fail because they did not comply with the requirements of the statute of wills. The deeds failed because they were undelivered and had no independent legal effect. As the deeds were never valid inter vivos conveyances, they did not come within the scope of RCW §11.02.090. * * *

The Legislature enacted RCW §11.02.090 to eliminate the uncertainty and litigation that often arose when various commonly used inter vivos agreements contained provisions that were intended to have effect at death. M. Reutlinger & W. Oltman, at 352; see Uniform Probate Code §6-201, Comment. The statute does not itself validate any such instrument. * * *

The unchallenged facts are that the deeds were not delivered during O'Brien's lifetime and therefore they were not valid inter vivos conveyances. As the conveyances were never valid, they did not come within the scope of RCW §11.02.090.

Chapter 17
ASSURING GOOD TITLE

§17.3   THE RECORDING ACTS

§17.3.3   Persons Protected by the Recording Acts
B.   BONA FIDE PURCHASERS WITHOUT NOTICE
p. 1194, insert the following note:

6.   Gates Rubber Co. v. Ulman, 214 Cal. App.3d 356, 262 Cal. Rptr. 630 (1989), held that where a lease was recorded and the tenant's possession was consistent therewith, the buyer did not have constructive notice of an *un*recorded option to purchase.   This seems to be a sensible exception to the *Cohen* rule, doesn't it? When the lease is recorded, notice from the tenant's possession should extend only to those things inconsistent with the recorded lease.

Chapter 18
LEGAL REGULATION OF THE SALE AND
FINANCING OF REAL PROPERTY

§18.1 THE REAL ESTATE PROFESSIONALS AND THEIR CONDUCT

§18.1.1   The Real Estate Broker and Agent

page 1253, insert the following note:

5.   The scope of liability for defects in sold homes remains controversial, but seems to be expanding.   See Ditcharo v. Stepanek, 538 So.2d 309 (La. App. 1989) (broker could be held liable for failing to disclose known termite infestation); Johnson v. Geer Real Estate Co., 239 Kan. 324, 720 P.2d 660 (1986) (broker liable for failing to disclose that house used septic tank rather than sewer system).   But see Murray v. Hayden, 211 Cal.App.3d 311, 259 Cal. Rptr. 257 (1989) (broker had no duty to inspect for concealed defects); Herbert v. Saffell, 877 F.2d 267 (4th Cir. 1989) (same, applying Maryland law); Hoffman v. Connall, 108 Wash.2d 69, 736 P.2d 242 (1987) (no broker's liability for innocent misrepresentation or failure to verify the seller's statements).